iPod
The Missing Manual
Eighth Edition

iPod: The Missing Manual, Eighth Edition

BY J.D. BIERSDORFER WITH DAVID POGUE

Published by O'Reilly Media, Inc., 1005 Gravenstein Highway North, Sebastopol, CA 95472.

O'Reilly books may be purchased for educational, business, or sales promotional use. Online editions are also available for most titles (*safari.oreilly.com*). For more information, contact our corporate/institutional sales department: 800.998.9938 or corporate@*oreilly.com*.

Executive Editor: Peter Meyers

Editor: Peter McKie

Production Editor: Nellie McKesson

Illustrations: Rob Romano, Lesley Keegan, Nellie McKesson, and J. D. Biersdorfer

Indexer: Fred Leise

Cover Designers: Randy Comer, Karen Montgomery, and Suzy Wiviott

Interior Designer: Ron Bilodeau

Print History:

October 2009: First Edition.

Images on pages xvi, 2, 3, 4, 6, 7, 23, 50, and 250 appear courtesy of Apple, Inc.

FEB 03 2010

ISBN-13: 978-0-596-80431-2

[F]

Contents

Chapter 7

Chapter 8

About the Creative Team

Peter McKie (editor) still has his second-generation iPod, now lying in pieces after his replacement battery and third-party hard drive finally bit the dust. He has moved on, however, to a sleek new iPhone. He has a master's degree in journalism from Boston University. Email: *pmckie@oreilly.com*.

Nellie McKesson (production editor) lives in Brighton, Mass., and spends all her spare time on her burgeoning t-shirt business (*www.endplasticdesigns. com*). Email: *nellie@oreilly.com*.

Acknowledgements

I would like to thank David Pogue for suggesting this book to me way back in 2002, and then being a terrific editor through the mad scramble of the first two editions—and for providing his cheerful expertise for this edition. Also thanks to editors Peter Meyers and Peter McKie for guiding me through the past six updates. Thanks to Nellie McKesson, Fred Leise, Lesley Keegan, Chris Stone, and the Missing Manual folks at O'Reilly, and to Apple for courteously providing the iPod images and to the assorted other iPod accessory companies who made their digital photography available. Thanks also to The Charms for letting us use their album art on the book's cover.

I'd also to thank all my friends and family (especially and most importantly, Betsy Book) for putting up with me at that time every year when Apple announces new iPods and I disappear into my computer for several weeks, muttering incoherently and cranking up the show tunes and bluegrass playlists to a hearty volume level.

The Missing Manual Series

Missing Manuals are witty, superbly written guides to computer products that don't come with printed manuals (which is just about all of them). Each book features a handcrafted index and RepKover, a detached-spine binding that lets the book lie perfectly flat without the assistance of weights or cinder blocks.

Recent and upcoming titles include:

Access 2007: The Missing Manual by Matthew MacDonald

AppleScript: The Missing Manual by Adam Goldstein

AppleWorks 6: The Missing Manual by Jim Elferdink and David Reynolds

The Missing Credits

About the Authors

J.D. Biersdorfer is the author of *Netbooks: The Missing Manual* and co-author of *The Internet: The Missing Manual, iPhoto '09: The Missing Manual*, and the second edition of *Google: The Missing Manual*. She's been writing the weekly computer Q&A column for *The New York Times* since 1998 and has covered everything from 17th-century Indian art to the world of female hackers for the newspaper. She's also written articles for the *AIGA Journal of Graphic Design, Budget Travel, The New York Times Book Review*, and *Rolling Stone*. She studied in the Theater & Drama program at Indiana University and now spends her limited spare moments playing the banjo and watching BBC World News. Email: *jd.biersdorfer@gmail.com*.

David Pogue (co-author) is the weekly tech columnist for the *New York Times*, an Emmy-winning correspondent for *CBS News Sunday Morning*, weekly CNBC contributor, and the creator of the Missing Manual series. He's the author or co-author of 47 books, including 22 in this series and six in the *"For Dummies"* line (including *Macs, Magic, Opera*, and *Classical Music*). In his other life, David is a former Broadway show conductor, a piano player, and a magician.

Links to his columns and weekly videos await at *www.davidpogue.com*. He welcomes feedback about his books by email at *david@pogueman.com*.

CSS: The Missing Manual, Second Edition, by David Sawyer McFarland

Creating a Web Site: The Missing Manual, Second Edition, by Matthew MacDonald

David Pogue's Digital Photography: The Missing Manual by David Pogue

Dreamweaver 8: The Missing Manual by David Sawyer McFarland

Dreamweaver CS4: The Missing Manual by David Sawyer McFarland

Excel 2007: The Missing Manual by Matthew MacDonald

FileMaker Pro 10: The Missing Manual by Geoff Coffey and Susan Prosser

Flash CS4: The Missing Manual by Chris Grover

Google Apps: The Missing Manual by Nancy Conner

iMovie '09 and iDVD: The Missing Manual by David Pogue and Aaron Miller

iPhone: The Missing Manual, Second Edition by David Pogue

iPhoto '09: The Missing Manual by David Pogue and J.D. Biersdorfer

JavaScript: The Missing Manual by David Sawyer McFarland

Living Green: The Missing Manual by Nancy Conner

Mac OS X: The Missing Manual, Leopard Edition by David Pogue

Mac OS X Snow Leopard: The Missing Manual by David Pogue

Netbooks: The Missing Manual by J.D. Biersdorfer

Office 2008 for Macintosh: The Missing Manual by Jim Elferdink

Palm Pre: The Missing Manual by Edward C. Baig

Photoshop CS4: The Missing Manual by Lesa Snider King

Photoshop Elements 8 for Mac: The Missing Manual by Barbara Brundage

Photoshop Elements 8 for Windows: The Missing Manual by Barbara Brundage

PowerPoint 2007: The Missing Manual by Emily Moore

QuickBooks 2010: The Missing Manual by Bonnie Biafore

Quicken 2009: The Missing Manual by Bonnie Biafore

Switching to the Mac: The Missing Manual, Leopard Edition by David Pogue

Windows XP Home Edition: The Missing Manual, Second Edition by David Pogue

Windows XP Pro: The Missing Manual, Second Edition by David Pogue, Craig Zacker, and Linda Zacker

Windows Vista: The Missing Manual by David Pogue

Word 2007: The Missing Manual by Chris Grover

Your Body: The Missing Manual by Matthew MacDonald

Your Brain: The Missing Manual by Matthew MacDonald

Introduction

Like the arrival of the Sony Walkman, which revolutionized the personal listening experience, Apple's introduction of the iPod in the fall of 2001 caught the world's ear. "With iPod, listening to music will never be the same again," intoned Steve Jobs, Apple's CEO. But even outside the Hyperbolic Chamber, the iPod was different enough to get attention. People noticed it, and more importantly, they bought it.

If you're reading this book, odds are you're one of those folks. Or maybe you've just upgraded to a new iPod—Nano, Touch, Classic, or Shuffle—and want to learn about all the new features. In any case, welcome aboard!

With today's iPods, you can watch Hollywood feature films and TV shows, play popular video games, display gorgeous full-color photos, and look up personal phone numbers. If you have an iPod Touch, you can also surf the Web, buy music wirelessly, and spend hours exploring the wonders of YouTube with no bulky computer necessary. You can quickly find out how to do all of that within these pages—and also learn everything you need to know about iTunes, the iPod's desktop software companion.

Three iPods can play video now: the latest Nanos, the Classic, and especially the smooth, sleek iPod Touch in all its widescreen glory. The latest Nanos can even record their own audio and video. And all models still crank out the music—including the tiny clip-on iPod Shuffle, the loudest lapel pin on the market. But no matter which iPod you have, it's time to load it up with music and other stuff that's important to you. Even the smallest model can hold hundreds of songs and play the Soundtrack of Your Life in any order you like.

Steve Jobs was right about the iPod. Things just haven't been the same since.

How to Use This Book

The tiny pamphlet that Apple includes in each iPod package is enough to get your iPod up and running, charged, and ready to download music.

But if you want to know more about how the iPod works, all the great things it can do, and where to find its secret features, the official pamphlet is skimpy in the extreme. And the iTunes help files that you have to read on your computer screen aren't much better: You can't mark your place or underline anything, there aren't any pictures or jokes, and you can't read them in the bathroom without fear of electrocution. This book lets you do all that, gives you more iPod info than the wee brochure, *and* it has nice color pictures.

About→These→Arrows

Throughout this book, and throughout the Missing Manual series, you'll find sentences like this one: "Open the View→Column Browser→On Top" menu. That's shorthand for a longer series of instructions that go something like this: "Go to the menu bar in iTunes, click the View menu, select the Column Browser submenu, and then slide over to the On Top entry." Our shorthand system helps keep things more snappy than those long, drawn-out instructions.

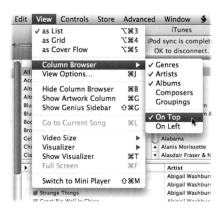

The Very Basics

To use this book, and indeed to use a computer, you need to know a few basics. This book assumes that you're familiar with a few terms and concepts:

- **Clicking.** To *click* means to point the arrow cursor at something on the screen and then to press and release the clicker button on the mouse (or laptop trackpad). To *double-click*, of course, means to click twice in rapid succession, again without moving the cursor at all. To *drag* means to move the cursor *while* pressing the button.

When you're told to *Ctrl+click* something on a PC, or *⌘-click* something on the Mac, you click while pressing the Ctrl or ⌘ key (both of which are near the Space bar).

- **Menus.** The *menus* are the words at the top of your screen or window: File, Edit, and so on. Click one to make a list of commands appear, as though they're written on a window shade you've just pulled down.

- **Keyboard shortcuts.** Jumping up to menus in iTunes takes time. That's why you'll find keyboard quickies that perform the same menu functions sprinkled throughout the book—Windows shortcuts first, followed by Mac shortcuts in parentheses, like this: "To quickly summon the Preferences box press Ctrl+comma (⌘-comma)."

If you've mastered this much information, you have all the technical background you need to enjoy *iPod: The Missing Manual*.

About MissingManuals.com

At our Web site, click the "Missing CD" link to reveal a neat, organized, chapter-by-chapter list of the shareware and freeware mentioned in this book. The Web site also offers corrections and updates to the book (to see them, click the book's title, then click Errata). You're invited to submit such corrections and updates yourself. To keep this book as up to date and accurate as possible, each time we print more copies, we'll make any confirmed corrections you've suggested.

We'll also note such changes on the Web site. And we'll keep the book current as Apple releases more iPods and software updates. While you're online, you can register this book at *www.oreilly.com*. Registering means we can send you updates about the book, and you'll be eligible for special offers like discounts on future editions of *iPod: The Missing Manual*.

Safari® Books Online

 Safari® Books Online is an on-demand digital library that lets you search over 7,500 technology books and videos.

With a subscription, you can read any page and watch any video from our library online. Read books on your cell phone and mobile devices. Access new titles before they're available for print, get exclusive access to manuscripts in development, post feedback for the authors. Copy and paste code samples, organize your favorites, download chapters, bookmark key sections, create notes, print out pages, and benefit from tons of other time-saving features.

O'Reilly Media has uploaded this book to the Safari Books Online service. To have full digital access to this book and others on similar topics from O'Reilly and other publishers, sign up for free at *http://my.safaribooksonline.com*.

1

Meet the iPod: Out of the Box and into Your Ears in 15 Minutes

I f you're like most people, you want to jump right in and get your spiffy new iPod up and running. You probably don't want to wade through any quick-start instructions longer than a couple of paragraphs, and you'd like plenty of color pictures, too.

Sure, Apple thoughtfully includes a little pamphlet of starter info with every iPod it sells. It's nicely designed as far as pamphlets go. But you may find that it doesn't go far enough. You want more help than a few line drawings and some haiku-like instructions can provide.

This book—and especially this chapter—is designed for you.

You won't get bogged down in a bland gray ocean of print here. You'll learn a bit about your particular iPod model and how to get it whistling sweet tunes in your ear in no time. If you want more information on in-depth iPodding or getting the most out of iTunes, you can find that stuff in chapters farther down the road.

But for now, let's get rolling with your new iPod. Ready?

Meet the iPod Nano

The iPod Nano may be Apple's mid-sized music player, but it's also one of its most versatile models. Sure, it can play songs, podcasts, and audio books like all the other iPods. And like the iPod Touch and iPod Classic, it can display photos, text notes, contacts, and calendars on its bright color screen. But unlike those 'Pods, which can merely *play* video, the Nano can also *shoot* video. It's one of the smallest camcorders ever.

If that's not enough, there's more: The 2009 Nano is the first iPod to include a built-in FM radio. That's right—you don't need a third-party attachment or any extra add-ons to pull live broadcasts out of the air and into your earphones. And unlike standard receivers, the Nano's radio can even pause live shows for a few minutes should someone start talking at you in the middle of a song.

You navigate through all these goodies using the Nano's smooth, touch-sensitive click wheel. With its 2.2-inch color screen and sharp 320 ×376 pixel resolution, the Nano can also play movies, TV shows, and video podcasts just like the bigger iPods, and it comes with its own selection of video games. But the Nano's perfect for gym workouts or that mad dash for the last train because it uses a flash memory chip to store everything. That means it's much more tolerant of jumping around than the traditional Classic iPod, with its big ol' hard drive tucked inside.

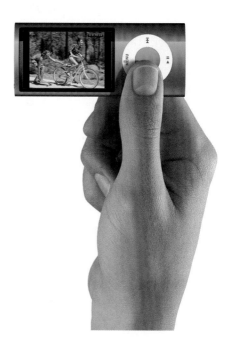

The Nano comes in two sizes: 8-gigabyte and 16 GB, all wrapped in scratch-resistant anodized alu-minum. And you're not stuck decid-ing between two colors when you buy a Nano, either—you get a rain-bow of nine choices: silver, black, purple, blue, green, yellow, orange, red, and pink. Oh, and if you like your music flowing all day long, you'll be glad to know the Nano's battery lasts up to 24 hours—you'll probably conk out before it does.

The Nano has a few other tricks under its aluminum hood. For one thing, it's got a built-in pedometer to measure your steps. It even reports how many calories you burn on your walk.

There's also an accelerometer (tilt sensor), which means the Nano senses movement and knows which way you're holding it. Turn it sideways to watch a movie, and the picture instantly spins around to orient itself for the wider view.

The accelerometer is shaking things up in another way, too—literally. Not in the mood for that song that just came on? Give your Nano a shake to have it shuffle up a new tune. And certain video games were made with the Nano in mind, making you tilt and move your way through a pixelated landscape in search of that next level.

The Nano is also one of the most accessible iPods ever for visually impaired listeners. An optional Spoken Menus feature recites the names of songs, albums, artists, and menus out loud, letting you navigate through this iPod's content with verbal cues. And for those of you tired of squinting, you can make the on-screen font size larger if you like.

At about a quarter of an inch thick and tipping the scales at a mere 1.3 ounces, who'd have thought it'd be this easy to fit a combination video camera/radio receiver/jukebox/movie theater/fitness trainer/handheld gaming console in your pocket?

Meet the iPod Touch

If an iPod Nano and Apple's iPhone ever had a kid, it would surely look something like the youngest iPod family member, the iPod Touch. The Touch gets its moniker from its responsive *touch screen*, the smooth front-side surface that lets you navigate through your music, videos, and photos with a tap or drag of your finger.

While it may have inherited its sensitivity from the iPhone, the Touch gets its stability from the same flash memory that's inside the Nano. No matter how hard you run or rock out, you'll probably never hear your music skip. You get about 30 hours of audio playback on a battery charge, or 6 hours of video.

Speaking of video, the iPod Touch sports the iPhone's eye-catching 3.5-inch widescreen display and 480×320 pixel resolution. Flip it sideways to see why it makes movies and TV shows look so good.

Apple gives you three Touches to choose from: an 8-gigabyte model, a 32-gigabyte version, or one that can store 64 gigs of your favorite stuff. That's 1,750 songs or 10 hours of iPod-friendly video on the 8 GB Touch; 7,000 songs or 40 hours of video on the 32 GB model; and a relatively whopping 14,000 songs and 80 hours of video on the big 64-gigabyte model.

But the Touch is much more than just a pretty face. In addition to all its regular iPod capabilities, like listening to music or showing off your latest photos, this iPod can reach right out and touch the Internet. Thanks to a built-in Wi-Fi chip and a small-but-powerful version of Apple's Safari Web browser, you can

catch up on all the latest news whenever you're in range of a Wi-Fi network. You use your fingertips to point your way around the Web—or fire up the Touch's onscreen keyboard when you have to enter text for a Web address or on a page.

And where there's Internet, there's email, stock-market updates, weather forecasts, and online maps. If that's not enough, there's a whole new world of possibilities in the iTunes App Store, where you can customize your iPod with additional software. Whether you're connected or not, you also get a handy notepad, your personal calendar, and your computer's address book, too.

If you hate leaving your computer for fear of missing something totally cool posted on YouTube, the popular video-sharing site, the Touch is there for you. This wireless iPod comes with its own one-click link to YouTube so you can keep up with the Web's funniest videos.

Oh, and one more thing…have you ever been listening to your iPod and wished you could buy even *more* music right there, no matter where you are? With the Touch (and a wireless network connection), you can. This little Internet iPod can step right up to the iTunes Wi-Fi Music Store (Chapter 7) and search, sample, and snap up tracks over the airwaves.

Note They may look an awful lot alike, but the iPod Touch and the iPhone have some distinct differences. For one thing, the iPod Touch is not a mobile phone. While this means Touch owners get to skip the AT&T Experience, it also means there's no ubiquitous cellphone network to use for online fun when your pool of Wi-Fi hotspots runs cold. There's also no integrated 2-megapixel camera. On the plus side, without the extra hardware inside, the Touch is much more svelte.

Meet the iPod Classic

With its solid, rectangular shape and horizontal screen, the faithful iPod Classic still looks the most like the original boxy white-and-chrome iPod that arrived on the scene in 2001. Less than a decade later, Apple has transformed that humble little 5-gigabyte music player with a black-and-white screen into a full-color, gorgeous portable media system that can play movies, TV shows, and video games—all while still fitting comfortably in the palm of your hand. And it's come a long way from those first 5 gigabytes: now you can stuff 160 gigabytes of music, photos, videos, and more onto it.

In those 160 gigabytes, you can fit 40,000 songs or 200 hours of video. And you don't have to stock up on the Duracells, either, because the iPod has a rechargeable battery that can play audio for 36 hours or video for 6 hours.

The iPod Classic comes in either silver or black. Unlike earlier iPods that sported hard glossy plastic on the front, Apple's latest version comes outfitted in a full metal jacket—anodized aluminum on the front and shiny stainless steel on the back.

Along with the click wheel—think of it as the iPod's mouse—the 2.5-inch color screen is the player's other main component. Capable of displaying more than 65,000 colors at a resolution of 320×240 pixels (translation: high-quality), the Classic's a great place to store and show off your latest vacation photos. In fact, you can have up to 25,000 pictures on your 'Pod. The screen also makes it a delight to catch up on that episode of *The Daily Show* you missed, or play a few rounds of solitaire while you listen to your favorite music or podcast.

The Classic comes with everything you need to hook it up to your Windows PC or Macintosh: a USB 2.0 cable. You also get those iconic see-what-I've-got white earphones. Once you get up and iPodding, you'll find that everyone and their grandmother wants to sell you other iPod accessories—all you have to do is stroll down to your favorite computer store and browse the ever-increasing selection of cases, cables, battery chargers, and more.

Meet the iPod Shuffle

The smallest member of Team iPod doesn't have a screen—but it doesn't need one, because it's designed for fuss-free music on the go. You don't have to worry about losing your Shuffle, because it clips right to your lapel or pocket—it's like jewelry you can rock out with. Take your pick of five standard Shuffle colors: blue, black, green, pink, and silver. You can get it with a 2-gigabyte memory chip (about 500 songs) or go for the 4-gigabyte model (1,000 songs); a special-edition 4-gigabyte version in shiny steel is also available. And even though it's called the iPod Shuffle, you don't have to shuffle your music; you can play your tracks in order with the nudge of a button (see below).

This petite 'Pod is so tiny, it doesn't even have room for a USB jack or navigation and volume controls—you control everything through the headphone jack. You plug a USB adapter into it to load music from iTunes and to charge the player, while a remote control built into the headphone cord handles volume control and music navigation chores.

The Shuffle, which offers about 10 hours of playing time, may not have a screen, but it includes Apple's VoiceOver technology, which audibly announces the name and artist of the song currently playing.

❶ Those trademark white Apple headphones plug into the headphone jack on the top of the Shuffle, but look closely—there's also a remote control right there on the cord.

❷ The + and – buttons on the remote raise and lower song volume. Click the gray center button to play and pause music. Click and hold the center button to hear artist and playlist names (see Chapter 6 for the scoop on playlists). Double-click the center button to skip to the next track or triple-click it to rewind.

❸ A little silver switch on top of the Shuffle turns it off and on, and flips between playing tunes in order (⟳) and shuffling them (⤫).

Install iTunes

Before you can have hours of iPod fun, you need to install Apple's iTunes multi-media, multifunction jukebox program on your computer. With iTunes, you also get Apple's QuickTime software—a video helper for iTunes. iPods once came with a CD packing all these programs, but these days you have to download everything yourself:

❶ **Fire up your computer's Web browser and point it to** *www.itunes.com/downloads.*

❷ **Click the "Download Now" button.** (Turn off the "Email me…" and "Keep me up to date…" checkboxes to spare yourself future marketing missives.) Wait for the file to download to your computer.

❸ **When the file lands on your hard drive, double-click the** *iTunesSetup.exe* **file.** If you use a Mac, double-click the *iTunes.dmg* file and then open the *iTunes.mpkg* file to start the installation. But if your Mac's younger than six years old, you probably already have iTunes installed. Go to Menu→Software Update and ask your Mac to see if there's a newer version of iTunes, just in case.

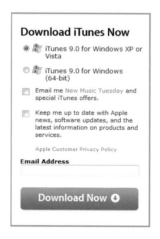

❹ **Follow the screens until the software installer says it's done.**

You may need to restart your computer after you install the software. Once that's done, you're ready to connect your new iPod to the computer.

> The hardware and operating-system requirements needed to run iTunes are listed below the Download Now button. If you have an older computer, it's worth a glance just to make sure your rig can handle the program. As for newer systems, iTunes runs fine on early versions of Microsoft's Windows 7.

Unpack iPod and Set It Up

If you haven't torn open the plastic box already, liberate your iPod from its box. The items you'll find inside vary depending on which iPod you purchased, but all of them come with:

❶ Apple's classic white headphones.

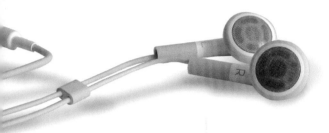

❷ A USB cable to connect the iPod to your computer. The iPod Nano, Touch, and Classic use the same white USB cable with the flat dock-connector port, while the iPod Shuffle has its own little USB adapter.

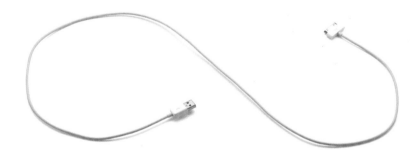

❸ A little pamphlet of basic quick-start information that's not nearly as fun or as colorful as this book.

What you want right now is the USB cable. Connect the small, narrow end to your computer's USB port and the wide, flat end (or the adapter, if you have a Shuffle) to the iPod. The first time you connect your iPod to a computer, iTunes' Setup Assistant walks you through a few steps to get your iPod ready to go.

The next step, if you want to hear some music, is to *get* some music.

Three Ways to Get Music for iTunes (and iPod)

Once you have iTunes running on your computer, you can start filling it with music. Chapters 4 and 5 have info on digital audio formats and technical settings you can tweak, but if you've got a brand-new iPod, odds are you don't care about *that* right now. No, you'd probably just like to load some music on your 'Pod. Here are three simple ways:

Import Existing Songs into iTunes

If you've had a computer for longer than a few years, odds are you already have some songs in the popular MP3 format on your hard drive. When you start iTunes for the first time, the program asks if you'd like to search your PC or Mac for music and add it to iTunes. Click "Yes" and iTunes will go fetch.

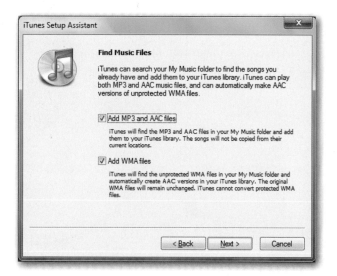

 Now, many Windows fans, if they do have existing music, may have songs in the Windows Media Audio (WMA) format. The bad news here is that iTunes can't play WMA files. The good news is that when iTunes finds WMA files, it can automatically convert them to an iPod-friendly format. Just be sure to turn on the last checkbox in the box above during iTunes setup. If you miss this step, you can always add WMA tracks by choosing File→Add to Library and selecting the songs you want; iTunes then converts them. One last thing to remember: the program can't convert copy-protected tracks you downloaded from other online music stores.

Import a CD

You can also use iTunes to convert tracks from your audio CDs into iPod-ready digital music files. Just stick a CD in your computer's disc drive after you start up iTunes. The program asks if you want to import the CD into iTunes. (If it doesn't ask, click the "Import CD" button at the bottom-right of the iTunes window.) If you're connected to the Internet, iTunes automatically downloads song titles and artist information for the CD (yes, strange as it may seem, music managers like iTunes don't get information about an album from the album itself, they search for it in a huge database on the Web).

Once you tell it to import music, iTunes gets to work and begins adding the songs to your library. You can import all the tracks from a CD, but if you don't want every song, turn off the checkbox next to the titles you want iTunes to skip. Chapter 4 has more about using iTunes to convert CDs.

Buy Music in the iTunes Store

Another way to get music for your iTunes library and iPod is to buy it from the iTunes Store. Click the iTunes Store icon in the list on the left side of iTunes. Once you land on the Store's main page and set up your iTunes account, you can buy and download songs, audio books, and videos. The content goes straight into your iTunes library and then onto your iPod. Chapter 7 is all about using the iTunes Store.

Get Stuff Onto the iPod Nano or Classic: The Quick Way

You don't have to do much to keep your iPod's music and video collection up to date with what's on your computer. That's because iTunes has a nifty *auto-sync* feature, which automatically makes sure that whatever's in your iTunes library also appears on your iPod once you connect it to the computer.

The first time you plug in your new iPod (after you install iTunes, of course), the iPod Setup Assistant leaps into action, asking you to name your iPod, and if you'd like to "Automatically sync songs to my iPod". If your answer's "yes," just click the Finish button. iTunes loads a copy of everything in its library that fits onto your iPod. That's it. Your iPod's ready to go.

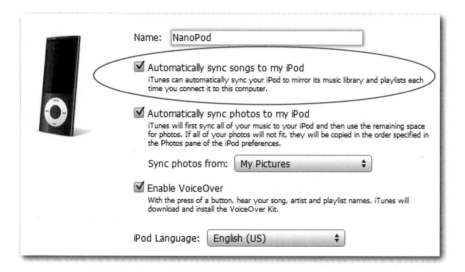

You can copy photos from your computer and turn on the talking VoiceOver menus here, too. But if you just want to stick with the music for now, Chapter 9 can fill you in on the photo business. If you generally like autosync but want more control over what goes onto your iPod, read on to find out how to make that happen.

 If you have a small-capacity iPod, you may already have more music than can fit on the player. If that's the case, *your* automatic option is the Autofill button at the bottom of the iTunes window. Skip ahead to page 14 to learn more about Autofill, which lets iTunes decide what to put on your iPod. And if you want to selectively sync certain playlists or artists, check out page 104 for the details.

Manually Load the iPod Nano or Classic

If you don't have enough room on your Nano or Classic for your whole iTunes collection, or if you plan to load music onto your iPod from more than one computer (say your work and home PCs), you'll want to *manually manage* your songs and other stuff. To put your iPod on manual right from the get-go, turn off the checkbox on the iPod Setup Assistant screen next to "Automatically sync songs…" (If you've already done the Setup thing, see page 106 for how to come back to Manual Land.) iTunes now refrains from automatically dumping everything onto your iPod. "But," you ask, "*how* do I get the music on there by myself?" It's easy. You just drag it:

❶ **In iTunes, click the Music icon under "Library".** Click the button circled below to see a list of all the songs in your music library. You can also click Ctrl+B (⌘-B) to go into Column Browser view, where iTunes lists your music by genre, artist, and album.

❷ **Click the songs or albums you want to copy to your iPod.** Grab multiple song titles or albums by holding down the Control or ⌘ key.

❸ **Drag your selection onto the iPod icon.** The number of songs you're dragging appears inside a red circle.

You can manually place any items in your iTunes library—audio books, movies, whatever—onto your iPod this way.

Fill Up Any iPod Quickly

Most people's entire music library is too big to stuff onto the wee Shuffle or even the 8-gigabyte Nano or Touch. If you love all your music and don't want to spend time cherry-picking tracks to load up your iPod, you can Autofill it to the brim with a full serving of tunes.

If you have a Shuffle and this is the first time you're plugging it into your PC, the iPod Setup Assistant appears. Leave the "Automatically choose songs…" checkbox turned on, click Done, and presto: iTunes grabs a random collection of songs from your library and copies them onto your tiny iPod. After that, each time you connect your Shuffle, a small panel appears at the bottom of iTunes, inviting you to fill up your iPod with the click of the Autofill button.

Although Autofill used to be a Shuffle-only feature, other iPods can use it as well, as long as you set them to manually manage music. To use Autofill with a Nano, Touch, or Classic, connect the iPod and click the flippy triangle next to its icon in the iTunes Source list—the left-most column in iTunes. The Autofill bar appears at the bottom of the screen. Click the Autofill button to load up.

With the Autofill From pop-up menu, iTunes can snag songs from your entire library or just a particular playlist (see Chapter 6). Click the Settings button for options to have iTunes pick random tracks or select highly rated songs more often. ("Ratings?" you say? Check out Chapter 5 for the details.)

After you Autofill for the first time, when you return for another batch of songs, you can turn on the checkbox next to "Replace all items when Autofilling" to have iTunes wipe the first batch of songs off your iPod and substitute new tracks.

Once iTunes fills up your iPod, you see an "iPod sync is complete" message at the top of the screen. Click the Eject button next to your iPod's icon, and then unplug the player from the computer.

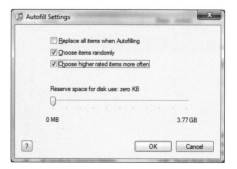

Manually Load Your iPod Shuffle

If *you* want to decide what goes onto your Shuffle, opt for manual updating instead of letting iTunes choose. As with any other iPod on manual control, you drag songs and playlists you want on your 'Pod from your iTunes library and drop them on the Shuffle's icon in the Source list.

When you click the Shuffle's icon and it displays your song list, feel free to re-arrange individual songs in the order you want to hear them—just drag them up or down. The info down at the bottom of the iTunes window tells you how much space you've got left on your Shuffle if you're looking to fill it to the rim. To delete songs from the Shuffle, select one or more tracks and then press the Delete key on your keyboard.

You can also mix and match your song-loading methods. Start by dragging a few favorite playlists over to the Shuffle, and then click Autofill to finish the job. Just make sure the "Replace all items when Autofilling" checkbox isn't turned on or iTunes will wipe off the tracks you personally added.

> **Note** Earlier versions of the iPod Shuffle used to be rather monogamous—that is, they only wanted to work with one iTunes library at a time and would threaten to erase and replace their contents if you added music from a different computer. The free-spirited iPod Shuffles of 2009, however, let you manually add music from multiple computers, just as you can with any other ol' iPod.

Get Stuff on the iPod Touch: The Quick Way

As with every iPod model that's come before it, the iPod Touch offers the simple and effective *autosync* feature. Autosyncing automatically puts a copy of every song, podcast, and video in your iTunes library right onto your player. In fact, the first time you connect your iPod Touch to your computer, the iPod Setup Assistant offers to copy all the music in your iTunes library over to your new player. If you opt to do that, your iPod is already set for autosync.

If you've added more music since that first encounter, the steps for loading the new goods onto your Touch couldn't be easier:

❶ Plug the USB cable into your Windows PC or Macintosh.

❷ Plug the flat end of that same cable into the bottom of the iPod Touch.

❸ Sit back and let iTunes leap into action, syncing away and doing all that heavy lifting for you.

You can tell the sync magic is working because iTunes gives you a progress report at the top of its window that says "Syncing iPod Touch…" (or whatever you've named your player). When iTunes tells you the iPod's update is complete, you're free to unplug your Touch and take off.

Autosync is a beautiful thing, but it's not for everyone—especially if you have more than 8, 32, or 64 gigabytes worth of stuff in your iTunes library. (That may sound like a lot of room for music, but once you start adding hefty video files, that space disappears fast.) If that's the case, iTunes fits what it can on the iPod.

If autosync isn't for you, jump over to the next page to read about more selective ways to load up your Touch.

Manually Load Your iPod Touch

If you opt out of autosyncing your iPod Touch, you now need to go ahead and choose some songs for it. Until you do, the Touch just sits there empty and for-lorn in your iTunes window, waiting for you to give it something to play with.

Manual Method #1

❶ Click the iPod Touch icon on the left side of the iTunes window. This opens up a world of syncing preferences for getting stuff on your iPod.

❷ Click the Music tab, then turn on the "Sync Music" checkbox.

❸ Click the button next to "Selected playlists, artists, and genres" and check off the items you want to copy to your iPod. (No playlists yet? See Chapter 6.)

❹ Click the Apply button at the bottom of the iTunes window.

Manual Method #2

❶ This one's for those into fine-grained picking and choosing: Click the Summary tab and turn on "Manually manage music and videos." Now you can click the songs, albums, or playlists you want and drag them to the Touch icon in the iTunes Source pane.

Manual Method #3

❶ Every item in your iTunes library has a checkmark next to its name when you first import it. Clear that checkmark next to whatever you *don't* want on the Touch. (If you have a big library, hold down the Control [⌘] key while clicking any title; that performs the nifty trick of removing *all* checkmarks. Then go and check the stuff you *do* want.)

❷ Click the iPod Touch icon under "Devices" in the Source list, and then click the Summary tab.

❸ At the bottom of the Summary screen, turn on the checkbox next to "Sync only checked songs and videos" and then click the Sync button.

Disconnect Your iPod from Your Computer

Got iTunes installed? *Check.*

Got music in the iTunes library? *Check.*

Got the iPod connected and the music you want copied onto it? *Check.*

Next up: Disconnect the iPod from your computer so you can enjoy your tunes. Resist the impulse to yank the USB cable out of the iPod without checking it first. If you can see menus or the battery icon on your 'Pod, you can safely unplug it.

But if you see the image shown at left, you need to *manually* eject the iPod from your computer. iTunes gives you two easy ways to do that:

❶ Click the little Eject icon next to the name of your iPod in the iTunes Source list.

❷ If your iPod's already selected in the Source list, choose Control→Eject iPod or press Ctrl+E (⌘-E).

With either method, the iPod's screen announces it's ejecting and displays an "OK to Disconnect" progress bar as it breaks its connection with the computer. Once all the gray screens go away and you see the regular menus again, you can safely liberate your iPod.

Charge Your iPod the First Time

Right out of the box, your iPod's battery probably has enough juice to run for a little while without you having to charge it up. Eventually, though, you'll need to go in for an electrical fill-up. All you need to do is plug the iPod back into your computer with the USB cable (the iPod charges itself by drawing from your PC or Mac's power). Just make sure you have your computer turned on and that it isn't asleep.

It takes only a few hours to fully charge your iPod's battery, and even less time to do what Apple calls a *fast charge*, which fills up 80 percent of the battery's capacity. That should be plenty of gas in your iPod's tank for a quick spin.

Here's how much time each iPod needs for both a fast and a full charge:

	Fast Charge	**Full Charge**
iPod Nano	1.5 hours	3 hours
iPod Touch	2 hours	4 hours
iPod Classic	2 hours	4 hours
iPod Shuffle	2 hours	3 hours

If you're traveling and don't want to drag your laptop with you just to charge your iPod, you can buy an AC adapter for it. Chapter 2 has more information on that.

Control the iPod Nano or Classic with the Click Wheel

Smack in the iPod's belly is the *click wheel,* your way around the iPod's contents. It's called a click wheel because you can actually click down on the four buttons evenly arranged around the ring. And the iPod's on-screen menus spin by as you move your thumb around the circle. There's also a big button in the wheel's center, which you'll push a lot as you tell your iPod to do your bidding. Here's what each button does, going clockwise from the top.

❶ **Menu.** Tap this button to return to any screen you just viewed. For example, if you visited Music→Playlists→My Top Rated, you'd press Menu twice to return to the Music menu. If you keep tapping Menu, you eventually wind up on the iPod's main menu.

❷ **Next/Fast-Forward.** Press this button to jump to the next song in a playlist (Chapter 6), or hold it down to advance quickly within a song.

❸ **Play/Pause.** Just like on a CD player, this button starts a song; push it again to pause the music.

❹ **Previous/Rewind.** Press this button to play the song directly before the current track, or hold it down to "rewind" within a song.

❺ **Select.** Like clicking a mouse button, press Select to choose a highlighted menu item. When a song title is highlighted, the Select button begins playback.

Other iPod Ports and Switches

On the outside, the iPod isn't a very complicated device. There's really just a Hold switch and two jacks to plug in cords. Here's what you do with 'em.

❶ **Hold Switch.** At the top of the Classic, over on the left side, is a little sliding switch marked Hold. This is a control that deactivates all the iPod's front buttons. Turning on the Hold switch stops your iPod from popping on if the buttons accidentally get bumped. The Nano's tiny Hold button is also on the top-left edge; the Touch doesn't have a Hold button, since it locks its screen when you press its Sleep/Wake button on top.

❷ **Headphone Jack.** Your new iPod comes with its own bright white headphones, and they plug in right here. If you don't like Apple's headphones, you can use another style or brand, as long as the other headphones use the standard 3.5-millimeter stereo miniplug.

❸ **Dock Connector.** The flat port on the iPod's bottom is called the Dock Connector. This is where you plug in the USB cable so you can connect your iPod to a computer for battery-charging and music and video fill-ups. (The Nano's headphone jack is also on the bottom.)

Basic Finger Moves for the iPod Touch Screen

Until the iPod Touch and the iPhone arrived on the scene, iPods were controlled by a wheel or control ring on the front of the player. The Classic and the Nano still work that way, but if you have an iPod Touch, you don't need a steering wheel to get around the iPod—you just tap the icons and menus directly on the screen to navigate around the device.

There are four moves you'll use most often when navigating the Touch screen:

- **Tap.** Just take the tip of your finger and directly touch the icon, song title, or control you see on the screen. The iPod Touch isn't a crusty old calculator, so you don't have to push very hard. A gentle press will do.

- **Drag.** Keep your fingertip pressed down on the screen and slide it around to scroll to different parts of the screen. You can do things like move volume sliders on music tracks or scoot over to different parts of a photo by dragging.

- **Flick.** Lightly and quickly whip your finger up or down a vertical list of songs on the iPod Touch screen, and watch them whiz by in the direction you flicked. The faster you flick that finger, the faster the text on-screen scrolls by. You can also flick side-to-side in Cover Flow view (Chapter 3) or in a photo album to see images parade triumphantly across your screen.

- **Slide.** A slide is sort of like a drag, but you use it mainly when your iPod presents you with a special on-screen button, such as when you need to unlock the iPod Touch's main screen when you first turn it on.

 The iPod Touch relies on the human touch—skin-on-glass contact—to work. If you have really long fingernails, a Band-Aid on the tip of your finger, or happen to be wearing gloves, you're going to have problems working the iPod Touch. You can't use a pencil eraser or pen tip, either. You can, however, find a special stylus to work with the Touch; for example, Pogo (*tenonedesign.com*) makes one for $15.

Special Buttons on the iPod Touch

The iPod Touch has the same headphone port on top and dock-connector jack on the bottom as other iPods. But because most of its controls are behind its sensitive screen, the Touch has only a couple of physical buttons on the outside.

One of these is the volume rocker on the left side. Pressing the top nib increases the sound on either the tiny little external speaker or an attached pair of headphones; the bottom nib lowers the volume.

For your pushing pleasure, the Touch comes with two other buttons:

- **Home.** Forget clicking your heels together three times—just push this indented button on the bottom of the Touch and you'll always return home. The iPod's Home screen is where all your tappable icons for Music, Photos, Safari Web browsing, and more hang out. If you ever wander deep into the iPod and don't know how to get out, push the Home button to escape. You can also push it to wake up the iPod Touch from sleep.

- **Sleep/Wake.** Press the thin black button on top of the Touch to put it to sleep and save some battery power. If you've got a song playing, no problem: a sleeping Touch still plays—it's just the display that goes dark.

Find the Music on Your iPod—and Play It

Now that you've got some songs on your iPod, you're ready to listen to them. Plug your headphones into the headphone jack and press any button on the front of the iPod if you need to turn it on.

Find Music on Your Nano or Classic

After you pick a language, the first menu you see says "iPod" at the top of the screen. Here's how to start playing your tunes:

❶ **On the iPod menu, highlight the Music menu.** Run your thumb over the scroll wheel to move the blue highlight bar up and down.

❷ **Press the round center button to select Music.**

❸ **On the Music menu, scroll to whichever category you want to find your song.** Your can select musc by artist, album, song, genre, and so on. Scroll to the one you want and press the center button to see your songs sorted by your chosen method.

❹ **Scroll through the list on the iPod's screen.** Say you decided to look for music by artist. You now see a list of all the singers and bands stored on your iPod. Scroll down to the one you want and press the center button. You'll see a list of all the albums you have from that artist.

Music
Cover Flow
Genius Mixes
Playlists
Artists
Albums
Songs
Genres
Composers
Audiobooks
Search

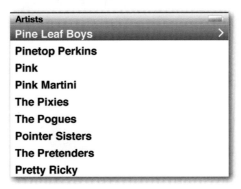

❺ **Scroll to the album you want to hear.** Press the Select or Play/Pause button to start playing the album.

You can find anything on your iPod by scrolling around and pressing the center button to select the item you want to hear, watch, read, or play. If you end up on a screen where you don't want to be, press the Menu button to retrace your steps. In fact, you can keep pressing the Menu button to reverse course and go all the way back to the iPod's main menu.

Press the Play/Pause button to pause a song that's playing. If a song's not playing and you don't touch the iPod's buttons for a few minutes, it automatically puts itself to sleep to save battery power.

Find Music on Your iPod Touch

"Hey!" you say, "I have an iPod Touch! How do I find my music since I don't have a scroll wheel?" Here's what you do.

❶ Tap the Music button on the Home screen.

❷ You see five tappable buttons at the bottom of the Music screen. These let you see your music sorted by Genius Mix, playlists, artists, or songs. (There's also a More button at the end that lets you sort by album, genre, and other categories.)

❸ Tap the Songs button and then scroll (by flicking your finger) down to the song you want to play. You can also hold down the alphabet bar on the right and then slide your finger slowly to better control the scroll. Tap the song's title to hear it play.

2:05 PM

Dr. & Mrs. Van der Trampp
Room to Breath
Sieve of Eratosthenes

Dr. & Mrs.
Van der
Trampp

Sieve of Eratosthenes

3:11 -1:59
4 of 7

Bopping Around the iPod Classic, Nano, and Shuffle

The standard iPod is a simple device to operate—five buttons and a click wheel quickly take you to all your songs, movies, games, audio books, and everything else parked on your 'Pod. Even though it doesn't have a mouse, the player's controls work just like those on a desktop computer: you highlight an item on-screen and click the center button to select it.

Performing this action either takes you to another menu of options or triggers an action—like playing a song, calling up your calendar, or checking the time in Paris. This chapter shows you what lies underneath all the menus on your iPod Classic or Nano and what each item does. Shuffle owners will find special coverage of their screenless wonders sprinkled throughout. The iPod Touch, unique among iPods for its lack of buttons and wheel-free controls, gets its own chapter right after this one.

Turn the iPod On and Off— or Put It On Hold

Classic or Nano, the iPod has only five buttons and one switch—none of them labeled Off or On. It's not hard to do either, even without official buttons.

- To turn your iPod on, tap any button on the front and it wakes right up, ready to play music or movies.

- To turn the iPod off, press the Play/Pause button for a few seconds until the screen goes dark. To preserve battery power, an inactive iPod automatically shuts itself down after a couple of minutes.

- For a one-click trip to Naptown from the iPod's main menu, add the Sleep option to your menu choices. Choose iPod→Settings→Main Menu→Sleep. (On the Nano, that's iPod→Settings→General→Main Menu→Sleep.)

The only drawback to the button-click turn-on is that, if a button gets bumped, say, in a purse or backpack, the iPod can turn on and run its battery down without you knowing it. Then you end up with a drained iPod right before that long commute home.

That's where the iPod's *Hold switch* comes in handy. It's on the top of the Classic, the current Nano, and older iPods. (On older Nanos, it's on the bottom.) Just slide it over so the orange bit underneath shows, and you've deactivated your iPod's front buttons. That'll keep you from accidentally sucking the life out of your battery. As an added bonus, if you stash your 'Pod in your pocket to listen to tunes as you walk down the street, you won't inadvertently jump to the next song with each step.

 The control clicker on the iPod Shuffle's headphone cord keeps its Play button up by your face—where it's less likely to get accidentally bumped. Still, if you want to keep the iPod Shuffle from accidentally turning on, just flick the tiny switch near the headphone jack to Off.

Navigate the iPod's Menus

Like any modern computer program, the iPod's user interface is a series of menus and sub-menus. The top-level, or main, menu just says "iPod" at the top of the screen. No matter how deeply you burrow into the player's submenus, you can always get back to this main menu by repeatedly pressing the Menu button on the click wheel.

In fact, think of iPod navigation like this: Press the round center button to go deeper into menus and press the Menu button to back out, retracing your steps along the way.

The contents of your iPod menu varies a bit depending on which model you have—except for the Shuffle, of course, which doesn't have a screen or menus. Here's the basic lineup if you have a song currently playing:

• **Music**	• **Extras**
• **Videos**	• **Settings**
• **Photos**	• **Shuffle Songs**
• **Podcasts**	• **Now Playing**

The 2009 Nanos include two menu items older Nanos and Classic iPods don't have: Video Camera (Chapter 8) and Radio (discussed later in this chapter).

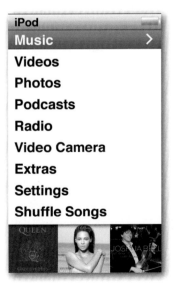

The next few pages give you a little more information about each menu. And just as the iPod and iTunes give you choices about your music, so you can decide what you want displayed on your main menu. If you like the sound of that, check out "Customize Your iPod's Menus" later in this chapter.

What's in the Music Menu

In the Music menu you'll find a one-stop shopping center for your iPod's audio-related options, including tunes, audio books, and podcasts.

- **Cover Flow.** A feature so cool it gets its own page, over there on the right. (Even though it's listed on the menu, the Nano has its own motion-sensitive shortcut to it.)

- **Genius Mixes.** Instructions on how to use your iPod's very own music mixmaster. Chapter 6 explains the genius of Genius in greater detail.

- **Playlists.** A *playlist* is a customized list of songs you create. Chapter 6 has loads more on creating playlists.

- **Artists.** This menu groups every tune by the performer's name.

- **Albums.** Your music, grouped by album.

- **Songs.** All the songs on your iPod, listed alphabetically.

- **Genres.** Your music, sorted by type: rock, rap, country, and so on.

- **Composers.** Your music, grouped by songwriter.

- **Audiobooks.** Your iPod's spoken-word content.

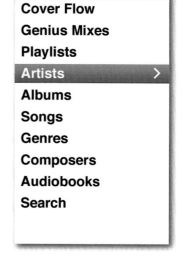

- **Search.** When you have a ton of tunes and don't feel like scrolling through your collection, use the Search function to scroll-and-click the first few letters using a tiny on-screen keyboard. Songs that match your entries pop up in their own list.

Even without using the Search function, the Music menu's sub-menus make it easy to find specific music. For example, to see a list of all songs on your iPod sorted by artist, select Artists from the Music menu. The next screen presents you with an alphabetical list of bands and singers.

Cover Flow on the iPod

The iPod offers a number of ways for you to browse your music collection, like scrolling through lists grouped by artist, album, or song. But if you want to see all your album covers parade majestically across your screen, choose iPod→Music→Cover Flow and then turn the scroll wheel. On the Nano, you can also hold the iPod sideways, in "landscape" view, to switch to Cover Flow.

Cover Flow on the iPod looks pretty much like the Cover Flow view in iTunes (Chapter 4), except, for some reason, it actually looks *cooler* on the iPod. It's also quite helpful to see what songs you have from each particular album sliding by. Here's how:

When the cover of the album you want to hear appears in the center of the iPod's screen, press the Select button. The artwork animatedly flips around to reveal the track names and times for each song. Scroll down the list and click the Select button again to play the chosen song.

If you don't have any artwork attached to your music files, Cover Flow can be a little bland because it just displays a default gray musical-note icon. Flip to Chapter 5 if you want to get a rolling start building up your cover-art collection.

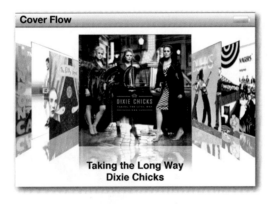

What's in the Videos Menu

Your iPod is also a personal movie player. Before you grab the popcorn, here's what you'll find on its menu of video setting and sorting options:

- **Camera Videos.** Movie clips shot with the iPod Nano's own video camera live here. Needless to say, this is a Nano-only menu item.

- **Movies.** Go here to find any full-length feature films you bought from the iTunes Store, as well as your own home movies (Chapter 8).

- **Rentals.** If you opted to rent a movie instead of buying it outright, you'll find it waiting for you in this menu.

- **TV Shows.** A menu for iTunes Store-purchased episodes and personally recorded shows.

- **Music Videos.** A list of your collected music-video clips.

- **Video Playlists.** Just like music, you can create playlists of videos in iTunes.

- **Settings.** You can configure your TV playback options. For example, you can set your iPod to play video in widescreen format or adjust it for full-screen viewing. An option to turn on closed-captioning is here, too.

Playing a video works just like playing a song: browse, scroll, and select. Chapters 7 and 8 tell you how to buy, sort, and organize your iPod's video collection using iTunes.

 Newer iPod Nanos place "Rentals" second on the menu list, between Camera Videos and Movies. If you haven't rented any movies, you won't see the menu item.

What's in the Photos Menu

Ready to turn your iPod into a pocket photo viewer? Once you stock your iPod with images (Chapter 9 has instructions), the Photos menu lets you adjust picture-viewing preferences—including slideshow settings for picture collections—and call up your actual pix.

All Photos

Click here to view your iPod's entire photo library; individual albums are listed by name below the Settings menu. Chapter 9 shows you how to summon your pictures on-screen.

Settings

- **Time Per Slide.** Linger up to 20 seconds on each photo, or manually click through each picture.

- **Music.** Select a playlist as your soundtrack, or choose silence.

- **Repeat.** As with playlists, slideshows can repeat—if you want 'em to.

- **Shuffle Photos.** Toggle the setting to On to randomly display each photo in a slideshow.

- **Transitions.** Options here include a classic Hollywood fade, a dissolve, and many more.

- **TV Out.** To display your slideshow on a connected TV, select On or Ask. For slideshows on the iPod, choose Off or Ask. (Off does what it says; Ask nags you to pick between TV and iPod before the show starts.) Nano and Classic owners only get the Off setting till they've actually plugged in a video-ready cable.

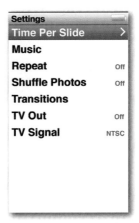

- **TV Signal.** When using a TV in North or South America, or East Asia, select NTSC; most other places use the PAL standard.

What's in the Podcasts Menu

When podcasts first appeared online several years ago, they were mostly audio files: radio-like shows to download and play on your iPod. But podcasts are not just about audio these days—there are plenty of video podcasts out there for the watching, too. If you want to dive in and get some shows right now, Chapter 7 explains how to download and subscribe to podcasts from the iTunes Store.

There are a couple of really great things about podcasts. For one, pretty much all of them are still free, so you have a wealth of fresh content available to put on your iPod every day. For another, you can find plenty of nightly and weekly news programs from the major TV networks here—*Face the Nation*, *Meet the Press*, *This Week*, *Washington Week*, and so on—all blissfully commercial-free and ready to get you up to date with the world.

Go to iPod→Podcasts to see the shows you've downloaded and synced up through iTunes. The iPod's menu sorts the podcasts by the name of the show, like *Ask a Ninja* or *BBC Digital Planet*, with the total number of episodes on your iPod listed. If you haven't yet listened to an episode, a blue dot appears next to the name—which makes it easy to find the new stuff.

What's in the Extras Menu

Here lie all the goodies that make the iPod more than just a music player:

- **Alarms.** Have the iPod wake you up with a beep—or put you to sleep with a timer setting that lets you drift off to Dreamland with music.

- **Calendars.** This menu holds a copy of your personal daily schedule, synced from iCal or Microsoft Outlook.

- **Clocks.** With its built-in clock and ability to display multiple time zones, the iPod is probably the most stylish pocket watch you'll ever see.

- **Contacts.** Any phone numbers and addresses you ported over from your computer reside here.

- **Fitness.** The pedometer (Chapter 10) lives in this Nano-only menu.

- **Games.** Test your capacity for trivia with iQuiz, kill time with a round of Klondike solitaire, travel the Maze, or shoot things in the Vortex. Games from the iTunes Store, like Ms. Pac-Man and Sudoku, also land here.

- **Notes.** The iPod has a built-in text reader program that you can use to read short documents and notes.

- **Screen Lock.** For stuff that's nobody's business—address book, schedule, photos, and so on—you may want to password-protect your 'Pod.

- **Stopwatch.** The iPod can serve as your timer for keeping track of your overall workout or your multiple laps around the track.

- **Voice Memos.** The Nano's homemade audio recordings can be found in this menu. Classic owners with an optional microphone attachment can find their recordings at iPod→Voice Memos.

Chapter 10 has more information on many of these features.

 Note The Classic and the Nano show these menu items in a slightly different order. The Nano goes for the alphabetical approach profiled in the text above.

What's in the Settings Menu

The Settings menu has more than a dozen options for tailoring your iPod's look and sound.

- **About.** Look here for your iPod's serial number; the number of songs, videos, and photos on it; your model's hard drive size; and how much free disk space is left. Click the center button to get to all three screens of info.

- **Shuffle.** Turn this feature on to shuffle songs or albums.

- **Repeat.** Repeat One plays the current song over and over; Repeat All repeats the current album, playlist, or song library.

- **EQ.** Apply more than 20 different equalizer presets for acoustic, classical, hip hop, and other types of music. Chapter 5 has more on equalization.

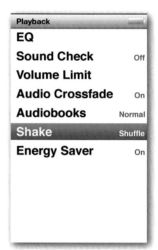

- **Sound Check.** Turning on Sound Check helps level out songs of differing volumes. Chapter 5 has more info.

- **Volume Limit.** Keep your (or your child's) eardrums from melting by setting a maximum volume limit—and locking it.

- **Audio Crossfade.** On the Nano, turning this setting on means never having to hear a gap between songs as the iPod fades out of one tune and into the next.

- **Audiobooks.** This setting lets you speed up or slow down a narrator's voice.

- **Shake.** Put this setting to Shuffle on the Nano. Then give it a gentle shake the next time you're playing a song and want to switch randomly to another track. The Nano emits a boop tone and serves up a new tune.

- **Energy Saver.** This feature turns off the Nano's screen if you're not currently pressing buttons—and saves you a little battery juice.

> The Nano groups music-oriented settings like EQ, Sound Check, and Audio Crossfade into a Playback submenu on the main Settings menu. Other settings, like Clicker, Backlight, and Main Menu—all the stuff that lets you fuss with the look and sound of the Nano's text screens—are grouped under the General submenu.

- **Clicker.** Some people think the Clicker noise during a long scroll sounds like ants tap-dancing. Others like the audio cue. Decide for yourself and turn the sound off or on here.

- **Rotate.** If you don't want Cover Flow kicking in when you hold your Nano sideways, turn it off here.

- **Backlight.** Specify how long your screen's backlight stays on each time you press a button or turn the dial—from 2 Seconds to Always On.

- **Brightness.** If your iPod movies seem a bit dim (and not just because of Hollywood's standards), use this setting to brighten the screen.

- **Font Size.** On the Nano, you can make the tiny screen type slightly bigger by switching from Standard to Large.

- **Main Menu.** Customize which items appear in your iPod's main menu here.

- **Music Menu.** Customize which items appear in your Music menu here, like Radio—for when you have Apple's optional FM Radio Remote.

- **Sort Contacts.** This setting lets you change the sort order of the contacts in your iPod's address book (first name first or last name first).

- **Date & Time.** Adjust your iPod's date, time, and time zone settings here.

- **Radio Regions.** If you travel the world with your Nano, you can use this menu to home in on the FM signals in your geographic area.

- **Language.** The iPod can display its menus in most major European and Asian languages. Pick one here.

- **Legal.** The Legal menu contains a long scroll of copyright notices for Apple and its software partners. It's not very interesting reading unless you're studying intellectual-property law.

- **Reset All Settings.** This command returns all your iPod's customized sound and display settings to their original factory settings.

Other Menus: Shuffle Songs and Now Playing

One—sometimes two—other items live down at the bottom of the iPod's main menu.

Shuffle Songs

The mystical, magical qualities of the iPod's Shuffle Songs setting (*"How does my little PeaPod always know when to play my Weird Al Yankovic and Monty Python songs to cheer me up?"*) have become one of the player's most popular features since the early days of iPodding. So Apple moved Shuffle out to the main menu. Just scroll and select it to shuffle your songs.

Now Playing

When you have a song playing—but have scrolled back to the main menu to do something else while jamming—the Now Playing item appears at the very bottom of the screen. Highlight this command and press Select to call up your song's Now Playing screen and get back to the music at hand.

Press the iPod's center button quickly when you're on the Now Playing screen to get a new mini-menu each time you hit the button, like the scrubber bar (page 43) or the chance to rate the song (Chapter 5).

Customize Your iPod's Menus

The iPod has a handy personalization feature: the ability to arrange both your Main Menu and Music Menu screens so that only the items you like show up there. For example, you could insert the Calendar option onto the iPod's main screen so you don't have to dig through the Extras menu to get at it. Or put your Playlists menu right out there on the main screen so you don't waste time getting to your latest musical inspiration.

To customize your Nano's main menu, start from the main iPod screen and choose Settings→General→Main Menu. On the iPod Classic, go to Settings→Main Menu. You see a list of items that you can choose to add or eliminate from the main screen: Music, Playlists, Artists, and so on.

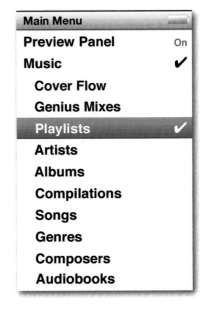

As you scroll down the list, press the center button to turn each one on or off. You might, for example, consider adding these commands:

- **Clock,** for quick checks of the time.

- **Games,** for quick killing of time.

- **Contacts,** to look up phone numbers and call people to pass the time.

To see the fruits of your labor, press Menu twice to return to the main screen. Sure enough, in addition to the usual commands described in this chapter, you'll see the formerly buried menus right out front, ready to go.

Now that you've got your Main Menu screen squared away, you can do the same type of customization on your iPod's Music screen by choosing Settings→Music Menu.

 Tip You can see more menu items and less eye candy on the skinny Nano's main screen by turning off the Preview Panel—that strip of images at the bottom of the window. Choose Settings→General→Main Menu→Preview Panel→Off. Your menu response time will get a lot peppier, too. As of now, the Classic's wider preview panel stays put on the right side of the screen.

Set the iPod's Clock(s)

When you choose Clocks from the iPod's Extras menu, you can set up clocks to track the time in multiple cities. This little timekeeper comes in handy if you forget your watch.

- To create a clock, choose Clocks and press the iPod's center button. A box appears with a choice of Add or Edit. Scroll to Add and click the center button to select it.

- To change the city a clock represents, click it with the iPod's center button and then select Edit. Pick the general region you want from the Region menu; then choose the new city on the next screen.

- To delete a clock from the list, select it, press the center button, and choose Delete.

- To make adjustments for things like Daylight Saving Time, the date, the time zone—or to opt for the military-style 24-hour clock display—choose iPod→Settings→Date & Time.

 You can ask your iPod to display the current time in its title bar whenever music's playing. Just choose iPod→Settings→Date & Time→"Time in Title". Press the center button to toggle the "Time in Title" display on or off.

Use the iPod as an Alarm Clock

The iPod's alarm clock can give you a gentle nudge when you need it. To set your alarm:

❶ **Choose Extras→Alarms→Create Alarm. Press the center button.** The Alarm changes to On and you land on a screen full of choices.

❷ **Choose Date.** As you turn the wheel, you change the date for your wake-up call. Press the center button as you pick the month, day, minutes, and so on.

❸ **Choose Time.** Repeat the wheel-turning and clicking to choose the hour, minute, and the AM/PM setting for the alarm. When you get back to the Create Alarm menu, click Repeat if this is a standing alert. Choose the alarm's frequency: daily, weekly, and so on.

❹ **Choose Alert Sound.** It's time to decide whether you want "Beep" (a warbling R2-D2-like tone that comes out of the iPod's built-in speaker) or music from a selected playlist. If you choose music, it plays through your headphones (assuming they haven't fallen out) or to an external set of speakers if you have some (unless you have a 2009 Nano with its own tiny external speaker).

❺ **Choose Label.** What's alarming you—a class, a meeting, time to take a pill? Pick a name for your alarm here.

If you wake up early and want to turn off the alarm, go to Extras→Alarms→ [Name of Alarm]→Alarm and press the center button to toggle it off. You can also delete any alarm with the Delete option at the bottom of the menu.

Search for Songs on the iPod

As your music collection grows, scrolling to find a specific song or album can leave you thumb-weary. Sometimes, you may not even remember if you *have* a certain song on your iPod. The Search feature, available on iPods released in the past few years, lets you drill down through your massive library and locate specific songs, albums, and so on with a few spins of the click wheel. It works like this:

❶ Choose iPod→Music→Search.

❷ On the screen that appears, use the click wheel to highlight a letter from the alphabet. Press the center button to select the letter.

❸ The iPod immediately presents a list of matching titles, winnowing it further as you select more letters. Use the iPod's Rewind/Previous key as a Backspace button to wipe out letters you don't want.

❹ Once the title you want appears on-screen, click the Menu button (to jump up to the results list) and then scroll down to select your song.

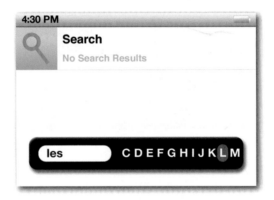

> **Tip** iPod Shuffle owners, you can have the iPod *recite* your playlists so you can pick the one you want to hear. If you haven't already done so, turn on the Shuffle's VoiceOver feature—connect the Shuffle to your computer, click its icon in the iTunes Source list, and click the Summary tab. Turn on the checkbox for Enable VoiceOver, and click Apply. Once VoiceOver syncs up audio menus for your Shuffle's content, you can hear more than just the music.
>
> To hear an audio menu of your playlists, click and hold down the center button on the headphones until you hear a beep. The Shuffle begins to announce your playlists by name. Click the center button to select the one you want to hear. To get out of the playlists audio menu, click and hold the center button for a second.

Jump Around Within Songs and Videos

Sometimes, you just have to hear the good part of a song again or watch that scene in the movie once more because it was so cool the first time. If that's the case, the iPod gives you the controls to do so.

Hold down the Rewind/Previous and the Fast-forward/Next buttons on either side of the click wheel to zip back and forth through a song or video clip.

If you want to get to a specific time in a song or video, press the iPod's center button and then use the wheel to scroll over to the exact spot in the track's on-screen timeline. For an audio file, a small diamond appears in the timeline when you press the center button so you can see where you are in a song.

This jump-to-the-best-part technique is called *scrubbing*, so if a fellow iPodder tells you to scrub over to 2:05 in a song to hear a great guitar solo, the person's not talking about cleaning the bathtub.

 Need some soothing sounds at the end of a long day—but don't want the iPod on all night if you drift off? Have it sing you to sleep with the Sleep Timer function. Choose Extras→Alarms→Sleep Timer and then pick the amount of time you'd like: 15, 30, 60, 90, or 120 minutes. (You can also choose to turn the timer *off* here as well.) Once you pick your time, press Play and relax. The Sleep Timer item in the Alarms menu displays a countdown of time left, but hopefully, you'll be too sleepy to notice.

Adjust the iPod's Volume

The clicker on the Shuffle headphones has plus (+) and minus (–) buttons to pump up (or down) your music's volume. The volume knob on the larger iPods is virtual. With a song or video playing, run your thumb over the click wheel; the timeline bar on the bottom switches to a volume-level indicator.

If you want to protect your hearing, use the Volume Limit setting to lock in a maximum volume. Parents who worry that their kids are blasting music too loudly can set a Volume Limit and lock it with a numeric password:

❶ Go to iPod→Settings→Volume Limit (on the Classic), or iPod→Settings→Playback→Volume Limit (on the Nano).

❷ On the next screen, use the click wheel and the volume bar to select a maximum volume level.

❸ Press the Play/Pause button to set it and to move to the next screen. (On the Nano, press the center button and choose either Done or Lock on the next screen. If you pick Lock, the next step is for you.)

❹ The iPod's Screen Lock display appears and you can dial in a secret four-number password; anyone who wants to change the setting will have to enter the password first.

On the iPod Shuffle, you set your volume limits for the player on the *iTunes* side. Connect the Shuffle to your computer, click its icon in the Source list, and click the Summary tab. Scroll down on the Summary screen to the Options area and turn on the checkbox for "Limit maximum volume." Use the slider on-screen to increase or decrease the Shuffle's loudness potential; you can also click the lock icon here to prevent little hands from making big changes to the setting. When you're done, click the Apply button.

Charge Your iPod Without Your Computer

The USB 2.0 cable (or USB adapter, if you have a Shuffle) that comes with your iPod has two jobs:

- To connect your iPod to iTunes.

- To draw power from your computer to charge up the iPod's battery.

There may be times, however, when your iPod's battery is in the red and you're nowhere near your computer. You many not even be near an electrical outlet, but on the road. Then it's time to turn to other options, including:

- **Using an Apple iPod USB Power Adapter.** This tiny white cube has a jack to plug in your iPod's USB cable (and connected iPod) into the back end. The front of the adapter has a set of silver prongs that plug into a regular electrical outlet. You can find the AC adapter for around $29 in iPod-friendly stores or online at *http://www.apple.com/ipodstore*.

- **Getting a car charger that connects to the standard 12-volt power outlet found in most cars.** Several companies make auto chargers for the iPod for around $20, and you can find the hardware at stores that sell iPod gear, Apple Stores (including *http://www.apple.com/ipodstore*) and specialty iPod-accessory Web shops like DLO (*http://www.dlo.com*).

DLO's AutoCharger for iPod

Tip If you find the iPod's backlight doesn't stay on nearly as long as you'd like, you can change the amount of time it shines. Choose Settings→General→Backlight (on the Nano), or Settings→Backlight (on the Classic). Scroll to the amount of time you'd like to see the light: increments between 2 and 30 seconds, or Always On. That last one's a real battery killer, though, as all that illumination needs power.

Play FM Radio on the iPod Nano

Forget about those boxy transistor radios of yore—your sleek new iPod Nano can also pull down an FM signal from the airwaves and bring live broadcasts right to your ears. For stations transmitting RDS (Radio Data System) information, the Nano even displays the name of the song, the artist, and the station's call letters on-screen. One thing: you need to listen to the radio through the headphones, because the antenna's in the cord. Here's how it all works:

- **Play and Tune the Radio.** To get started, choose iPod→Radio. The radio screen appears, with an old-fashioned-looking FM dial along the bottom of the screen; press the center button if you don't see it. Slide your finger or thumb along the Nano's click wheel to move up and down the dial. You can also press the Previous or Next buttons to jump from station to station. (Hold down these same buttons to seek and scan along the dial, listening to five-second samples of each station. Press the center button if you want to stop and listen to a station.)

- **Add Favorite Stations.** When you land on a station you really like, press the center button and choose "Add to Favorites" from the menu. You can now jump to your favorite stations by pressing the Previous or Next buttons, but note that adding favorites disables the seek and scan functions when you press these buttons. To delete a favorite station, tune into it (or choose iPod→Radio→Favorites→[Station]), hold down the center button, and choose "Remove From Favorites."

- **Pause Live Radio.** To pause a broadcast, press the Play/Pause button. A progress bar at the bottom displays how long you've been in Pause mode. Press Play/Pause again to resume listening where you left off. Like TiVo, you can fast-forward or rewind through the audio stored in the progress bar—just hit either side of the click wheel.

- **Tag Songs.** If you see a little tag icon (circled above), the station supports iTunes Tagging. When you hear a song you *have* to have, press the center button to tag it. When you sync your Nano to your computer, the songs appear in a Tagged playlist in the Store area of the Source list. You can listen to previews there—and *buy* the songs, naturally.

When you have the radio screen up, press the Menu button to get to the Radio menu. Here, you can see tagged and recent songs, pick a geographical listening region, turn Live Pause on or off—and play or turn *off* the radio.

Play Games on an iPod

The iPod is a personal entertainment machine on many levels. All iPod Classic models have three games: iQuiz, Klondike, and Vortex, while the Nano has Klondike, Maze, and Vortex. You can also buy and download old-school video games like Ms. Pac-Man, Sudoku, and more from the iTunes Store (Chapter 7). To find any of your games, go to iPod→Extras→Games.

Klondike

The iPod has a Vegas-style Klondike solitaire game. To play, you get a row of seven card piles, on which you're supposed to alternate black and red cards in descending numerical order. Use the click wheel to pass the hand over each card stack. Click the center button when you get to the card you want to move to the bottom of the screen. Then scroll the hand to the pile where you want to place the card, and click the center button again to make the play. Click the face-down card (upper-left) for three new cards to play.

Maze

The Nano's accelerometer gets a workout in the Maze, a game that has you tilting the iPod around in every direction as you try to work a ball through a series of increasingly complex mazes. You don't have all day to wave the Nano around—you have to make it through the puzzle before the timer runs out.

iQuiz

Complete with colorful flashing graphics and a cheesy, 70's-style game show soundtrack, iQuiz picks your brain with contemporary multiple-choice questions in several trivia categories: music, movies, and TV. The game brings its own questions to the screen, but also taps into your iPod to find out how much you know about your own music library.

Vortex

Most computers and handheld devices wouldn't be complete without some brick-bashing version of the old Pong-against-the-wall game. Vortex scales up the basic concept of Brick to 360 degrees of smashing 3-D fun. Use the scroll wheel to move the bat around the edges of the circular Vortex and audibly smash through the rotating bricks. If you have an older video-playing iPod, Vortex is available for purchase in the games area of the iTunes Store.

Some Idiot Set the iPod Menus to Greek

Changing the iPod's on-screen language to an unfamiliar alphabet is a favorite trick of jealous co-workers and older brothers. Fortunately, you have a couple of ways to get the iPod back to English.

First, click the Menu button until you get back to the iPod's main menu screen. You'll see "iPod" in English at the top, and the menu listings in whatever language your wisenheimer pal picked out for you. Then follow these steps:

❶ **Scroll down to the sixth line on your iPod Classic or the eighth line on a 2009 Nano.** You've just highlighted the Settings menu; click it.

❷ **Scroll all the way down to "Reset Settings," which conveniently appears in English.** Here, you can make a decision:

Option 1: The *third* menu item from the bottom (that is, the menu item two rows up from "Reset Settings") is the Language setting. Scroll up there to get to the language list and then choose English.

Option 2: If you're tired of your iPod settings, you can wipe them out and start over. Click Reset All Settings. The next screen gives you a choice: Cancel or Reset.

Lock Up Your Pod

When you turn your iPod's Screen Lock feature on, the screen displays a safe's door icon that stubbornly refuses to go away until you enter your combination. To activate this protective layer:

❶ Choose Extras→Screen Lock.

❷ On the Lock screen, pick the numbers for your secret code. Using the click wheel, navigate to each box. By spinning the wheel, pick a number from 0 to 9. Press the center button to enter a number and continue until you fill all four boxes. Confirm the combination by re-entering the sequence again on the next screen. You can also press the Menu button to bail out without locking the screen up.

❸ Now, when you want to lock your 'Pod, choose Extras→Screen Lock→ Lock. You also have the option to reset your code on this screen.

The iPod displays the Lock screen—even when it's asleep or connected to a computer—until you click the center button and enter the correct combination with the click wheel. If you enter the wrong digits, the lock icon stubbornly refuses to leave the screen.

 Note This lock's not foolproof: You (or someone else) can always get into the iPod by connecting it to the computer that it normally synchronizes with.

3

Touring the Touch

Traditional iPods may have their click wheels and buttons, but the iPod Touch brings a whole new level of control to your fingertips. In fact, your fingertips *are* the way you control this very special iPod. Instead of scrolling and clicking through menu after menu, the iPod Touch gives you a set of icons on its Home screen. Tap one and you instantly drop into the place you want to be—whether that's on the Web, amongst your favorite tunes, or in your photo collection.

In addition, the Touch comes preloaded with colorful little programs to let you keep tabs on the weather, the stock market, and even your email. But you're not limited to this standard-issue software, either—thanks to the iTunes App Store, you can turn your iPod into a personalized little pocket computer with its own games, utility programs, ebooks, and more.

This chapter gives you a close-up look at where to find everything on your iPod Touch, and how to customize it to your personal preferences. And, because playing music on this iPod is truly a hands-on experience, you'll learn everything you need to know to get your tunes cranked up and responding to your every tap.

Turn the Touch On and Off

The iPod Touch has only three physical buttons on the outside of its case. The Sleep/Wake button is the skinny black one on the top-left edge (circled).

Press this tiny sliver of a button once to put the Touch to sleep—that is, into Standby mode. Press it again to turn the screen on, so it's ready for action.

This small button also works as an On/Off switch to shut down your iPod completely; press it until the screen goes black and a red arrow commanding you to "Slide to power off" appears. Drag the red arrow to the right to power down your 'Pod. Press the Sleep/Wake button again when you're ready to turn the Touch back on.

The Home Button and Home Screen

The Home button is the one and only *real* button on the front of this iPod. Push it to summon the Home screen, which is your gateway to everything the iPod Touch does.

Having a Home button is a wonderful thing. It means you can never get lost. No matter how deeply you burrow into the Touch software, no matter how far off-track you find yourself, one push of the Home button takes you back to the main screen. Unlike other iPods, with their menu buttons and retraceable paths through submenus, the Home button is the *only* way out of some screens.

Pressing the Home button also wakes up the iPod from Standby mode. That's sometimes easier than finding the Sleep/Wake switch on top of the Touch.

 Tip The Home button is also a "force quit" button. If you press it for six seconds straight, whatever program you're running completely shuts down. It's a good failsafe maneuver when a particular program seems to be acting up.

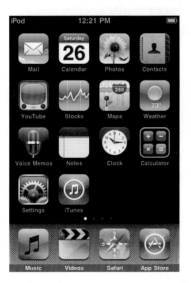

On the Home screen, you find all your Touchable icons, divided into two groups. The top part of the screen holds all your personal-information applications, including your email app, a calendar program, your photo albums, and an address book. Icons for a clock, calculator, Voice Memos, YouTube, and the iTunes Store are here, too. The Settings icon lets you set your preferences for many of these programs.

Want to rearrange the icons *on* the Touch? Press down on an icon until it wiggles, and then drag it to a new location. Press the Home button to make the icons sit still again. Once you fill up the Home screen with icons and applications, swipe your finger to the left to see your next screen full of icons. Swipe that finger the other way to go back to the first screen of icons.

The bottom row of icons is where the fun really begins. Here you find shortcuts to all the music and movies you copied from your computer to your iPod, plus the World Wide Web via Safari. And, thanks to that blue App Store icon, you're only a wireless network away from getting even more stuff.

What's in the Music Menu

Tap the Music icon and the Touch instantly transports you into a land of lists—lots of lists. The first four icons at the bottom of the screen (circled) represent your starter lists, as follows:

- **Genius.** Tap here to go right to those Genius Mixes that iTunes cooked up for you (Chapter 6).

- **Playlists.** A *playlist* is a group of songs you group together in a sequence that makes sense to you. One playlist might consist of party tunes; another might hold romantic dinner music. Chapter 6 tells you how to create them.

  Scroll the list by dragging your finger or flicking it. To see what songs are in a playlist, tap its name. (The > symbol in an iPod menu always means, "Tap to see what's in this list.")

- **Artists.** This list identifies all the bands, orchestras, or singers in your collection. Even if you have only one song from a certain performer, it shows up here. Once again, you drill down to the list of individual songs by tapping an artist's name. At that point, tap any song to play it.

- **Songs.** Here's an alphabetical list of every song on your iPod. Scroll or flick through it, or use the index at the right side of the screen to jump to a letter of the alphabet. Tap anything to begin playing it.

These four lists—Genius, Artists, Songs, and Albums—are only suggestions. On *old-school* click-wheel iPods, of course, you can slice and dice your music collection in all kinds of other listy ways: by album, genre, composer, and so on. You can do that on the iPod Touch, too; there just isn't room across the bottom row to hold more than four list icons at a time.

> **Tip** Here's a universal Touch convention: Anywhere the Touch asks you to *drill down* from one list to another—from a playlist to the songs inside, for example—you can backtrack by tapping the blue button in the upper-left corner of the screen. Its name changes to tell you what screen you came from (Playlists, for example).

To view some of the most useful secondary lists, tap the fifth and final icon, labeled "More". The More screen appears, listing a bunch of other ways to view your collection:

- **Albums.** That's right, it's a list of all the CDs from which you derived your music collection, complete with miniature pictures of the album art. Tap an album's name to see the list of songs you put on your 'Pod.

- **Audiobooks.** One of the great joys of life is listening to digital "books on tape" you bought from Audible.com (Chapter 7). They show up in this list. (Audio books you've ripped from CDs don't automatically show up here—only the ones you've downloaded from Audible.)

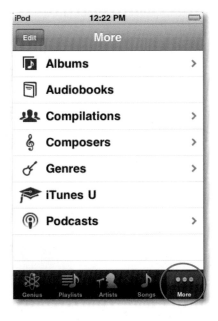

- **Compilations.** A *compilation* is one of those albums that has songs from different performers. You're supposed to turn on the Compilation checkbox manually, in iTunes (in the Preferences box's Advanced tab), to identify songs that belong together this way. Then, all the songs that belong to compilations show up in this list.

- **Composers.** Here's your whole music collection sorted by composer.

- **Genres.** Tap this item to sort your collection by musical genre (that is, by style): Pop, Rock, World, Soundtrack, Gospel, or whatever.

- **iTunes U.** College lectures, educational videos, and other academic pursuits from the iTunes U campus in the iTunes Store live here.

- **Podcasts.** Here are all your podcasts (Chapter 7), listed by creator. A blue dot indicates that you haven't yet listened to some episodes by a certain podcaster. Similarly, if you tap a podcast's name to drill down, you see the individual episodes, once again marked by blue "you haven't heard me yet" dots. (Half a dot means you started listening and stopped, with the remaining time listed under the episode title.)

> **Tip** At the bottom of any of these lists, you'll see the total number of items *in* that list: "76 Songs," for example. At the top of the screen, you may see the Now Playing button, which opens up the playback screen of whatever's playing.

What's in the Videos Menu

Tap this icon for one-stop browsing of all the video on your iPod Touch, organized by category:

- **Movies.** All your full-length feature films, downloaded movie trailers, and even your own filmmaking efforts live in this menu.

- **TV Shows.** When you're ready to catch up on your TV-watching, check this menu for your iTunes Store-purchased episodes and personally recorded shows.

- **Music Videos.** Music video clips, many of which are now offered as bonus material on iTunes album purchases, hang out here.

- **Video Podcasts.** Podcasts aren't just audio-only these days; look here for the full-blown video productions. (You see only one listing for each podcaster, along with the number of episodes you've got.)

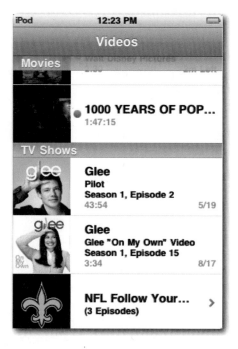

A handy thumbnail photo next to each video gives you a hint as to its content, and you also see the total playing time of each 'cast.

You can probably guess, at this point, how you start playing one: by tapping its name. But don't forget to rotate the Touch 90 degrees; all videos play in landscape orientation (the wide way). See Chapter 8 for more on video.

What's in the Photos Menu

The iPod Touch makes an extremely handsome—and portable—pocket photo album and slide carousel. Once you send copies of your favorite digital pictures from your computer to your iPod Touch, they land here in the Photos menu, all within easy reach of the Home screen.

Once you tap Photos, you see all your pictures grouped into one collection known as the Photo Library. If you choose to sync up specific photo albums from Adobe Photoshop Elements, iPhoto, or whatever compatible picture program you use, the Touch lists each album separately. The gray number in parentheses tells you how many pictures you have in the albums.

Tap the name of any library or album to see its pictures. To learn how to set up all this photo fun on your Touch, Chapter 9 has the scoop.

Tip See that Saved Photos album at the top of the picture up there? That's where the Touch stores photos you grab from the Web and email messages. To save a photo from a Safari page or a Mail attachment, press your finger on the picture until a Save Image button slides up from the bottom of the screen. Tap the button and the Touch deposits your photo in this Saved Photos album. Any screenshots you take on the Touch (see Chapter 9 for the Tip on that) land here as well.

What's in the Settings Menu

The iPod Touch is a powerful little media machine, and the Settings menu is where you go to fine-tune the player's preferences to your liking. Here's what you find by tapping the Settings icon on the Home screen:

- **Wi-Fi.** See what network you're connected to (or not), and turn the iPod's Wi-Fi antenna on or off here.

- **Brightness.** Sensors automatically detect the light in a room and adjust the Touch screen's brightness, but you can override that here.

- **General.** Here are the settings for the Touch's keyboard, sound effects, screen wallpaper, and auto-lock timer. Controls for network settings and Location Services (the Touch's GPS-like ability to plot your position on a map) are here, too. Newer Touch models can now use stereo Bluetooth headsets for wireless, tangle-free audio streams from iPod to ears, but you need to turn on the Bluetooth feature here. You'll also find the About screen, which tells you your iPod's serial number and how much stuff you have on it. If you're worried about who can see your iPod's contents, you can assign a four-digit number to unlock this screen in the Passcode settings. In the International area, you can choose the iPod screen's display language or pick an on-screen keyboard designed for typing in French, German, Italian, Japanese, and several other languages. You can also reset all the settings you've been fiddling with in the General area—and even erase all the iPod's content.

- **Music.** You can shuffle music by shaking the iPod (or not), turn the Equalizer and Sound Check features (Chapter 5) off or on, and set limits for your maximum volume here.

- **Video.** The Touch can remember where you stopped that video you were watching thanks to a setting here. You can also toggle Closed Captioning on or off. The TV Out settings for pumping the video signal from your iPod and into a TV set are here as well.

- **Photos.** Here's where you set how long each photo in a slideshow stays on-screen. You can pick artsy on-screen transitions like "Cube" or "Ripple" between images—and put the whole show on a constant repeat loop (just like TV shows on low-budget cable networks). To keep things interesting, you can also choose to randomly shuffle all the photos during your slideshow.

- **Store.** You can see the settings for the iTunes account used to purchase applications, music, and video from Apple's online digital shopping mall—and sign out of it if you don't want your account name displayed.

- **Mail, Contacts, Calendars.** Tap here to set up an email account right on the Touch. You can adjust all other Mail-related preferences here, too (like how often the Touch looks for new messages), and you can delete unwanted accounts. Scroll further down for the Contacts settings, where you can change the sort order of the first and last names of people in your Touch's address book. In the Calendars area, you get Time Zone controls to make sure your events are set for your own zone, and a toggle to turn new invitation alerts on or off. Chapter 10 has more on syncing contacts and calendars.

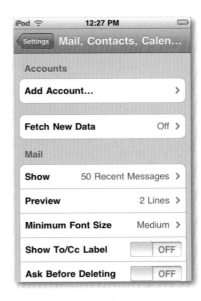

- **Safari.** The search and security preferences for the Touch's Wee Wide Web browser are located on this screen. Choose between Yahoo or Google as your default search engine, and whether you want the Autofill feature to fill in Web-site usernames and passwords for you. On the security front, you can enable a warning if you hit a fraudulent Web site, block pop-up ads and cookies, or clear out all the accumulated Web-page data left over from your surfing by clearing the cache. Chapter 11 has more on this.

- **Nike + Pod.** If you use the Nike + iPod kit in your daily workouts, tap the On button here to place a shortcut on the Touch's Home screen. You can also adjust your preferences for spoken feedback, measuring in miles or kilometers, and your personal "Power Song" to get you motivated.

- **Individual application settings.** Certain apps like Facebook and Stanza have their own settings screens as well. Tap an app to see and adjust the settings for that particular program.

Other Icons on the Touch Home Screen

The Music, Videos, and Photos icons on the Touch Home screen definitely get a workout, but there are several other icons awaiting your gentle tap as well:

- **Mail.** Tap here to check your email—or send some messages.

- **Safari.** Take a Web journey, no computer needed. Tap the Safari icon to fire up the browser; check out Chapter 11 to learn how to use it.

- **Calendar.** You can take a copy of your schedule with you from your computer's copy of iCal, Entourage, or Outlook. Chapter 10 tells you how.

- **Contacts.** Keep in touch on your Touch with the iPod's address book. See Chapter 10 for instructions on syncing old contacts or making new ones.

- **YouTube.** Wirelessly watch video from one of the world's most popular Web sites. See Chapter 8 for more on YouTube and other iPod video.

- **Stocks.** Check your portfolio and see how the market's doing. Tap the tiny ❶ in the bottom corner to spin the screen around and add your own ticker symbols to your palm-sized big board.

- **Maps.** Get directions or even *find yourself*. Chapter 11 shows the way.

- **Weather.** Current temperatures and forecasts for your favorite cities. Tap ❶ to flip the screen and add new towns. Swipe a finger across the screen to cycle through them.

- **Voice Memos.** Turn your Touch into an audio recorder. Chapter 10 tells you how.

- **Clock.** You can have one clock in your pocket— or keep time in several cities around the world at once. Chapter 10 has the details.

- **Calculator.** Tap the Calculator icon to get a big bright math machine, ready to divide and conquer for you. Hold the Touch sideways in its landscape mode to get a scientific calculator for when you need to do trigonometry on the go.

- **Notes.** Tap here to add a memo to yourself using the Touch keyboard.

- **iTunes.** The happy purple icon leads to shopping fun—without wires. Chapter 7 tells you what to expect once you get there.

- **App Store.** Tap here for games, ebooks, and more to tickle your Touch.

Set Up and Check Your Mail

When inside a Wi-Fi hotspot, the Touch is also a traveling email machine that lets you check, write, and send messages. And just as there are two ways to get apps on the Touch, there are two ways to get your email account settings in place on your mini musical computer.

- **Sync mail settings with iTunes.** You get email on your computer, right? If you're using a dedicated program like Apple Mail or Microsoft Outlook, you can copy those account settings over to the Touch. Connect the Touch to your computer, click its icon in iTunes, and then click the Info tab. Scroll down to Mail Accounts and put a check in the box next to "Sync selected mail accounts." Pick the accounts you want to tote around on the Touch. Click 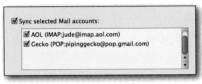 Sync or Apply to copy the settings—but not your computer-based messages—over to the Touch, where you can check mail on the run.

- **Set up mail accounts on the Touch.** Tap the Mail icon. If you use Exchange, MobileMe, Gmail, Yahoo, or AOL, tap the appropriate icon. If you don't use any of those, tap Other. On the next screen, type in your name, email address, password, and a short description ("Personal Gmail", say). If you tapped Other, be prepared to type in the same settings you got from your Internet provider when you signed up for the account. Click Save and the  Mail program goes out and gets your new messages. Need help sorting through email geekery like the difference between IMAP and POP? Check out this book's Missing CD page at *www.missingmanuals.com*.

Mail on the Touch looks and works pretty much like any other email program. Here's the layout:

❶ **Mailboxes.** Your incoming, outgoing, and drafts (saved messages-in-progress) live here.

❷ **Check for new mail.** Tap the circular arrow to see if you have fresh messages.

❸ **Write a new message.** Tap the icon in the bottom-right corner to fire up a new message. Fill in the address, your thoughts, and tap Send.

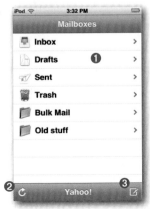

Fancier Fingerwork for the iPod Touch

Now that you've mastered the old tap, drag, flick, and slide (see Chapter 1 for a refresher), there are two more iPod Touch moves to add to your repertoire. The player uses these maneuvers in its more visually oriented programs, like the Safari Web browser, and in Photos and Movies.

Finger Spread and Pinch

Tiny Web page type can be hard to read, or maybe you want to take a closer look at a certain photo. To zoom in, put your thumb and index finger together, place them on what you want to see, and make a spreading motion across the screen to zoom in on that area. To zoom out, pinch your fingers closer together on-screen. Chapter 11 is all about using the Web on the Touch, and Chapter 9 shows you how to give your photos (and fingers) a workout.

Double-Tap

You may be used to double-clicking a computer mouse, but on the iPod Touch, one tap usually does it. Still, there are at least two places within the Touch where double-tapping pays off:

- In the Safari Web browser or in Photos, tap the screen twice to quickly zoom in and magnify the area you just tapped.

- When watching a video, tap the screen twice to toggle back and forth between screen aspect ratios—the full-screen view (below, left) where the edges of the frame get cropped off, or the widescreen, letterboxed view (right), which movie lovers favor because it's what the director really intended a scene to look like.

Cut and Paste By Touch

Since it arrived in 2007, one of the most sought-after features for the iPod Touch was the power to cut, copy, and paste text and images. In mid-2009, Apple made it happen. Here's how to move text and images around from place to place—or program to program—on your 'Pod:

❶ To cut or copy from text you can edit (like an outgoing email or a note you create), double-tap the word to highlight it. A Cut | Copy | Paste box pops up. To select more words, drag the blue dots on either end of the selected word to highlight the text. Then tap the Cut or Copy command.

❷ For pages you *can't* edit (like incoming emails), hold your finger down until a magnifying glass and insertion-point cursor appear. Drag it to the text you want to copy. When you lift your finger, a Select or Select All box appears. Select gives you the blue dots you can drag to highlight more text or photos. Select All highlights all the text. Lift your finger to get a Copy button. A Web page is a little different: When you lift your finger there, you go right to the Copy button.

❸ Tap the place in the file you want to paste the text—or jump to a different program completely and tap within it to get the Paste button.

❹ Tap the Paste button to copy the text into the new location, file, or program.

Make a mistake and wish you could undo what you just did? Give the Touch a quick shake and tap the Undo Edit button that appears on-screen.

Want to copy a photo or video so you can email it? Hold your finger down until the Copy button pops up. Tap it, create an email, and tap the message body to get a Paste button. Tap it and paste away.

> **Tip** The Notes program on the Touch is a handy place to stash text when you find something from a Web page or email message that you want to keep. If you use Outlook 2003 or 2007 for Windows or the Mail program that comes with Mac OS X 10.5.7, you can sync your notes back and forth between Touch and computer. Just connect the Touch to the computer, click its icon in the iTunes Source list, and click the Info tab. Scroll down and turn on the Sync Notes checkbox, then click Apply.

Customize Your Touch Menus

The Touch Music menus described earlier in this chapter showed how you can sort your collection by every conceivable criterion. But what if you're a huge podcast nut? Are you really expected to open up the More screen every time you want to see your list of podcasts? Or what if you frequently want access to your audiobooks or composer list?

Fortunately, you can add icons for these lists to the bottom of the main iPod Touch screen, where the four starter categories (Playlists, Artists, Songs, and Albums) now appear. That is, you can replace or rearrange the icons that show up here, so that the lists you use most frequently are easily available.

To renovate the four starter icons, tap the More button and then tap the Edit button (upper-left corner). You arrive at the Configure screen.

Here's the complete list of music-and-video sorting lists: Genius, Playlists, Artists, Songs, Albums, Audiobooks, Compilations, Composers, Genres, iTunes U, and Podcasts. As you can see, there's a lot to choose from.

To replace one of the four starter icons at the bottom, use a finger to drag an icon from the top half of the screen downward, *directly onto* the icon you want to replace. It lights up to show the success of your drag. Lift your finger and the new icon replaces the old one.

Don't worry, you won't lose the old icon; the Touch keeps copies of all of the icons in the Edit window.

When you release your finger, you'll see that the new icon has replaced the old one. Tap Done in the upper-right corner.

Oh, and while you're there on the Configure screen: You can also take this opportunity to *rearrange* the first four icons at the bottom. Drag them around with your finger. It's fun for the whole family.

Cover Flow in Motion

Anytime you use the iPod Touch for music, whether you're playing songs or just flipping through your lists, you can rotate the Touch 90 degrees in either direction—so it's in landscape orientation—to turn on Cover Flow. *Nothing* gets oohs and ahhhs from the admiring crowd like Cover Flow.

In Cover Flow, the screen goes dark for a moment—and then it reappears, showing two-inch-tall album covers, floating on a black background. Push or flick with your fingers to make them fly and flip over in 3-D space, as though they're CDs in a record-store rack (remember those?).

If you tap one (or tap the little ❸ button in the lower-right corner), the album flips around so you can see the "back" of it, containing a list of songs from that album. Tap a song to start playing it; tap the ‖ in the lower-left corner to pause. Tap the back (or the ❸ button) again to flip the album cover back to the front and continue browsing.

To turn off Cover Flow, rotate the iPod upright again.

So what, exactly, is Cover Flow for? You could argue that it's a unique way to browse your collection, to seek inspiration in your music without having to stare at scrolling lists of text. But you could also argue that it's just Apple's engineers showing off.

> **Tip** With all the audio and video files—not to mention email messages, contacts, calander appointments, and other stuff—on your Touch, you may be wishing for a quick way to find a specific item. Wish no more. On the Home screen, just swipe your finger to the right instead of to the left to get a handy Search box.

The Now Playing Screen: The Basics

Whenever you have a song playing, the Now Playing screen appears, filled with information and controls for your playback pleasure. For example:

- **Return arrow.** At the top-left corner of the screen, the fat, left-pointing arrow means, "Return to the list from whence this song came." It takes you back to the list of songs in this album, playlist, or whatever.

- **Song info.** Center top: the artist name, track name, and album name. Nothing to tap here, folks. Move along.

- **Song list.** At the top-right corner, you see a three-line icon that seems to say "list". Tap it to view a list of all songs on *this* song's album.

Return to list

Songs on this album

Swipe to return to list

Volume slider

Tip You can also issue spoken commands to the iPod and have it obey with the Voice Control feature—if you have a 32- or 64-gigabyte Touch from late 2009. To use it, hold down the Home button until the Voice Control screen appears and beeps. Then speak your commands clearly into the headphone mic. Sample commands include "Play artist [Beyoncé]" or "Play album [Rubber Soul]." Say "Shuffle" to shuffle or "Genius" to hear similar tracks. "Play" and "Pause" work as commands and you can even ask "What's playing?" To turn off Voice Control, say "Stop" or "Cancel."

On the screen that appears, you're offered three enjoyable activities. You can jump directly to another track by tapping its name. You can check out the durations of the songs on this album. And you can *rate* a song, ranking it from one to five stars, by tapping its name and then tapping one of the five dots at the top of the screen.

If you tap dot number 3, for example, then the first three dots all turn into stars. You've just given that song three stars. When you next sync your Touch with your computer, the ratings you applied magically show up on the same songs in iTunes.

To return to the Now Playing screen, tap the upper-right icon once again. (Once you tap, that icon looks like the album cover.) Or, for a bigger target, double-tap any blank part of the screen.

- **Album art.** The touch fills most of the screen with a bright, colorful shot of the original CD's album art. (If none is available—if you're listening to a song *you* wrote, for example—you see a big gray generic musical-note picture.)

Tip You can double-tap the big album art picture to open the track list, too. It's a bigger target.

The Now Playing Screen: Song Maneuvers

Once you're on the Now Playing screen, a few controls await your fingertip—some obvious and some not so obvious.

- **Play/Pause (▶/II) button.** The Pause button looks like this II when the music is playing. If you do pause a song, the button turns into the Play button (▶).

- **Previous, Next (I◀◀, ▶▶I).** These buttons work exactly as they do on any other iPod. That is, tap I◀◀ to skip to the beginning of this song (or, if you're already at the begin-ning, to skip to the previous song). Tap ▶▶I to skip to the next song.

If you hold down one of these buttons instead of tapping, you rewind or fast-forward through a song. It's rather cool, actually—you hear the music speed by as you keep your finger down, without turning the singer into a chipmunk. The rewinding or fast-forwarding accelerates if you keep holding down the button.

- **Volume.** Drag the round, white handle of this scroll bar (bottom of the screen) to adjust song volume. (You can also use the Volume rocker on the left side of the Touch, if you've got a second-generation model.)

> **Tip** "Okay," you're saying to yourself, "These playback controls are all well and good when I'm on the Now Playing screen—but what if I'm browsing my photos and I want to skip over this one track I hate? Do I have to tap my way back through the Home screen to Music so I can skip ahead to the next song?"
>
> Not at all. Tap the Home button twice to bring up a mini-control panel where you can get to the playback controls, no matter where you are in the non-musical parts of the Touch. You can adjust the volume, pause, move to the next or previous track, and even see what's playing. If you need to get back to the Music menu, tap the Music button in the corner to go there immediately.

Of course, you probably didn't need a handsome full-color book to tell you what those basic playback controls are for. But there's also a quartet of *secret* controls that don't appear until you tap on an empty part of the screen (for example, on the album cover, but only when your 'Pod is vertical—remember, if you tap an album cover in horizontal mode, you get the track list):

- **Loop button.** If you *really* love a certain album or playlist, you can command the iPod to play it over and over again, beginning to end. Just tap the Loop button (⟳) so that it turns blue (⟳).

- **Scroll slider.** This slider (top of the screen) reveals three useful statistics: how much of the song you've heard, in "minutes:seconds" format (at the left end), how much time remains (at the right end), and which slot this song occupies in the current playlist or album.

  To operate the slider, drag the tiny round handle with your finger. (Just tapping directly on the spot you want to hear doesn't work.)

- **Genius playlist.** Tap the ✳ icon to make a Genius playlist based on this song. Chapter 6 has the details.

- **Shuffle button.** Ordinarily, the iPod plays the songs in an album sequentially, from beginning to end. But if you love surprises, tap the ⤫ button so it turns blue. Now you'll hear the songs on the album in random order.

  To hide the secret buttons, tap an empty part of the screen once again.

  By the way, there's nothing to stop you from turning on *both* Shuffle *and* Loop, meaning that you'll hear the songs on the album played endlessly, but never in the same order twice.

Tip If you're looping an album and hear a song you love, tap the Loop button a second time to endlessly loop *just that song*. A tiny number icon appears on the blue loop graphic, like this ⟳, to let you know that you've entered this mode. Tap a third time to turn off looping.

Install (and Uninstall) New Apps

Programs from the App Store give your Touch all sorts of new powers. If you're anxious to try some out, here are two ways to trick out your Touch:

- **Buy apps in the iTunes Store.** Click the App Store link on the main Store page. After you shop, connect the Touch to your computer, and sync 'em up. Chapter 5 explains the fine art of syncing.

- **Buy apps on the Touch.** When you've got a Wi-Fi connection, tap the blue App Store icon on the Home screen and browse away. At the top of the Featured screen, you can see what's new and hot—or what the iTunes Genius thinks you might like. At the bottom of the screen, you can find apps grouped by category or by the Top 25 apps in the Store. A Search icon (🔍) awaits if you're looking for something specific. When you find an app you want, tap the price icon; it turns into a Buy Now button. Hit that, type in your iTunes Store name and password (even if it's a free application), and the download begins. After

the program finishes loading and installing, tap its icon to launch your new app and start using it.

It's a fact of life: sometimes apps don't work out. They're not what you thought they'd be, they're buggy and crashy (it happens), or they're taking up too much precious Touch space. Here are two ways to uninstall an app:

- **Remove apps in iTunes.** Connect the Touch to your computer, click its icon in the iTunes window, and click the Applications tab. In the list, deselect the apps you want to remove and then click Sync to uninstall them.

- **Remove apps on the Touch.** On the Home screen, press and hold the unwanted application's icon until an X appears in the wiggling icon's corner. Tap the X, confirm your intention to delete, and wave goodbye to that app. Press the Home button to return to business as usual.

 See a red circled number on the App Store icon? You've got updates waiting for that number of apps; tap the icon to see what they are. Tap the name of the program you want to update, tap the Price button (don't worry, updates are free), and then tap Install. The program upates after you type in your Store password.

Manage Apps in iTunes

Earlier in this chapter, you learned how to rearrange the icons on the Home screen of your Touch. And after reading the previous page, you may now have a *ton* of groovy new app icons all over your Touch—but not in the order you'd like them. Sure, you can drag wiggling icons all over your nine pages of Home screen, but that can get a little confusing and frustrating if you accidentally drop an icon on the wrong page.

Fortunately, iTunes 9 lets you arrange all your Touch icons from the comfort of your big-screen computer:

❶ **Connect the iPod to your computer.** Click its icon in the Source list.

❷ **Click the Applications tab.** You now see all your applications—plus giant versions of all the separate pages of your Touch Home screen, all lined up vertically on the right side.

❸ **Select the icons you want to move.** Once you click an icon you want to move on the large screen, drag it to the desired page thumbnail displayed along the right side of the screen to move it there. It's much easier to group similar apps on a page this way—you can have, say, a page of games or a page of online newspapers. You can even change the four permanent icons in the gray bar on the bottom of the Touch screen.

❹ **Click Apply or Sync.** Wait just a moment as iTunes rearranges the icons on your iPod Touch, so they mirror how you have them in iTunes.

iTunes Basics

If you read Chapter 1 to find a speedy way to get your iPod set up and ready to play, you've already dipped a toe into the iTunes waters. But as you may have guessed, beneath its pretty surface, iTunes is a deep well of media-management wonders.

Even without buying music from the online iTunes Store, you can use the program to import music from your CD collection and add personal ratings, lyrics, and artwork to your song files. Once you check everything into your iTunes library, the program makes it easy to browse and search through all your treasures—and automatically mix your music.

Yes, iTunes is a powerful program. So powerful, in fact, that this chapter will focus on its most basic and useful functions—like what the controls do and how to import music from CDs. If you want to learn more about fine-tuning your library, Chapter 5 covers more advanced iTunes features. Chapter 6 tells you how to create customized song playlists, Chapter 7 is all about blowing your bucks in the iTunes Store, and Chapter 8 spotlights the video side of iTunes.

But enough of the introductory blah-blah. Turn the page if you want to get to know iTunes better.

The iTunes Window: An Introduction

iTunes is your iPod's best friend. You can do just about everything with your digital music here—convert songs on a CD into iPod-ready music files, buy music, listen to Internet radio stations, watch video—and more.

Here's a quick tour of the main iTunes window and what all the buttons, controls, and sliders do.

The Source panel on the left side of iTunes displays all the audio and video you can tap into at the moment. Click any item listed in the Source column to display its contents in the main window, like so:

❶ Click any icon in the Library group to see what's in your different media libraries. As you add movies, music, and other stuff to iTunes, click the appropriate icon to find what you're looking for—a song, a TV show, and so on. Programs you buy for the iPod Touch land here under Applications. Want to change the items you see listed? Press Ctrl+comma (⌘-comma) to call up iTunes Preferences menu and then click the General tab. In the "Show:" area, turn on (or off) the checkboxes for, say, Ringtones or iTunes U, as you see fit.

❷ In the Store area, click the shopping-bag icon to shop for new stuff in the iTunes Store or the green curled-page icon to see the list of things you already bought. The Downloads icon (a green down-arrow) shows items you're downloading from the store, or files ready for you to snag.

❸ If you have a music CD in your computer's drive, it shows up in the Devices area, as will a connected iPod. Click the gray Eject icon next to the name to safely pop out a disc or disconnect an iPod.

❹ In the Shared area, browse the media libraries of other iTunes fans on your network. You can stream music if you see a blue stacked playlist, or copy music and videos between machines with the Home Sharing feature turned on.

❺ iTunes keeps all your custom song lists—whether the iTunes Genius automatically generated them or you lovingly handcrafted them—in the Genius and Playlists sections. The iTunes DJ feature, which quickly whips up party mixes, lives here too.

❻ When you click an item in the Source list—Music, in this case—iTunes' main window displays all the things in that category. Three columns above the main song list let you browse through the genres, artists, and albums in your collection. Naturally, this part of the window is called the Column Browser. It's shown here in the top position, but you can display your chosen browser categories as a series of vertical columns on the left side of the iTunes window by choosing View→Column Browser→On Left.

The outer edges of the iTunes window are full of buttons and controls:

❼ Play and pause your current song or video—or jump to the next or previous track. The volume slider adjusts the sound.

❽ The center of the upper pane shows you what song's playing. To the right of that you have handy buttons to change views within the main part of the window and a search box for finding songs fast.

❾ At the bottom-left corner are shortcut buttons for (from left to right) making a new playlist, shuffling or repeating your playlists, and displaying album artwork or videos.

❿ The lower-right corner of iTunes is where the Genius controls hang out. When you have a song selected, click the whizzy electron-shaped icon to create a Genius playlist (Chapter 6) based on that song. The boxed-arrow icon toggles the Genius Sidebar panel on (it's stocked with "Buy these songs" suggestions to help round out your library), and off (to leave you in peace).

Change the Look of the iTunes Window

Don't be misled by the brushed-aluminum look of iTunes: You can push and pull various window parts like salt-water taffy.

- Adjust how much of the iTunes Browser—the three-pane quick-browse area that opens and closes when you press Ctrl+B (⌘-B)—by dragging the tiny dot at the top of the song list window up or down. The same keyboard shortcut toggles the browser off and on. (You can also put the browser on the left; see page 75.)

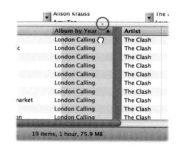

- iTunes divides the main song list into columns that you can sort or re-arrange. Click a column title (like Name or Album) to sort the list alpha-betically. Click the column title again to reverse the sort order. Change the order of the columns themselves by dragging them, as shown above.

- To adjust a column's width, drag the right-hand vertical divider line. (You may need to grab the line in the column title bar.)

- To resize all the columns so their contents fit precisely, right-click (Control-click) any column title and choose Auto Size All Columns.

- To add (or delete) columns, right-click (Control-click) any column title. From the pop-up list of column categories (Bit Rate, Date Added, and so on), choose the column name you want to add or remove. Checkmarks indicate currently visible columns.

- Click the black triangle in the first column to display or hide album covers alongside song titles. If you don't have any artwork for the song, iTunes displays the generic Gray Musical Note icon. If you find life has too many gray areas already, the next chapter tells you how to add album artwork to your files.

Change the Size of the iTunes Window

Lovely as iTunes is, it takes up a heck of a lot of screen real estate. When you're working on other things, you can shrink it down. In fact, iTunes can run in three size modes: small, medium, or large:

❶ *Large.* This is what you get the first time you open iTunes. (Hate the music hard-sell from the Genius Sidebar on the right? Close the panel by clicking the square button in the lower-right corner.)

❷ *Medium.* Windows folks: Switch back and forth between large and medium by pressing Ctrl+M (Shift-⌘-M) or choosing View→Switch to Mini Player.

❸ *Small.* To really scrunch things down, start with the medium-size window. Then drag the resize handle (the diagonal lines in the lower-right corner) leftward. To expand it, just reverse the process.

Tired of losing your mini-iTunes window among the vast stack of open windows on your screen? You can make the iTunes mini-player *always* visible on top of other open documents, windows, and assorted screen detritus. Open iTunes Preferences (Ctrl+comma [⌘-comma]), click the Advanced tab, and turn on the checkbox next to "Keep Mini Player on top of all other windows." Now you won't have to click frantically around the screen trying to find iTunes if you get caught listening to your bubblegum-pop playlist.

Import Specific Songs From Your CDs

In Chapter 1 you learned how iTunes simplifies converting (also called *ripping*) songs from your compact discs into small iPod-ready digital files: You basically just pop a CD into your computer's disc drive and iTunes walks you through the process. If you're connected to the Internet, iTunes downloads song titles and other album info. A few minutes later, you've got copies of those tunes in iTunes.

If you want time to think about *which* songs you want from each CD, no problem. Simply summon the Preferences box (Ctrl+comma [⌘-comma]), click the General tab, and then change the menu next to "When you insert a CD:" to "Show CD."

 Tip If you know you want all the songs on that stack of CDs next to your computer, just change the iTunes CD import preferences to "Import CD and Eject" to save yourself some clicking.

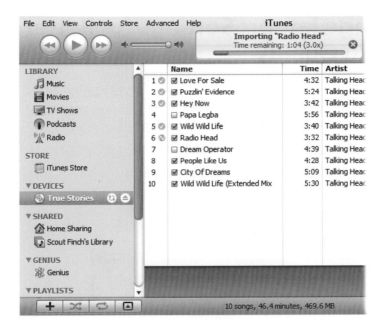

So now, if you don't want to rip an entire album—who wants anything from Don McLean's *American Pie* besides the title track?—you can exclude the songs you *don't* want by removing the checkmarks next to their names. Once you pick your songs, in the bottom-right corner of the screen, click the Import CD button.

You can Ctrl+click (⌘-click) any box to deselect all the checkboxes at once. To turn them all on again, Ctrl+click (⌘-click) a box next to an unchecked song. This is a great technique when you want only one or two songs in the list; turn off *all* the checkboxes, and then turn on only those *two* tracks.

As the import process starts, iTunes moves down the list of checked songs, converting each one to a file in your Music→iTunes→iTunes Media→Music folder for Windows 7 or Home→Music→iTunes→iTunes Music on a Mac OS X system. An orange squiggle next to a song name means that iTunes is currently converting the track. Feel free to switch to other programs, answer email, surf the Web, or do any other work as iTunes rips away.

Once iTunes finishes up, each imported song bears a green checkmark, and the program signals its success with a melodious little flourish. Now you have some brand-new songs in your iTunes music library.

Change Import Settings for Better Audio Quality

iPods can play several different digital audio formats: AAC, MP3, WAV, AIFF, and a format called Apple Lossless. Feel free to safely ignore that last sentence, as well as the rest of this page, if you're *happy* with the way your music sounds on your iPod or a pair of external speakers.

If you find the audio quality lacking, you can change the way iTunes encodes, or *converts*, songs during the CD conversion process. iTunes gives you two main options in its import settings box (Edit [iTunes for Macs]→Preferences→General, and then click the Import Settings button to get there): They are:

- **Audio format (use the drop-down menu beside "Import Using").** Some formats tightly compress audio data to save space. The tradeoff: lost sound quality. Highly compressed formats include AAC (iTunes' default setting) and MP3. Formats that use little or no compression include WAV and AIFF, sound better, but take up more space. Apple Lossless splits the difference: Better sound quality than AAC and MP3, but not as hefty as WAV or AIFF.

- **Bit rate (beside "Setting").** The higher the number of bits listed, the greater the amount of data contained in the file (in other words, your files take up more storage space). The advantage? Better sound quality.

To see a song's format and other technical information, click its title in iTunes, press Ctrl+I (⌘-I), and then click the Summary tab in the Get Info box.

Three Ways to Browse Your Collection

Instead of just presenting you with boring lists of songs and albums, iTunes gives you three options for browsing your media collection—some of them more visual than others. Click the View button at the top of iTunes to switch among views.

- **List View** presents the traditional way of displaying song titles. Press Ctrl+B (⌘-B) on the keyboard to toggle on and off the browser that shows vertical (or horizontal) panes grouping your music by genre, artist, and album. Press Ctrl+Alt+3 (Option-⌘-3) to jump back to List View from another view.

- **Grid View** presents your collection in a nifty array of album covers and other artwork. You can sort the grid by album, artist, genre, or composer. There's a lot you can do in Grid View, so flip the page for more. Press Ctrl+Alt+4 (Option-⌘-4) to switch to the Grid.

- **Cover Flow.** If you *really* like album art, this view's for you. Ctrl+Alt+5 (Option-⌘-5) is the shortcut. In the top part of iTunes, your collection appears as a stream of album covers. To browse them, press the left- and right-arrow keys on the keyboard or drag the scroll bar underneath the albums to see them whiz by. If that's not enough visual stim-

ulation for you, click the little Full Screen button by the slider bar to turn your whole screen into Cover View, complete with playback controls.

Get a Birds-Eye Look at Your Collection with Grid View

Although it's been around since iTunes 8, Grid View is still probably the most eye-catching way to see your media library. It's like laying out all your albums on the living room floor—great for seeing everything you've got, without the hassle of having to pick it all back up. More picturesque than List View and not quite as moving as Cover Flow, Grid View is the middle road to discovering (or rediscovering) what's in your iTunes library.

iTunes offers four ways to see your collection: grouped by album, artist, genre, or composer. Click each named tab to see the music sorted by that category. (If you don't see the tabs, choose View→Grid View→Show Header.) Here's how to work the Grid:

- Hover your mouse over any tile on the grid to get a clickable Play icon that lets you start listening to the music.

- Double-click a cover in Albums view to display both the cover and song titles in List View.

- If you have mutliple albums under the Artists, Genres, or Composers tabs, hover your mouse over each tile to rotate through the album covers. If you want to represent the group using a particular album cover or piece of art, right-click it and choose Set Default Grid Artwork. You can do the opposite for art you *don't* want to see: right-click it and choose Clear Deafult Grid Artwork.

- Adjust the size of the covers and art by dragging the slider at the top of the window.

One thing about Grid View, though: It's pretty darn depressing unless you have artwork on just about everything in your collection. (If you don't, and you see far too many generic musical-note icons there, Chapter 5 shows you how to art things up.) And if you hate Grid View, don't use it—iTunes just defaults to whatever view you were using the last time you quit the program.

Search for Songs in iTunes

You can call up a list of all the songs with a specific word in their title, album name, or artist attribution just by clicking the Source pane's Music icon (under Library) and typing a few letters into the Search box in iTunes' upper-right corner. With each letter you type, iTunes shortens the list of songs it displays, showing you only tracks that match what you type.

For example, typing *train* brings up a list of everything in your music collection that has the word "train" somewhere in the song's information—maybe the song's title ("Mystery Train"), the band name (Wire Train), or the Steve Earle album (*Train A Comin'*). Click the other Library icons, like Movies or Audiobooks, to comb those collections for titles that match a search term.

Another way to search for specific titles is to use the iTunes Browser mentioned earlier in this chapter. If you can't see the browser pane, press Ctrl+B (⌘-B) to summon it. Depending on how you configured it in View→Column Browser, the browser reveals your music collection grouped by genre, artist, and album. Hit the same keys again (Ctrl+B [⌘-B]) to close the browser.

 Tip If you find List View deadly dull without art, a quick keyboad shortcut pops open the Artwork column next to the song titles from that album. Just press Ctrl+G (⌘-G) to jazz up the List window with graphics. After all, Grid View and Cover Flow can't have all the visual fun now, can they?

Shuffle Your Music in Many Ways

With its sometimes uncanny ability to randomly pluck and play songs that seem perfect together, iTunes' Shuffle feature has won over a huge number of fans, especially those who don't want to think about what to listen to as they noodle around the Internet. To start shuffling, click the twisty-arrows icon down on the bottom-left corner of the iTunes window.

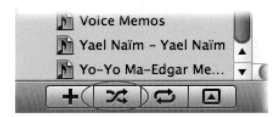

You're not stuck with a single shuffling method, either. Some days you may feel like mixing up your music song by song, and other days you may be more in the mood to change things up by album.

You can control just what you shuffle by choosing Controls→Shuffle and selecting Songs, Albums, or Groupings from the submenu. (As explained in the next chapter, Grouping is a way to keep cetain tracks together in your iTunes library, like separate classical-music movements that are part of a larger work in the Classical music category.)

Animate Your Songs: iTunes Visualizer

Visualizer is the iTunes term for an onscreen laser-light show that pulses, beats, and dances in perfect sync to your music. The effect is hypnotic and wild, especially when summoned midway through a sluggish day in the office.

Choose View→Visualizer to select from *iTunes Visualizer* (lots of Disco in Space moments) or *iTunes Classic Visualizer* (trippy psychedelic patterns a-go-go). Mac users running OS X 10.5 or later even get three more colorful themes to choose from: *Lathe*, *Jelly*, and *Stix*.

❶ To summon the scenery, choose View→Show Visualizer. The show begins immediately. To see a tiny onscreen menu of even more controls for Visualizer or Classic Visualizer, press the / key and then the letter of the desired command listed on screen. It's a great way to fiddle.

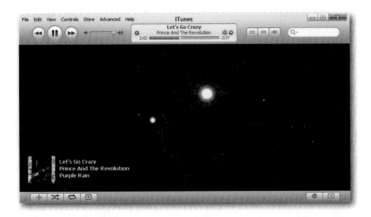

Tip The keyboard shortcut for turning the Visualizer off and on is Ctrl+T (⌘-T).

❷ If you find the iTunes window too constraining for all this eye candy, you can play it full screen by going to the Preferences box (Ctrl+comma [⌘-comma]) and clicking the Advanced tab. Put a check in the box next to "Display visualizer full screen."

True, you won't get a lot of work done, but when it comes to stress relief, visuals are a lot cheaper than a hot tub.

5

iTunes Power Moves

Now that you've seen how easy iTunes makes converting your favorite CD tracks into small, great-sounding files, it's time to get down to some serious listening and tune-tweaking. With iTunes, you can do things like assign star ratings to songs and albums, share music and videos with other folks on your network, and even add album artwork to your tracks.

You'll also learn how to use iTunes as an editor: the program gives you the tools to change song formats, edit out boring on-stage banter on live recordings, and apply preset or customized equalizer settings to tracks. Once you get everything tuned to your liking, you'll learn how to add, delete, and manually manage the music on your iPod.

Finally, you'll learn how iTunes can help with a vital—but often ignored—part of music management: backing up your catalog for safe-keeping in case your hard drive croaks and takes all your songs with it.

You're the Critic: Rate Your Music

Although there's no way to give a song two thumbs up in iTunes, you *can* assign an album or each song in your collection a rating of from one to five stars. Then you can use the ratings to produce nothing but playlists of the greatest hits on your hard drive.

If you assign an album a single rating, *all* the songs on the album get the same number of stars. If you rate just a few tracks on an album but not all of them, the album rating reflects the average of the *rated* songs—so an album with two five-star songs and a bunch of unrated tracks gets a five-star rating.

❶ To add ratings, first make sure you turn on the Album Rating and/or Rating columns in the iTunes View Options box (Ctrl+J [⌘-J]).

❷ Highlight the row that has the song you want to rate by clicking it. iTunes displays five dots in the Rating column (in the iTunes main window). When you click a dot, iTunes turns it into a star. Now either drag the mouse across the column to create one to five stars, or click one of the dots itself to apply a rating (click the third dot, for example, and iTunes gives the song three stars).

❸ Once you assign ratings, you can sort your song list by star rating (click the Album Rating or Rating column title), create a Smart Playlist of only your personal favorites (File→New Smart Playlist; choose Album Rating or Rating from the first drop-down menu), and so on.

You can even rate songs on your iPod, and iTunes records the ratings the next time you sync up.

To rate a song on your iPod, start playing it and tap the Select button a few times until you see dots on-screen. Use the scroll wheel to transform the dots into the number of stars you feel the song deserves. Your star ratings also show up on the iPod's Now Playing screen.

> **Tip** If you're more menu-oriented, you can add stars from up top in the iTunes menu. With a track selected, choose File→Rating, slide over to the submenu, and apply the number of stars you feel the song deserves. This is also the place to go if you inadvertently rated a song: Choose None to return a song to its pristine, unrated condition.

Listen to Internet Radio

Not satisfied with being a mere virtual jukebox, iTunes also serves as an international radio—without the shortwave static. You can tune in everything from mystical Celtic melodies to Zambian hip hop. Computers with high-speed Internet connections have a smoother streaming experience, but the vast and eclectic mix of music is well worth checking out—even with a dial-up modem. Just click the Radio icon in iTunes' Source list to see a list of stations.

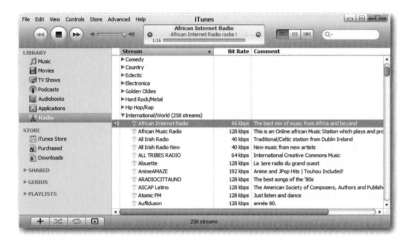

If you find your radio streams constantly stuttering and stopping, summon iTunes' Preferences box (Ctrl+comma [⌘-comma]). Click the Advanced icon or tab on the right side of the box. Then, from the Streaming Buffer Size pop-up menu, choose Large. Click OK. You may have to wait a little longer for the music to start, but iTunes will pre-load enough data to reduce the stutters.

Once you listen to all the stations listed in iTunes, hit the Internet. You can find more radio stations at *www.shoutcast.com*. Windows 7 and Mac OS X users can play them through iTunes by clicking the yellow Tune In button. (If this is your first time at Shoutcast, a prompt asks how you want to hear the stream—click the button for iTunes.) XP users, save the offered *.pls* file to your desktop and then drag and drop it on "Playlists". Click the resulting "tunein-station" playlist.

Tip Radio stations do a great job of making song volumes even from song to song—and you can do the same with iTunes. Open the Preferences box (Ctrl+comma [⌘-comma]). Click the Playback icon or tab and turn on the box for Sound Check. You also need to turn on Sound Check on your iPod. On the Nano's main screen, choose Settings→Playback→Sound Check and click the Select button. On the Classic, choose Settings→Sound Check. On the iPod Touch choose Settings→Music and then tap Sound Check "On". The next time you connect your iPod to your computer, iTunes makes the necessary audio adjustments.

Share Your iTunes Music and Videos

Now that you've built a fabulous media collection, you may feel like sharing it. You can, under one condition: Your fellow sharers need to be on the same computer network. For instance, family members on your home network: kosher. Cousin Ferdinand, living in another state: not kosher.

The power to share music—that is, stream it between computers—has been with iTunes for years. But you can do much more than stream songs with the new *Home Sharing* feature in iTunes 9. With Home Sharing, you can actually *copy* music and video files from one computer to another.

Sounds great, doesn't it? Home Sharing does have its limits, though. For starters, you can only share content among five computers. Each also needs:

- A network connection (either wired or wireless).

- A copy of iTunes 9 installed.

- The name and password of the same iTunes Store account or App Store account (see Chapter 7 if you need one).

One you have all these things in hand, it's time to share:

❶ In the iTunes Source list, click the Home Sharing icon. On the screen that appears, type in an iTunes account name and password. (If you don't see the cute little house-shaped Home Sharing icon in the Source list, choose Advanced→Turn On Home Sharing. If you get told to authorize the computer for that iTunes account, choose Store→Authorize Computer.)

❷ Click the Create Home Share button.

❸ Repeat these steps for every computer you want to share with on the network (up to four others).

Once you set up all the computers, each of their iTunes libraries appears in everyone's Source list. Click the triangle beside the house icon for the library you want to explore. After iTunes hits the network, icons for that library's contents appear in your own iTunes window. Click, say, a shared Music icon and then a song title in your iTunes window to hear it.

In addition to streaming audio files, you can also stream video—which can get skippy. This is where the power to *copy* files off of one machine and onto your own comes in handy.

Copy Files With Home Sharing

You can copy files between shared iTunes libraries two ways: *manually* or *automatically*. The manual method is good when you want to occasionally raid someone's media collection for random albums or videos. But if everyone listens to the same audiobook or just has to have every new album that comes into the house, the automatic method saves time and effort.

- **The manual method.** In the shared library, select the title (or titles—Ctrl+click [⌘-click]) of the audio or video files you want to copy to your PC or Mac. Click the Import button in the bottom-right corner of the iTunes window and wait as your selections pour into your own library. If you only want to see items in the shared library that you *don't*  have, jump down to the Show pop-up menu at the bottom-left of the iTunes window and choose "Items not in my library".

- **The automatic method.** With the shared library on-screen, click the Settings button at the bottom-right of the iTunes window. Turn on the checkboxes next to the types of content, like Music, that you want to automatically hoover onto your own machine. Click OK.

But what if you don't want to share *everything* in your library, just some of it? Or if you want to password-protect your stuff from siblings or other annoyances? That's where the Sharing preferences box comes to the rescue.

Call up the iTunes Preferences box (Ctrl+comma [⌘-comma]) and then click the Sharing tab. Turn on "Share my library on my local network." You can choose to share your entire collection or just selected playlists. (You can also tell your computer to look for other people's music here.)

Turn on the checkbox for "Require password" if you want to secure your library; if your network buddies opt for this, too, you'll need their passwords to play. Finally, click the General tab in this same preferences box. Whatever you type in the Library Name box will show up in your friend's iTunes Source list.

Change a Song's File Format

Sometimes you've got a song in iTunes whose format you want to change—you might need to convert an AIFF file before loading it onto your iPod Shuffle, for example. First, head over to Edit→Preferences (iTunes→Preferences), click the General tab, and then the Import Settings button. From the Import Using pop-up menu, pick the format you want to convert *to* and then click OK.

Now, in your iTunes library, select the song you want to convert and choose Advanced→Create MP3 Version (or AIFF, or whatever format you just picked).

If you have a whole folder or disk full of potential converts, hold down the Shift (Option) key as you choose Advanced→"Convert to AAC" (or your chosen encoding format). A window pops up, which you can use to navigate to the folder or disk holding the files you want to convert. The only files that don't get converted are protected ones: Audible.com tracks and older tracks from the iTunes Store that still have copy-protection built in. If you bought a song after January 2009, though, odds are you have a high-quality iTunes Plus track (see page 159) that's delightfully free of such restrictions.

The song or songs in the original format, as well as the freshly converted tracks, are now in your library.

> **Tip** Although you have intentionally created a duplicate of a song here, you may have other unintended dupes from home sharing, ripping the same album twice, or other accidental moments of copying. To find these duplicates—and recover a little hard drive space—choose File→Show Duplicates. iTunes dutifully rounds up all the duplicates in one window for you to inspect and possibly delete. Just make sure they are true duplicates, not, say, a studio and a live version of the same song. Click the Show All button to return the window to your full collection.

Set Up Multiple iTunes Libraries

There's Home Sharing and then there's home, sharing. Many families have just one computer. If everyone's using the same copy of iTunes, you soon get the Wiggles bumping up against Wu-Tang Clan if you have iTunes shuffling the music tracks, or when you autosync multiple iPods. Wouldn't it be great if everyone had a *personal* iTunes library to have and to hold, to sync and to shuffle—separately? Absolutely.

To use multiple iTunes libraries, follow these steps:

❶ **Quit iTunes.**

❷ **Hold down the Shift (Option) key on your PC or Mac keyboard and launch iTunes.** In the box that pops up, click Create Library. Give it a name, like "Tiffany's Music" or "Songs My Wife Hates."

❸ **iTunes opens up, but with an empty library.** If you have a bunch of music in your main library that you want to move over to this one, choose File→"Add to Library".

❹ **Navigate to the music you want and add it.** If the songs are in your original library, they're probably in Music→iTunes→iTunes Media→Music (Home→Music→iTunes→iTunes Music), in folders sorted by artist name. Choose the files you want to add.

To switch between libraries, hold down the Shift (Option) key when you start iTunes, and you'll get a box that lets you pick the library you want. (If you don't choose a library, iTunes opens the last one used.) Tracks from CDs you copy go into whatever library's open. And now that you have those songs in this library, you can switch back to the other one and get rid of them there.

> **Tip** Can't remember which iTunes library you're in at the moment? That nice, thoughtful iTunes 9 displays the name of it at the top of the iTunes window.

Improve Your Tunes with the Graphic Equalizer

If you'd like to improve the way your songs sound, you can use iTunes' graphic equalizer (EQ) to adjust various frequencies in certain types of music. You might want to boost the bass tones in dance tracks to emphasize the booming rhythm, for example.

To get the equalizer front and center, choose View (Window)→Equalizer and unleash some of your new EQ powers.

❶ Drag the sliders (bass on the left, treble on the right) to accommodate your listening tastes (or the strengths and weaknesses of your speakers or headphones). You can drag the Preamp slider up or down to compensate for songs that sound too loud or too soft. To create your own presets, click the pop-up menu and select Make Preset.

❷ Use the pop-up menu to choose one of the canned presets for different types of music (Classical, Dance, Jazz, and so on).

You can apply equalizer settings to an entire album or to individual songs.

❸ To apply settings to a whole album, select the album's name (either in Grid View or in the iTunes browser pane). Then press Ctrl+I (⌘-I) and click "Yes" if iTunes asks whether you're sure you want to edit multiple items. In the box that pops up, click the Options tab and choose your preferred setting from the Equalizer Preset pull-down menu.

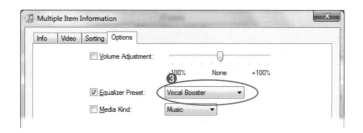

Equalization is the art of adjusting the frequency response of an audio signal. An equalizer emphasizes, or boosts, some of the signal's frequencies while lowering others. In the range of audible sound, *bass* frequency is the low rumbly noise; *treble* is at the opposite end of the sound spectrum, with high, even shrill, notes; and *midrange* is, of course, in the middle, and it's the most audible to human ears.

❹ You can apply equalizer presets to specific songs as well. Instead of selecting the album name in the iTunes window, click the song name, and then press Ctrl+I (⌘+I). Click the Options tab and choose a setting from the Equalizer Preset menu.

❺ Finally, you can change the EQ settings right from your song lists by adding an Equalizer column. Choose View→View Options and turn on the Equalizer checkbox. A new column appears in your track lists, where you can select EQ settings.

 The iPod itself has more than 20 equalizer presets you can use on the go. To set your iPod's Equalizer to a setting designed for a specific type of music, on the Nano choose iPod→Playback→Settings→EQ. (On the Classic, it's iPod→Settings→EQ.) Scroll down the list of presets until you find one that matches your music style, and then press the Select button. Your iPod now lists the preset's name next to "EQ" on the Settings menu. The process works pretty much the same way on the iPod Touch, except that you find the EQ choices at Settings→Music→EQ.

Change a Song's Start and Stop Times

Got a song with a bunch of onstage chitchat before it starts, or after the music ends? Fortunately, you don't have to sit there and listen. You can change a song's start and stop times so you hear only the juicy middle part.

To change a track's stop time, play the song and observe the iTunes status display window. Watch for the point in the timeline where you get bored. Then:

❶ Click the track you want to adjust.

❷ Choose File→Get Info (Ctrl+I [⌘-I]) to call up the song's information box.

❸ Click the Options tab and take a look at the Stop Time box, which shows the full duration of the song.

❹ Enter the new stopping point for the song, as you noted earlier.

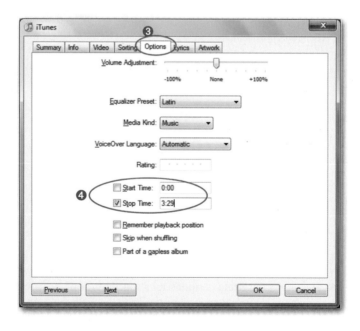

You can perform the exact same trick at the beginning of a song by adjusting the number in the Start Time box. The shortened version plays in iTunes and on your iPod, but the additional recorded material isn't really lost. If you ever change your mind, go back to the song's Options box and return the song to its full length.

Edit Song Information

Tired of seeing so many tunes named *Untitled*? You can change song titles in iTunes—to enter a song's real name, for example, or to fix a typo—a couple of ways.

In the song list, click the text you want to change, wait a moment, and then click again. The title now appears highlighted and you can edit the text—just like when you change a file name on the desktop.

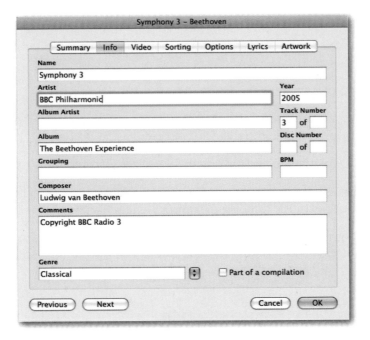

Another way to change a song's title, artist name, or other information is to click the song in the iTunes window and press Ctrl+I (⌘-I) to summon the Get Info box. (Choose File→Get Info if you forget the keyboard shortcut.) Click the Info tab and type in the new track information.

Too much work? You can always try Advanced→Get CD Track Names and see what comes up, although the Gracenote database iTunes uses may not know the title, either, if it's something deeply obscure or homemade.

> **Tip** Once you've got a song's Get Info box on-screen, use the Previous and Next buttons to navigate to other tracks grouped with it in the iTunes song list window. That way, you can rapidly edit all the track information in the same playlist, on the same album, and so on, without closing and opening boxes the whole time.

Edit Album Information

You don't have to adjust your track information on a song-by-song basis. You can edit an entire album's worth of tracks simultaneously by clicking the Album name in the iTunes column browser (or on its cover in Grid View) and pressing Ctrl+I (⌘-I) to bring up the Get Info box.

Ever careful, iTunes flashes an alert box asking if you really want to change the info for a bunch of things all at once. Click Yes.

You can make all sorts of changes to an album in the four-tabbed box that pops up. Here are just a few examples:

❶ Fix a typo or mistake in the Album or Artist name boxes.

❷ Manually add an album cover or photo of your choice to the whole album by dragging it into the Artwork box.

❸ Click the Options tab and change the Equalizer preset for all the songs.

❹ Have iTunes skip the album when you shuffle music—great for keeping winter holiday music out of your summer barbecue album rotation.

❺ Tell iTunes to play back the album without those two-second gaps between tracks by choosing the "Gapless album" option. (Perfect for opera and *Abbey Road*!)

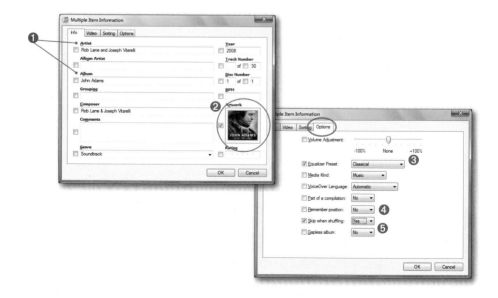

Fetch Missing Album Covers

Songs you download from the iTunes Store often include artwork—usually a picture of the album cover. iTunes displays the picture in the lower-left corner of its main window (you may need to click the Show Artwork icon at the lower-left). Covers also appear in both the Grid and Cover Flow views. But even if you rip most of your music from your own CD collection, you're not stuck with artless tracks. You can ask iTunes to head to the Internet and find as many album covers for you as it can.

You need a (free) iTunes Store account to make this work, so if you haven't signed up yet, flip ahead to Chapter 7 to learn how. To make iTunes go fetch, choose Advanced→Get Album Artwork. Since Apple has to root around in your library to figure out what covers you need, you get an alert box warning you that the company will be getting (and then dumping) personal information from you (but it's not laughing at your Bay City Rollers tracks).

Then go fetch yourself a sandwich while iTunes gets to work. If you have a huge library, this may take a little while. When iTunes finishes, though, you should have a healthy dose of album art whizzing by in Cover Flow view or filling up the Grid in the middle of the iTunes window.

If iTunes can't find certain album covers on its own, it displays a list of the missing artwork. You can use this helpful list to hunt for and place the art yourself, as described next….

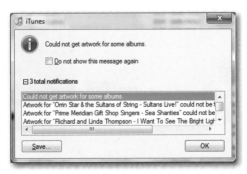

Tip Some albums in the iTunes Store go beyond cover artwork. Albums with the new iTunes LP feature often include performance videos, animated lyrics, photos, liner notes, and more. Check out Chapter 7 for the scoop on iTunes LP.

Replace Album Covers Manually

Despite its best intentions, sometimes iTunes can't find an album cover (or retrieves the wrong one). If that happens, take matters into your own hands by manually adding your own album artwork—or a photo of your choice. If Pachelbel's *Canon in D* makes you think of puppies, you can have baby dachshund photos appear in iTunes every time you play that song.

❶ To add your own art to a song, pick a photo or image—JPEG files are the most common.

❷ If you found the cover on Amazon (*hint*: a great source!), save a copy of it by dragging it off the Web page and onto your desktop or by right-clicking (Ctrl-clicking) it and choosing the "Save Image" option in your Web browser.

❸ With your image near the iTunes window, select the song and click the Show Artwork button in the bottom-left corner of the iTunes window.

❹ Drag the image into the iTunes Artwork pane to add it to the song file.

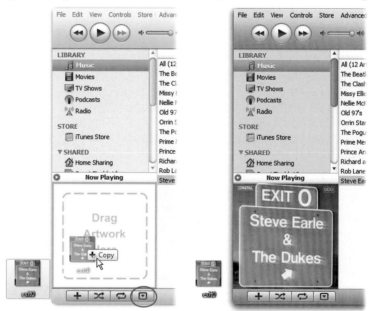

> **Tip** You can also click a song title, type Ctrl+I (⌘-I) to bring up the Get Info box, and then click the Artwork tab. Then just click the Add button to call up a navigation box that lets you choose an image from your hard drive.

Find and Add Lyrics to Your Song Files

You can save lyrics with a song file just as you do album art. To add lyrics, select a song in iTunes and press Ctrl+I (⌘-I) to call up the Get Info box. Then click the Lyrics tab.

Here, you can either meticulously type in a song's verses or look them up on one of the hundreds of Web sites devoted to cataloging them. Once you find your words, getting them into iTunes is a mere cut 'n' paste job away. If you want to add lyrics to all the songs on an album, or have several to add on the same playlist, click the Next button (circled). That advances you to the next song, thereby saving yourself repeated keystrokes invoking the Get Info command.

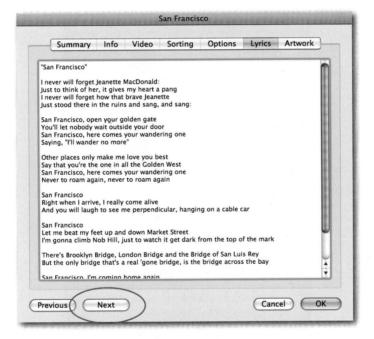

View Lyrics on the iPod

Now that you've spent all that time grooming your song files and adding lyrics, wouldn't it be great if you could take the fruits of your labor with you? The good news is, you can—all the info in an iTunes song file transfers over when you sync your iPod. Except, of course, in the case of iPod Shuffles, which lack the whole screen thing needed to view images and text.

When you're out strolling with your iPod and have a song playing, press the center button to cycle through all the information about the song. After four or five taps, the lyrics appear on the iPod's screen, making it a handheld karaoke machine you can sing along with as you go down the street. Got an iPod Touch? Just tap the album cover on your screen to see the lyrics.

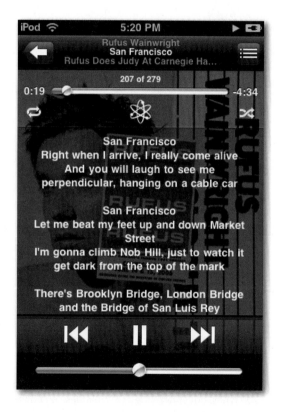

Tip As you click through iPod screens to get to your lyrics, check out the shortcut to shuffling songs that Apple has slipped into the menus. Right before you get to the lyrics screen, you get an option to shuffle songs or albums.

What iTunes Can Tell You About Your iPod

iTunes not only lets you decide which songs and videos end up on your iPod, it also helps keep your iPod's own internal software up to date, see how much space you have left on your player, and change your music, video, and podcast synchronization options.

When you connect your iPod to your computer, it shows up in the iTunes Source list (in the Devices area), Click the iPod icon to see all your options. Each tab at the top of the screen lets you control a different kind of content, like music, photos, or games.

Here, on the Summary screen, iTunes tells you:

❶ The size of your iPod, its serial number, and whether it's formatted for Windows or the Mac.

❷ Whether your iPod has the latest software (and if it's having problems, you get the chance to reinstall it).

❸ Whether iTunes is set to automatically synchronize with your iPod or whether you need to update its contents manually. (Automatic means everything in iTunes ends up on your iPod—space permitting, of course; manual means you get to pick and choose.) If you have one of the new Nanos, you can turn on spoken-word prompts to hear your Nano recite things like menu names, song titles, and so on.

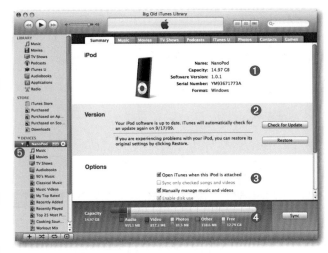

❹ The bar at the bottom of the window identifies the different media types filling up your iPod using color. Click the bar to see the information displayed in numbers of items, the amount of drive space used, or the number of days' worth of a particular type of media.

❺ Click the flippy triangle next to the iPod in the Source list to see its contents and playlists.

Adjust Your iPod's Syncing Preferences with iTunes

Once your iPod's connected and showing up in iTunes, you can modify all the settings that control what goes on to (and comes off of) your media player. Thanks to iTunes 9's long, scrollable screen full of checkboxes and lists in most categories, it's easier than ever to get precisely what you want on your 'Pod.

So where do you start? See those tabs all in a row toward the top of iTunes? Click each one to see the preferences for that type of media. Here's what you'll find in the tabs (they vary slightly depending on the type of iPod you have):

❶ **Summary.** Key iPod hardware info here: Drive capacity, serial number, and software version (and a button to update the same when Apple releases a new version). The Options area lets you choose syncing preferences and whether you want to turn your iPod into a portable data drive for carrying around big files.

❷ **Music.** Click this tab to synchronize all your songs and playlists—or just the ones you listen to the most. Keep scrolling down; you can sync by artist and genre as well.

❸ **Movies.** Full-length movies can take up a gigabyte or more of precious 'Pod space, so iTunes gives you the option to load all, selected, or even just unwatched films.

❹ **TV Shows.** As with movies, you can selectively choose which TV shows (or episodes thereof) you bring along on your iPod.

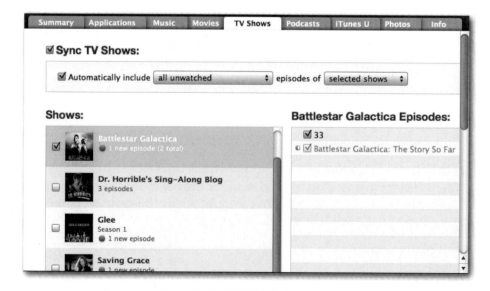

⑤ **Podcasts.** Your pal iTunes can automatically download the podcasts you've *subscribed* to through the iTunes Store (Chapter 7); here, you can decide which ones you want to listen to on the go.

⑥ **iTunes U.** This tab lets you selectively sync up all the university lectures and other educational content you download from the iTunes Store.

⑦ **Photos.** The Nano, Touch, and Classic can all display little copies of your digital photos. Click this tab to select where you want iTunes to look for photos (like in iPhoto or Photoshop Elements) and which photo albums you want to bring with you.

⑧ **Contacts.** It's not just an all-purpose media player! The iPod is happy to carry copies of all the addresses and phone numbers listed in your computer's address book (from Microsoft Outlook, the Mac OS X Address Book, and other programs). Scroll down the screen and you find an option to grab Outlook or iCal calendars, too.

This tab is called **Info** on the iPod Touch. Along with notes, contacts, and calendars, you can sync up Web browser bookmarks and email account settings from your computer. If you're a MobileMe subscriber, you can add the Touch to your collection of über-synced computers and iPhones to keep your info current across all your Internet-connected hardware.

⑨ **Games.** You get a few basic built-in iPod games in your Extras menu, but if you've purchased *Pac-Man* or *Bejeweled* from the iTunes Store, decide here which ones to move to your iPod.

If you have a Touch, this tab is called **Applications**. It's where you select how many of those cool little programs you downloaded from the iTunes App Store to sync up with your iPod.

Tip The iPod Nano, Shuffle, the 32- and 64-gigabyte Touch models, and iTunes have features for the visually impaired to navigate audio content by verbal cues instead of on-screen menus. In iTunes, on the iPod's Summary screen, turn on the checkbox next to "Enable spoken menus for accessibility". On the Nano, scroll to iPod→Settings→General→Spoken Menus. Triple-click the Home button to activate VoiceOver on the Touch. And if you want to control iTunes using the Mac's built-in VoiceOver software or one of the many screen-reader programs for Windows, pay a visit to *http://www.apple.com/accessibility/itunes/ipodtouch.html* for the details.

Load Songs Onto an iPod from More than One Computer

iTunes' *Autosync* feature makes keeping your iPod up-to-date a total breeze, but there's a big catch: You can sync your iPod with only *one* computer. Lots of people have music scattered around multiple machines: a couple of different family Macs, an office PC and a home PC, and so on. If you want to load up your music from each of these sources, you have to change your iPod settings to *manual management*. That's easy to do. Just connect your iPod, select it in the Source list, and then click the Summary tab in the iTunes window. Then:

* Scroll down to the Options area and turn on the checkbox next to "Manually manage music and videos". Click the Apply button in the bottom-right corner of iTunes to make the change.

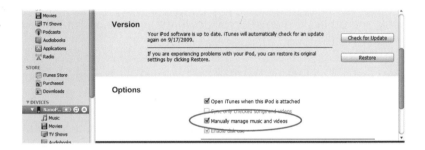

* Don't forget to manually eject your iPod from iTunes every time you want to remove it from your computer. (Manual update gives you total control, but as Uncle Ben said in *Spider-Man*, "With great power comes great responsibility.") Eject the iPod by either clicking the Eject button next to the iPod's name in the iTunes Source list or by pressing Ctrl+E (⌘-E) to properly free the player from the computer.

Tip Your iPod's Summary screen (in iTunes) shows whether your iPod is formatted for Windows or Mac. If you have a new Classic or Nano and want to use it with both a PC and a Mac, connect it to the PC first and have iTunes format the iPod for Windows. A Mac can read the Windows format just fine, but Windows won't recognize the Mac format without special software. The iPod Touch will talk to either computer, no matter which one you use it with first.

Manually Delete Music and Videos from Your iPod

People who choose to autosync their iPods don't have to worry about dumping stuff off their players. They can choose which playlists and media to automatically copy over to their iPod—or they can just delete unwanted items out of iTunes and resync their 'Pods to wipe the same files off the player.

But if you're a Manual Manager, you have to delete unwanted files yourself. (You can, however, have iTunes automatically update your podcast subscriptions for you; see Chapter 7 for more about podcasts.)

❶ To delete files from your iPod, connect it to the computer, and click the iPod icon in the Source list.

❷ Click the flippy triangle next to the iPod icon to get to the media library you want to clean up. If you want to delete songs, for example, click the Music icon.

❸ In the list that appears on the right side of iTunes, select the unwanted tracks and press the Delete key on the keyboard. This removes the files from your iPod, but doesn't whack them out of the iTunes library.

Where iTunes Stores Your Files

Behind its steely silver-framed window, iTunes has a very precise system for storing your music, movies, and everything else you add. Inside its own iTunes folder on your hard drive (which, unless you moved it, is in Music→iTunes [Home→Music→iTunes]), the program keeps all your files and song information. (If you're running Windows Vista, your iTunes folder is at User→<username>→Music→iTunes, and Windows XP users can find it at My Documents→My Music→iTunes.)

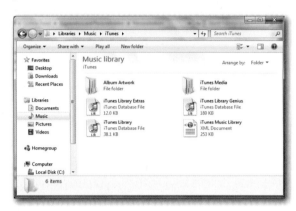

Your iTunes Library file, a database that contains the names of all the songs, playlists, videos, and other content you've added to iTunes, sits inside the iTunes folder. Be very careful not to move or delete this file if you happen to be poking around in the iTunes folder. If iTunes can't find it, it gives a little sigh and creates a new one—a new one that doesn't have a record of all your songs and other media goodies.

But even if you accidentally delete the Library file, your music is still on your computer—even if iTunes doesn't know it. That's because all the song files are actually stored in the iTunes *Music* folder, which is also inside the main iTunes folder. You may lose your custom playlist if your Library file goes missing, but you can always add your music files back (File→"Add to Library") to recreate your library.

 Tip Depending on whether or not you updated an older version of iTunes, your iTunes Music folder may actually be an iTunes Media folder. If you have a Media folder, iTunes neatly groups things like Games, Music, TV Shows, Movies, and other content in their own subfolders, making it much easier to find your downloaded episodes of *Mad Men* among all the song files. If you want to reorganize, media-style, choose File→Library→Organize Library and choose "Upgrade to iTunes Media organization."

Move the iTunes Music Folder to an External Drive

Media libraries grow large, and hard drives can seem to shrink, as you add thousands of songs and hundreds of videos to iTunes. You may, in fact, think about using a big external drive for iTunes storage. That's just dandy, but you need to make sure that iTunes knows what you intend to do.

If you rudely drag your iTunes Music folder to a different place without telling iTunes, it thinks the songs and videos in your collection are gone. The next time you start the program, you'll find a newly created, empty Music folder. (While iTunes remains empty but calm, *you* may be having heart palpitations as you picture your media collection vanishing in a puff of bytes.)

To move the Music folder to a new drive, just let iTunes know where you're putting it. Before you start, make sure iTunes has been putting all your songs and videos in the iTunes Music folder by opening the Preferences box (Ctrl+comma [⌘-comma]) and confirming the folder location. Then:

❶ Click the Advanced tab and turn on the check-box next to "Keep iTunes Music folder organized."

❷ Click the Change button in the iTunes Music folder location area and navigate to the external hard drive.

❸ Click the New Folder button in the window, type in a name for the iTunes library, and click the Create button.

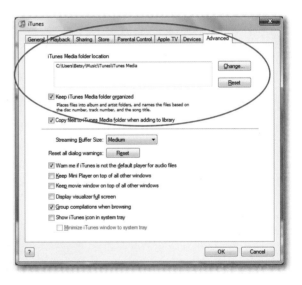

❹ Back in the Change Music Folder Location box, click the Open button.

❺ Click OK to close the iTunes Preferences box.

❻ Choose File→Library→Organize Library and then check "Consolidate files".

Ignore the ominous warnings from iTunes (*"This cannot be undone"*) and let iTunes heave a complete copy of your iTunes folder to the external drive. Once you confirm that everything is in the new library, trash your old iTunes folder and empty the Trash or Recycle Bin to get all those gigs of space back.

Copy Your Music from iPod to iTunes

To prevent rampant piracy across the seven seas of Musicdom, Apple originally designed the data transfer between iTunes and the iPod as a one-way trip—you could copy music *to* a connected iPod, but not *from* an iPod to your computer. This is still pretty much Apple's way, although you can now copy iTunes Store purchases from your iPod to iTunes; Chapter 7 has the details.

But there are times when perfectly honest people need to get their songs off of their iPod—like when your computer dies and takes your iTunes library with it.

The Web is full of tips and tricks for harvesting content off of an iPod and getting it back into iTunes, often by fiddling with system settings in Windows or Mac OS X. These methods can vary based on which iPod and which version of an operating system you have. Thankfully, there's also The Shareware Option. Several helpful folks have developed free or inexpensive programs to copy content from your iPod to your computer:

- **TouchCopy.** The program costs $25, but it works with Windows and Mac OS X—and on all iPod models. (*www.wideanglesoftware.com/touchcopy*)

- **YamiPod.** A free program that runs off of the iPod itself and exports music back to Windows, Mac, and Linux systems. (*www.yamipod.com*)

- **SharePod.** This freeware program for Windows can copy music and videos back to your PC and also edit playlists, artwork, and song tags (labels) as well. (*www.getsharepod.com*)

- **iPodAccess.** This one works with all iPods and is available for $20 in either Windows or Mac versions. (*www.findleydesigns.com/ipodaccess*)

- **Senuti.** The names makes sense when you realize it's iTunes spelled backward. Senuti, pictured at right, is an $18 shareware program for the Mac that lets you copy all (or just some) of the music on your iPod back to iTunes. (*www.fadingred.org/senuti*)

Back Up Your iTunes Files to Disc

If your hard drive dies and takes your whole iTunes folder with it, you lose your music and movies. This can be especially painful if you paid for lots of songs and videos from the iTunes Store, because Apple won't let you re-download new copies. Luckily, iTunes gives you a super simple way to back up your iTunes files onto a CD or DVD.

❶ In iTunes, choose File→Library→"Back Up to Disc".

❷ In the box that pops up, choose what you want to back up—everything, or just items you paid for in the iTunes Store. Later, after you've backed up for the first time, you can turn on a checkbox to back up only the stuff you added since the last backup.

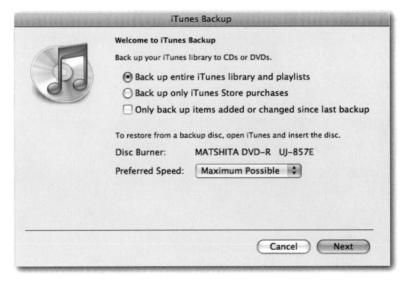

❸ Have a stack of discs ready to feed into your computer's disc drive. Depending on the size of your library, you may need several CDs (which store up to 700 megabytes of data each) or DVDs (which pack in at least 4.7 gigabytes of files per disc). You'll get nagged by iTunes to feed it a new disc once it fills up the current one.

If you ever need to use your backup copies, open iTunes and put in one of those discs to start restoring your files. Remember, there's nothing really exciting about file backups—until you have to use them to save the day.

6

The Power of Playlists

A *playlist* is a group of songs you gather from your iTunes library that you think go well together. You can include pretty much any tunes arranged in any order. For example, if you're having a party, you can make a playlist out of the current Top 40 radio hits and the dance music in your iTunes library. If you're in a 1960s Brit Girl Pop mood, you can whip together the hits of Dusty Springfield, Lulu, and Petula Clark. Some people may question your taste if you, say, mix tracks from *La Bohème* with Queen's *A Night at the Opera*, but hey—it's *your* playlist.

Creating playlists has become something of an art form, especially since the iPod arrived in 2001. You can find books filled with sample playlists. Academics around the world write papers about group dynamics and cultural identity after studying how people create playlists—and which ones they choose to share with others. You can publish your own playlists in the iTunes Store (see page 125) so others can bear witness to your mixing prowess. Some nightclubs even invite people to hook up their iPods so they can share their playlists with the dance-floor audience.

Even if you don't have time to make your own playlists, Apple lends you an expert hand. Its Genius feature lets you create one-click mixes of music that sound like they were actually meant to go together.

Now that you know what a playlist is and how people use them, it's time to get cracking and make one (or 42) of your own.

Make a New Playlist in iTunes

To create a playlist, press Ctrl+N (⌘-N). You can also choose File→New Playlist or click the + button at the bottom-left of the iTunes window.

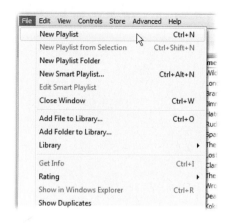

All freshly minted playlists start out with the impersonal name "untitled playlist." Fortunately, this generic name is highlighted and ready for editing—just type in a better name: Cardio Workout, Hits of the Highland Lute, or whatever you want to call it. As you add playlists, iTunes alphabetizes them in the Playlists area.

Once you create and name a spanking new playlist, you're ready to add your songs or videos. You can do this in several ways, so choose the method you like best.

Playlist-Making Method #1

❶ If this is your first playlist, open the playlist in its own window to make it easy to see what's going on: You get your full library in one window, and your empty playlist in the other. To make that happen, just double-click the new playlist's icon in the Source list. If this is your first playlist, iTunes pops up an intro screen. Ignore it and go to Step 2.

❷ Go back to the main iTunes window and drag the song titles you want from your library over to the new playlist window. (Make sure you click the Music icon in the Source list to see all your songs.) Drag songs one at a time, or grab a bunch by selecting tracks as you go: just Ctrl+click (⌘-click) each title.

Playlist-Making Method #2

❶ Some folks don't like multiple windows. No problem. You can add songs to a playlist by highlighting them and dragging the tunes to the playlist's icon right from the main iTunes window.

❷ Tip: If you create lots of playlists, you may need to scroll down to get to your new one.

Playlist-Making Method #3

❶ You can also pick and choose songs in your library and then create a playlist out of the highlighted songs. Select tracks by Ctrl+clicking (⌘-clicking) the titles.

❷ Then choose File→New Playlist From Selection, or press Ctrl+Shift+N (⌘+Shift+N). The songs you selected appear in a brand-new playlist. If all of them came from the same album, iTunes names the playlist after the album (but it also highlights the title box so you can rename it).

Don't worry about clogging up your hard drive. When you drag a song title onto a playlist, you don't *copy* the song, you just tell iTunes where it can find the file. In essence, you're creating a *shortcut* to the track. That means you can have the same song on several playlists, but only one copy of it on your PC.

That nice iTunes even gives you some playlists of its own devising, like "Top 25 Most Played" and "Purchased" (a convenient place to find all your iTunes Store goodies listed in one place—and one to *definitely* back up to a CD or DVD).

Change an Existing Playlist

If you change your mind about a playlist's tune order, drag the song titles up or down within the playlist window. Just make sure to sort the playlist by song order first (click the top of the first column, the one with the numbers listed in front of the song titles).

You can always drag more songs into a playlist, and you can delete titles if you find your playlist needs pruning. Click the song in the playlist window and then hit Delete or Backspace. When iTunes asks you to confirm your decision, click Yes. Remember, deleting a song from a playlist doesn't delete it from your music library—it just removes the title from that particular playlist. (You can get rid of a song for good only by pressing Delete or Backspace from within the iTunes library; select the Music icon under "Library" to get there.)

You can quickly add a song to an existing playlist right from the main iTunes window, no matter which view you happen to be using: Select the song, right-click (Control-click) it, and then, in the pop-up menu, choose "Add to Playlist". Scroll to the playlist you want to use and then click the mouse button to add the track to that playlist.

If you want to see how many playlists contain a certain song, select the track, right-click (Control-click) it, and choose "Show in Playlist" in the pop-up menu.

Add a Playlist to Your iPod

Adding that fabulous new playlist to your iPod doesn't take any heavy lifting on your part. In fact, if you set your iPod to autosync with iTunes, the only thing you need to do is grab your USB cable and plug in your iPod. Once iTunes recognizes the iPod, it copies any new playlists you created right over.

You can also tell iTunes to sync different playlists to different iPods—helpful if you're in a multiple-iPod-owning household and you all share the same computer and iTunes library. Just plug in your iPod, select it in the Source list, and then click the Music tab. In the Sync Music area, click the button for "Selected playlists" and then turn on the checkboxes for the playlists you want.

If you manually manage the syncing process, adding new playlists is a total drag—literally: Dragging is all you have to do. With your iPod connected, click the playlists icons you want to transfer and drag them onto the iPod's icon. That's it.

 Tip If you find your Source list is longer than the line for a Green Day concert, you can save some space by putting batches of song mixes, like "Dinner Party" or "Cardio Workouts", inside *playlist folders* within the Source list. Making a folder is easy—just choose File→New Playlist Folder. Once the new folder appears in the Playlists area of the Source list, give it a name and then drag a bunch of playlists onto the folder icon. To open the folder and crank up a certain playlist inside, click the flippy triangle next to the folder name to reveal the playlists. Click the triangle again to close the folder and shorten your Source list.

Delete a Playlist

The party's over and you want to get rid of that iTunes playlist. Start by clicking it in the Source list, then press the Backspace (Delete) key. iTunes presents you with a warning box, double-checking that you really want to vaporize the list. (Again, this maneuver just zaps the playlist itself, not all the stored songs you had in it. Those remain available in the main iTunes window.)

If you have your iPod set to autosync, any playlist you delete from iTunes will disappear from you iPod the next time you plug in and sync your player.

If you manually manage your iPod and all its contents, connect the player and spin open the flippy triangle next to its name in the Source list. That gives you a look at all its libraries and playlists. Click the one you want to dump and then hit the Backspace (Delete) key on the keyboard.

Make an On-The-Go Playlist on an iPod Nano or Classic

Sometimes you're out with your iPod and you get the urge to hear a bunch of songs on different albums one after the other. Good news: You can create playlists right on your iPod, and have them sync back into iTunes the next time you connect:

❶ Scroll through your iPod until you get to the title of the first song you want to add to a playlist.

❷ Hold down the iPod's center button for a few seconds until a new set of menus appears. Choose "Add to On-the-Go".

❸ Scroll to the next song and repeat the process.

❹ When you're done adding songs, press the iPod's menu button until you get to the Music menu; go to Playlists→On-The-Go. Under "On-The-Go", you see the number of songs you just compiled. Press the Select button to see the song titles.

❺ If you like what you see, scroll up to "Save Playlist" and click the center button. If you don't like what you see, choose "Clear Playlist" to dump the songs and start over.

Your freshly inspired playlist now appears in your Playlists menu as On-The-Go 1. The next one you make and save will be On-The-Go 2, and so on. When you reconnect your iPod to iTunes, you can click these names and change them to something peppier—or more descriptive.

Make and Edit On-The-Go Playlists on the iPod Touch

Nanos and Classics aren't the only iPods to supply you with playlist fun on the run. The iPod Touch has its own version of the On-The-Go playlist. To make one, all you need is some songs and a finger.

Here's how:

- **Create an On-The-Go playlist.** Tap the Music icon on the Touch Home screen. Tap Playlists. Near the top of the Playlists screen, tap On-The-Go.

  Now a master list of all your songs appears. Each time you see one worth adding, tap its name (or the ⊕ button). You can also tap one of the icons at the bottom of the screen, like Play-lists, Artists, or Albums, to find the stuff you want. At the top of every list is an "Add All Songs" option that does just what it says—adds all the songs listed to your OTG playlist.

  When you finish, tap Done. Your playlist is ready to play.

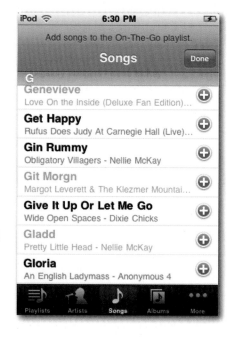

- **Edit the On-The-Go playlist.** On the Playlists screen, tap On-The-Go; on the next screen, tap Edit. Here your iPod offers you a Clear Playlist command, which (after a confirmation request) empties the list completely.

  You also see the universal iPod Touch Delete symbol (⊖). Tap it, and then tap the Delete confirmation button on the right side, to remove a song from the playlist.

  To add more songs to the list, tap the ⊞ button at the top-left. Each time you see a song worth adding, tap it. Finally, note the "grip strip" at the right edge of the screen (≡). With your finger, drag these handles up or down to rearrange the songs in your OTG playlist. When you finish editing your list, tap Done.

Make a Genius Playlist in iTunes

Playlists are fun to make, but occasionally you just don't have the time or energy. If that's the case, call in the expert—the iTunes Genius. With the Genius feature, you click any song you're in the mood for and iTunes crafts a playlist of 25 to 100 songs that it thinks go well with the one you picked.

The first time you use it, Genius asks permisson to go through your music collection and gather song information. Then it uploads that data to Apple. When your information has been analyzed (by software) and anonymously added to a big giant database of everybody else's song info (to improve the Genius's suggestions), the Genius is ready for duty. Here's the procedure:

❶ Click a song title in your libary.

❷ Click the Genius button ⊞ at the bottom-right of iTunes. If you're playing the song, click the Genius icon in the iTunes display window.

❸ iTunes presents you with your new playlist in a flash.

❹ Use the buttons at the top of the Genius window to adjust the number of songs in the playlist, refresh it with new songs if you want a different mix, and—best of all—save the playlist permanently.

The Genius doesn't work if it doesn't have enough information about a song— or if there aren't enough similar songs available to match it with. In that case, pick another tune. If you frequently add new music to your library and want to get it in the mix, inform the Genius at Store→Update Genius.

And if you happen to have the Genius Sidebar panel open in your iTunes window (Chapter 4), the Genius cheerfully presents you with a list of other songs that you can buy right there to round out your listening experience.

> **Note** If you declined iTunes' initial offer to activate the Genius, you can summon it again by choosing Store→"Turn On Genius". And if you're regretting your choice to invite the Genius into your iTunes home, kick him out for good by visiting the same menu and choosing "Turn Off Genius".

Make a Genius Playlist on the iPod

You may get so hooked on making Genius playlists in iTunes that you never want to leave your computer. Your friends will start to wonder where you are. Before your face ends up on a neighborhood "Lost" flyer, consider this: You can also make Genius playlists on the iPod itself when you're out and about. You just need to have the latest model Touch, Nano, or Classic.

To use your portable pocket Genius, though, you first have to set it up and upload your information from iTunes to Apple, as described on the previous page. But you've probably already done that by now, so here's how to make the Genius do your bidding when you're away from your computer.

❶ On a Nano or Classic, select a song and hold down the iPod's center button for a few seconds, until a menu appears; choose "Start Genius". On the Touch, tap Music→Playlists→Genius Playlist and then tap the song you want Genius to use as a starting point.

❷ If you don't like the resulting mix, select or tap the Refesh option atop the screen to get new tunes.

❸ If you love the work of Genius, select or tap the Save option at the top of the screen.

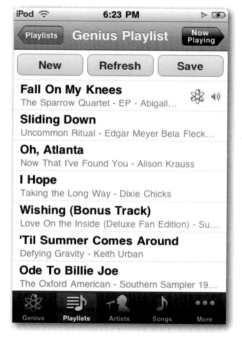

As in iTunes, Genius playlists are titled with the name of the song you originally chose as the foundation for your mix. When you sync the iPod with iTunes, the traveling Genius playlists get copied back over to iTunes.

 Tip If your currently playing song is totally the vibe you want for a playlist, you can summon the Genius from the iPod's Now Playing screen. On a Classic or Nano, tap the center button a couple times until you see the Genius option at the bottom of the screen, then flick the clickwheel over to Start and fire up the Genius. On the iPod Touch, just tap the screen to call up the playback controls (Chapter 3); then tap the electron-shaped Genius icon in the upper-middle part of the screen.

Genius Mixes in iTunes

Yes, the iTunes Genius feature takes almost all the effort out of making a play-list—all you do is click the Genius button. But if even a one-button click seems like too much effort, iTunes 9 makes computerized playlist creation even *easier*. Welcome to Genius Mixes.

The Genius Mix feature works like this: iTunes takes it upon itself to search your entire music library and then automatically compose (depending on the size of your library), up to 12 different types of song collections. Unlike a Genius playlist of tunes calculated to go well together, a Genius Mix is more like a radio station or cable-TV music channel based on *genre*. Depending on what's in your iTunes library, the Genius could present you with a hip hop mix, a country mix, a classical mix, and so on. In addition, the Genius Mix creates up to 12 playlists at once, all saved and ready to play, unlike the Genius's single mix that you have to save to preserve.

If you don't already see a square purple Genius Mix icon in your iTunes Source list, choose Store→Update Genius. Once activated, the Genius quietly stirs up its sonic concoctions from your music library.

To play a Genius Mix, click the Genius Mix icon in the Source list. The iTunes window reverts to Grid View and displays the different mixes it's created. Each is represented by a quartet of album covers from tracks in the mix. Pass the mouse cursor over the album squares to see the name of the mix or click the squares to start playing music.

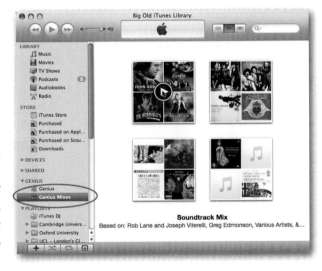

Like most traditional radio stations, you don't get to see a playlist of what's actually in a particular Genius Mix—it's all a surprise. If you don't care for a par-ticular song the Genius has included, you can always hit the forward button or tap the right-arrow key on the computer's keyboard to skip to the next track.

Genius Mixes can be another great way to effortlessly toss on some back-ground music at a party, and you may even hear songs you haven't played in forever. Want to take the Genius Mix with you? The next page explains how.

Genius Mixes on the iPod

As with most playlists, (except for those highly mobile On-the-Go kind) you need to copy Genius Mixes over to the iPod by way of iTunes. But there's one other little requirement: you have to copy the Genius Mixes over by *syncing* them through iTunes. People who manually manage music by dragging tracks from the iTunes Library onto the iPod can't physically drag a Genius Mix onto the player. For now, anyway.

People who autosync their entire libraries don't have to do anything to get the Genius Mixes onboard their iPod. For those who selectively sync, however, copying a Genius Mix takes just a few steps:

❶ Connect your iPod to your computer and click its icon when it appears in the iTunes Source list.

❷ Click the Music tab in the middle of the iTunes window.

❸ If you haven't done so, turn on the checkbox for Sync Music and click the button for "Selected playlists, artists, and genres." (If you selectively sync anyway, you've already done this step.)

❹ Turn on the checkboxes next to the Genius Mixes you want to copy to your iPod. Click Apply and/or Sync to transfer them to the player.

❺ To play a mix on your iPod Touch, tap Home→Music→Genius. Swipe your finger across the screen until you get to the mix you want, and then tap the Play triangle to fire it up. On a Nano or Classic, choose iPod→Music→Genius Mixes. Use the Next or Previous buttons on the iPod's click wheel to get to the mix you want to hear. The dots below the covers indicate how many Genius Mixes you have on your iPod. Press the Center or Play/Pause button to listen to the Genius Mix shown on the screen.

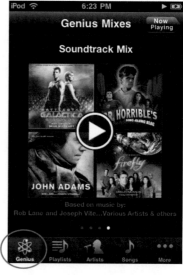

Publish Your Own Playlists (iMixes)

An *iMix* is a playlist you publish on the iTunes Store, so everyone on earth can see your masterwork. You can name it, write your own liner notes explaining your mixing inspiration, and put it out there for everyone to see. (You're not actually copying songs up to the store; you're just showing off your cool tastes, which Apple hopes will lead others to buy those songs.) Here's how:

❶ Start by signing into your store account.

❷ Then, in the iTunes Source list, select the playlist you want to publish. (If it contains any songs that Apple doesn't sell, they'll get knocked off the list—which may ruin your carefully constructed mix.)

❸ Click the arrow next to the playlist and click the Create iMix button in the box that pops up. You now find yourself in the iTunes Store.

❹ Click the Publish button after you fill in all the info about your playlist.

Once you click the Publish button, your playlist is released into the wild. Now other people can see your playlist, rate it, be inspired by it, or—and let's face it, here's the important thing from Apple's perspective—buy the songs for themselves.

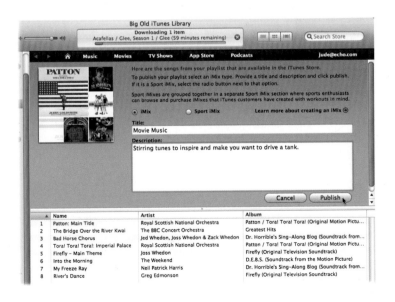

Smart Playlists: Another Way for iTunes to Assemble Your Playlists

As cool as the Genius is, sometimes you want a little more manual control over what goes into your automatically generated music mixes. That's where Smart Playlists rise to the occasion.

Once you give it some guidelines, a *Smart Playlist* can go sniffing through your music library and come up with its own mix. A Smart Playlist even keeps tabs on the music that comes and goes from your library and adjusts itself based on that.

You might tell one Smart Playlist to assemble 45 minutes' worth of songs that you've rated higher than four stars but rarely listen to, and another to play your most-often-played songs from the 1980s. The Smart Playlists you create are limited only by your imagination.

❶ **To start a Smart Playlist, press Ctrl+Alt+N (Option-⌘-N) or choose File→New Smart Playlist.** A Smart Playlist box opens: It sports a purple gear-shaped icon next to its name in the Source list (a regular playlist has a blue icon with a music note icon in it).

② Give iTunes detailed instructions about what you want to hear. You can select a few artists you like and have iTunes leave off the ones you're not in the mood for, pluck songs that only fall within a certain genre or year, and so on. To add multiple, cumulative criteria, click the plus (+) button.

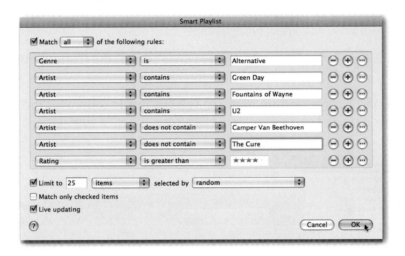

③ Turn on the "Live updating" checkbox. This tells iTunes to keep the playlist updated as your collection, ratings, and play count change. (The play count tells iTunes how many times you play a track, a good indicator of how much you like a song.)

④ To edit an existing Smart Playlist, right-click (Ctrl-click) the playlist's name. Then choose Edit Smart Playlist.

A Smart Playlist is a dialogue between you and iTunes: You tell it what you want in as much detail as you want, and the program whips up a playlist according to your instructions.

You can even instruct a Smart Playlist to pull tracks from your current Genius playlist. Just click the + button to add a preference, choose Playlist as another criteria, and select Genius from the list of available playlists.

> **Tip** When you press Shift (Option), the + button at the bottom of the iTunes window turns into a gear icon. Click this gear button to quickly launch the Smart Playlist creation box.

iTunes DJ: Get the Party Started

The standard iTunes song-shuffle feature can be inspiring or embarrassing, depending on which songs the program happens to play. The iTunes DJ feature lets *you* control which songs iTunes selects when it shuffles at your next wingding. It also shows you what's already been played and what's coming up in the mix, so you know what to expect.

❶ **Click the iTunes DJ icon in the Playlists area of the iTunes Source list.** Now you see a new pane at the very bottom of iTunes.

❷ **Use the Source pop-up menu to select a music source for the mix.** You can use either an existing playlist, the Genius, or your whole library.

❸ **If you don't like the song list that iTunes proposes, click the Refresh button at the bottom-right of the iTunes window.** iTunes generates a new list of songs for your consideration.

❹ **Click the Settings button at the bottom of the window.** In the Settings box, you can change the number of recently played and upcoming songs that iTunes

displays. If iTunes is DJ'ing your interactive music party, the Settings box also has a place to put a Welcome message for guests changing up your music with the Remote program on their iPhones and iPod Touches. (Page 251 has more information on the Remote app.)

❺ **Arrange the songs if you feel like it.** Back on the playlist, you can manually add songs, delete them from the playlist, or rearrange the playing order. To add songs, click the Source list's Music icon and then drag your selected tunes onto the iTunes DJ icon.

❻ **Click the Play button.** And let the music play on.

Three Kinds of Discs You Can Create with iTunes

If you want to record a certain playlist on a CD for posterity—or for the Mr. Shower CD player in the bathroom—iTunes gives you the power to burn. In fact, it can create any of three kinds of discs:

- **Standard audio CDs.** This is the best option: If your computer has a CD burner, it can serve as your own private record label. iTunes can record selected sets of songs, no matter what the original sources, onto a blank CD. When it's all over, you can play the burned CD on any standard CD player, just like the ones from Best Buy—but this time, you hear only the songs you like, in the order you like, with all the annoying ones eliminated.

- **MP3 CDs.** A standard audio CD contains high-quality, enormous song files in the AIFF format. An *MP3* compact disc, however, is a data CD that contains music files in the MP3 format. Because MP3 songs are much smaller than AIFF files, many more of them fit in the standard 650 or 700 MB of space on a recordable CD. The bottom line? Instead of 74 or 80 minutes of music, a CD full of MP3 files can store *10 to 12 hours* of tunes. The downside? Older CD players may not be able to play these CDs.

- **Backup CDs or DVDs.** If your computer can play and record both CDs and/or DVDs, you have another option: iTunes can back up your entire library, playlists and all, by copying it to a CD or DVD. (The disc won't play in any kind of player, of course; it's just a glorified backup disk for restoration when something goes wrong with your hard drive.) Chapter 5 tells you how to use data discs to back up your iTunes library.

To see if your disc drive is compatible with iTunes, select a playlist and click the Burn Disc button on the iTunes window to get the Burn Settings box. If your drive name is listed next to "CD Burner," iTunes recognizes it.

 Note: Even if you've got a DVD drive, you still see it listed next to the label "CD Burner."

Burn a Playlist to a CD

Making a CD out of your favorite playlist takes just a few simple steps with iTunes: Get your blank disc ready and click along.

❶ **Select the playlist you want to burn.** Check to make sure your songs are in the order you want them; drag any tune up or down to reorder.

❷ **When you're ready to roll, choose File→Library→"Burn Playlist to Disc" (or click the Burn Disc button at the bottom-right of the iTunes window).** When the Burn Settings box pops up, pick the type of disc you want to create (see the previous page for your choices).

❸ **Insert a blank disc into your computer's drive when prompted.** If your computer's got a CD platter that slides out, push it back in. Then sit back as iTunes handles things.

iTunes prepares to record the disc, which may take a few minutes. In addition to prepping the disc for recording, iTunes has to convert the files (if you're burning an audio CD) to the industry-standard format for CDs.

Once iTunes has taken care of business, it lets you know that it's now burning the disc. Again, depending on the speed of your computer and disc burner, as well as the size of your playlist, the recording process could take several minutes. When the disc is done, iTunes pipes up with a musical flourish. Eject the disc and off you go. But if you want to make a nice-looking CD cover…

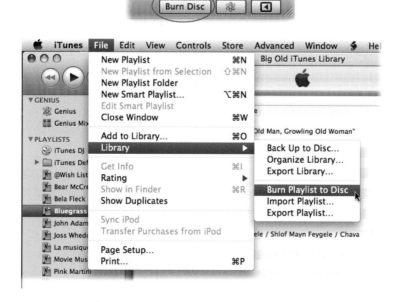

Print Playlists and Snazzy CD Covers

You used to have to do a lot of gymnastics just to print a nice-looking song list that would fit into a CD case. But with iTunes, all you need to do is choose File→Print, select a preformatted option, and then click the Print button.

The Print dialog box is *full* of choices.

- **CD jewel case insert.** You can print out a perfectly sized insert for a CD jewel case, complete with song list on the left and a miniature mosaic of all your album artwork on the right—or just a plain list of songs on a solid color background. (If you choose to make a CD insert, your resulting printout even comes with handy crop marks to guide your X-Acto blade when you trim it down to size.)

- **Song listing.** If you want something simpler, you can opt for a straight-forward list of all the songs on the playlist. This option is also great for printing out a list of all the podcasts you currently have in your iTunes library—just click the Podcasts icon in the Source list, click the "Song listing" option, and print away.

- **Album listing.** You can also print a list of all the albums that have contributed songs to your playlist, complete with album title, artist name, and the songs' titles and play times for each track culled from that album.

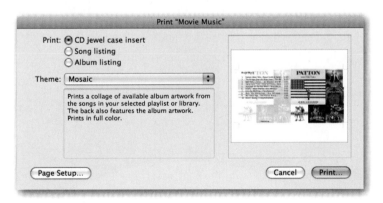

Want to use one of your own personal photos for the cover of your CD case? Start by adding the artwork of your choice to a track (Chapter 5). When you're ready to print, select that track on the playlist and then choose File→Print→"CD jewel case insert"→Theme: Single Cover to place your photo front and center. This method also works great if you're looking to create jewel-case inserts that look just like the ones that come with commercial CDs.

Shop the iTunes Store

People have been downloading music from the Internet since the 1990s, from sites that were legal and others that were, well, not so much. Music fans loved the convenience, but record companies saw potential profits slipping down millions of modem lines. They fought back by suing file-sharing services and other software companies for aiding and abetting copyright infringement.

The need for a legal music download site was obvious, but most early efforts resulted in skimpy song catalogs and confusing usage rights. Things changed dramatically in April 2003, when the iTunes Music Store went online to sell legal iPod-ready digital versions of popular songs for 99 cents a pop. In January 2009, Apple announced it was even doing away with restrictive copy protections built into most songs in the Store. This liberating act gave customers unlimited uses for their music and even the ability to play them on (gasp!) non-Apple players.

Now simply called the iTunes Store, you can find millions of songs, plus full-length movies, TV shows, audio books, podcasts, iPod Touch applications, video games, music videos, and more on its virtual shelves. It's all custom-tailored for the iPod, and best of all, once you buy a title, it's yours to keep. This chapter shows you how to find and use what you're looking for, and get more out of the Store.

Getting to the iTunes Store

Compared to paying for gas, fighting traffic, and finding a parking spot at the mall, getting to the iTunes Store is easy. All you need is an Internet connection and a copy of iTunes running on your computer. Once you're online and looking at iTunes, you can either:

❶ Click the iTunes Store icon in the Source list.

❷ Click the icon in the lower-right corner of the iTunes window (circled) to slide open the Genius Sidebar, where any *Buy* button or song title you click will sweep you into the Store. (This option's available only when you're playing your own music and *don't* have the iTunes Store selected.)

The first method lands you squarely on the Store's main page. You can start wandering around from there, clicking on what looks good.

The second method is targeted to your current song choice. If you're chilling out to some Etta Baker, the Genius Sidebar suggests other tracks you can buy, plus recommendations for works by similar artists.

Preview suggested songs by clicking the musical note icon in front of the track's title. The Buy button is there waiting for your impulse purchase, making it extremely easy to run up your credit-card tab.

If you have an iPod Touch and are in range of a wireless network connection, you have a third way to get to the Store: over the airwaves, as explained on the next page.

 Tip Long-time iTunes Store customers—especially those who are still paddling around the Net on dial-up modems—may be deeply dismayed to see the loss of the Shopping Cart feature in iTunes 9. The Shopping Cart, which let you pile up songs and then download them all at once at the end of your shopping session, has been loosely replaced with the Wish List feature, described later in this chapter.

Shop the iTunes Wi-Fi Store

Owners of the iPod Touch don't even *need* a computer to shop the iTunes Store—these lucky souls can tap their way right into the iTunes inventory over a wireless Internet connection. Many Wi-Fi–enabled Starbucks coffee shops also let you tap into the iTunes Store to browse and buy music, including whatever track is currently playing right there at Starbucks.

Now, to buy stuff when you're out and about—and in the mood to shop:

❶ Tap the purple iTunes icon on the iPod Touch's Home screen. Make sure you have a Wi-Fi connection; see Chapter 11 for guidance on making that happen.

❷ The Store appears on-screen. Tap your way through the categories like "New Releases" until you find an album or song that interests you. (Tap an album to see all its songs.)

❸ Tap a title for a 30-second preview.

❹ Tap the Music, Videos, Podcasts, or Search buttons at the bottom of the window for targeted shopping. Type in search terms with the Touch keyboard.

❺ To buy and download music or video, tap the price on screeen, then tap Buy Now.

❻ Type in your iTunes Store password and let the download begin. You can check the status of your purchase-in-progress by tapping the Downloads button, which also lets you pause your download if you need to. If you don't have an account, tap the Create New Account button on the Sign In screen and follow the steps. You can sign in and out of your account with a link at the bottom of the Store screen.

When the download's done, you now have some brand new material ready to play on your Touch—the new tracks are now on the Purchased playlist.

To get those freshly harvested songs or videos back into the iTunes library on your computer, sync up the Touch when you get home. The tracks pop up in a new iTunes playlist called "Purchased on Touchy" (or whatever you named your wireless iPod this week).

An Overview of the Store's Layout

The iTunes Store is jam-packed with digital merchandise, all neatly filed by category across the top of the main window: Music, Movies, TV Shows, and so on. Click a tab to go to a section of the store. You can also hover your mouse over a tab and click the triangle that appears; a pop-up menu lets you jump to a subcategory (Blues, Pop, and so on) within the selected section.

The main part of the iTunes Store window—that big piece of real estate smack in the center of your browser—highlights iTunes' latest audio and video releases and specials. Free song downloads and other offers appear here, too. This window is usually stuffed full of digital goodies, so scroll down the page to see featured movies, TV shows, apps, and freebies.

If you're looking for a specific item, use the Search box in the upper-right corner to hunt your quarry; enter titles, artist names, or other searchable info.

"Quick Links" along the right side of the window includes shortcuts to buying and redeeming iTunes gift certificates, Genius recommendations, a more advanced search feature, your account settings, technical support, and more.

As you scroll, you also see Top Ten lists along the right side of the screen showing you the hottest selling items in the Store at that very moment.

Navigate the Aisles of the iTunes Store

You navigate the iTunes Store aisles just as you'd navigate a Web site—by using links on the Store's page. Most artist and album names have links—click on a performer's name or an album cover to see a list of associated tracks.

Click the button with the small house on it (circled below) to jump to the Store's home page, or click the Back button in the upper-left corner (to the left of the house) to return to a previous page.

When you find a performer or album you're interested in, click the name to jump to a page with more information. Not only do you see a list of all the tracks on the album, you also see a list of other albums by the same artist, reviews from other iTunes users, and similar albums to buy. Double-click a track title to hear a 30-second snippet. Previews of audiobooks and videos are also available.

As you click around the name of the artist, show, album, or whatever you're looking at appears in the top right corner of the screen. If you get excited by something you've found in the Store and want to share it with friends—or want to drop a not-so-subtle hint for your birthday— click the black triangle next to any Buy link to get a pop-up menu that lets you post a link to your discovery on your Facebook or Twitter page.

Set Up an iTunes Store Account

Before you can buy any of the cool stuff you see in the Store, you need to set up an account with Apple. To do so, click the "Sign In" button on the upper-right corner of the iTunes window.

 Tip America Online members and existing customer can use their AOL screen names to log into the Store. If you are setting up a new account, however, the iTunes Store will walk you through setting up an Apple Account linked to your AOL address.

If you've ever bought or registered an Apple product on the company's Web site, signed up for an AppleCare tech-support plan, have a MobileMe membership, or used another Apple service, you probably already have the requisite Apple ID. All you have to do is remember the ID (usually your email address) and password.

If you've never had an Apple ID, click Create New Account. The iTunes Store Welcome presents you with the three steps you need to follow:

❶ Agree to the terms for using the Store and buying music.

❷ Create an Apple Account.

❸ Supply a credit card or PayPal account number and billing address.

As your first step to creating an Apple Account, you must read and agree to the long scrolling legal agreement on the first screen. The 26-page statement informs you of your rights and responsibilities as an iTunes Store and App Store customer. (It boils down to this: *Thou shalt not download an album, burn it to CD, and then sell bootleg copies of it at your local convenience store.* and *Third-party crashware apps are not our fault.*)

Click the Agree button to move on to step 2. Here, you create an Apple ID, password, and secret question and answer. If you later have to click the "Forgot Password?" button in the Store sign-in box, this is the question you'll have to answer to prove that you're you. Apple also requests that you type in your birthday to help verify your identity.

On the third and final screen, provide a valid credit card number with a billing address. Instead of a credit card, you can also use a PayPal account for iTunes purchases.

Click Done. You've got yourself an Apple Account. From now on, you can log into the iTunes Store by clicking the "Sign In" button in the upper-right corner of the iTunes window.

Change the Information in Your Apple Account

You can change your billing address, switch the credit card you have on file for Store purchases, or edit other information in your Apple Account without calling Apple. Just launch iTunes, click the Store icon in the Source list, and then sign in to your account by clicking the Sign In button in the upper-right corner of the screen.

Once you've signed in, you'll see your account name (email address). Click it. In the box that pops up, re-enter your password and click View Account. If you want to change your password or secret identity-proving question, click the Edit Account Info button. To change your billing address or credit card information, click the Edit Payment Information button. You can also deauthorize all the computers that can play songs purchased with this account (more on when and why you'd want to do *that* later).

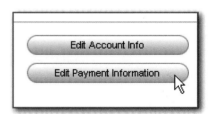

And there are other account settings you can change here, too, like the nickname that appears when you post a customer review in the Store. You can also turn on the My iTunes feature, which lets you put widgets and news feeds on your blog or Facebook profile showing all the things you've been snapping up in the Store lately.

 Note By the way, any changes you make to your Apple Account through iTunes affect other programs or services you then use with your account, like ordering pictures with iPhoto (Mac owners only).

Adjust Your Store Preferences

The iTunes Store aims to be your one-stop shopping hub for all your digital entertainment: music, movies, TV shows, audio lectures from major universities on universal themes in the *Harry Potter* novels, and so on. In fact, some people have even canceled their cable TV subscriptions, preferring instead to go à la carte with iTunes.

If you use iTunes' Season Pass feature, which lets you buy a whole season of a TV show in advance, or if you pre-order an album before it's released, you may never know when iTunes will decide to jump up and start downloading your pre-purchased content. This could be a little inconvenient if, say, your weekly Season Pass episode of *Gossip Girl* starts downloading on your big computer monitor while iTunes DJs your holiday party.

To control how iTunes behaves around your Internet connection, visit the Store tab of the iTunes Preferences box (Ctrl+comma [⌘-comma]). Here, you can decide if you want iTunes to automatically check for downloads, download pre-purchased content, or snag album covers on its own.

While the first three checkboxes concern the program's online activity, the last checkbox controls your view of the online wares. If you prefer an immersive shopping experience without the clutter of the Source list along the left side of the screen, turn on the checkbox for "Use full window for iTunes Store."

 Note Music, videos, and other content you download from the iTunes Store lands in their respective Source list libraries—songs in the Music library, *Heroes* episodes in TV Shows, and so on. Those paid-for music and videos also live on the Purchased playlist in the Source list, a one-click trip to see where all your spare cash went.

Find Music by Genre

The main page of the iTunes Store can be a bit overwhelming, especially if you just want to slip in and buy a few Gregorian Chant music tracks or browse the latest additions to the Classical section. To quickly find music by genre, hover your cursor over the Music tab at the top of the Store window until a down-arrow appears. Click it to reveal a drop-down menu.

On this handy menu, twenty different musical genres await you, from Alternative to World, with Hip-Hop/Rap, Latino, Jazz, Reggae, and Rock in between. You'll also find sections for Music Videos and Children's Music.

Select one of the genres and the middle section of the Store window displays the latest albums in that category, including the newest releases and songs recently added to iTunes' ever-growing catalog. At the same time, the Top Sellers list in the right-hand column changes to reflect the most popular downloads for that genre

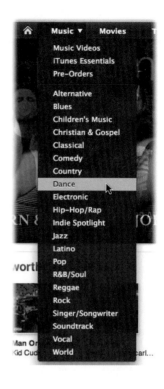

Buy a Song or Album

Click any album name to see a list of the songs on the record. To purchase any of them, click the Buy Song button in the Price column. As of 2009, tracks cost 69 cents, 99 cents, or $1.29, depending on the age and popularity of the song. In most cases, you also have the option to buy the whole album (use the Buy Album button). Album prices vary as well, but tend to range from $8 to $12.

When you download an album, or even just one song, it's accompanied by a color picture of the album cover, which appears in iTunes when you're playing the song, or on the color screen of your iPod. Albums designated as "iTunes LPs" have even more multimedia extras, like videos and liner notes.

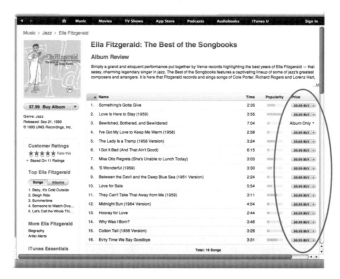

Once you click that Buy Song button, an alert box appears asking if you really want to buy the item you just clicked. Click the glowing Buy button to confirm your purchase decision, or Cancel if you suddenly remember that your credit card is a bit close to the limit this month. Once you click Buy, the download begins and you soon have a new bit of music in your iTunes library.

> **Tip** Buy three songs off an album and wish later you'd just bought the whole thing? If it's within six months of your original purchase, click the Complete My Album link on the main Store page. You get whisked into a screen that lets you download the rest of the tracks—all for a price that's less than paying for each remaining song.

Buy Movies or TV Shows

To buy video content, just click the link on the Store's main page for the type you want—a movie or a TV show. Apple's full-length movie library is small but growing. You'll see titles like *Twilight*, *Iron Man*, and a handful of Pixar classics like *WALL-E* and *Monsters, Inc.* Compared to little ol' song files, movies can take up a ton of hard drive space—a full gigabyte or more—so be prepared for a download time of 30 minutes or more, depending on your Internet connection.

 Tip If you want to watch a movie but not own it, check the flick's Store page to see if it's available for rental. Rentals cost less than $5 and download just like regular iTunes Store–purchased movies that you can play on your iPod or computer. You have 30 days to start watching the rental and 24 hours to finish it, but it means never having to wait for Netflix—or slog to the video store in the rain.

Dozens of old and new TV classics are also available, including episodes from *Mad Men*, *The Daily Show*, and *The Office*. You can buy single episodes or entire seasons at once. Sign up for a Season Pass and you get each new show automatically as it's released. TV shows are big files, too: one 30-minute episode of *30 Rock* in standard definition for instance, is close to 300 megabytes.

Once you purchase and download the files from the iTunes Store—just click the Buy button next to the title you want—they land in your iTunes Library.

Many videos in the iTunes Store come in high-definition as well as standard definition. The HD versions look great on the computer or when played via Apple TV. When you download a high-def show, you also get a standard-definition version of it to play on the iPod. (See Chapter 8 if you want to do that.)

Buy Audio Books

Some people like the sound of a good book, and iTunes has plenty to offer in its Audiobooks area. You can find verbal versions of the latest bestsellers. Prices depend on the title, but are usually cheaper than buying a hardback copy—which would be four times the size of your iPod anyway. Click any title's name and then the Buy Book button; the rest of the process works just like buying music.

If audio books are your thing, you can find even more of them—all iTunes- and iPod-friendly—at Audible. com (*www.audible.com*), a Web store devoted to selling all kinds of audio books, recorded periodicals like *The New York Times,* and radio shows. To purchase Audible's wares, though, you need to go to the site and create an Audible account. The Audible site has all the details, plus a selection of subscription plans to choose from.

If you use Windows, you'll need to download a small piece of software from Audible called Audible Download Manager; details and instructions for the past several versions of Windows are at *http://tinyurl.com/lm2963*. Mac fans don't need to worry about that, as the Audible files land directly in iTunes when you buy them.

Buy iPod Games

The iTunes Store first started selling games when the original video iPods appeared on the scene. The store offers dozens of titles for sale designed to work with older video iPods as well as the iPod Classic and video-playing Nanos. To find them, just visit the App Store menu at the top of the Store window and choose iPod Click Wheel Games.

Gaming classics like Ms. PAC-MAN, Tetris, and Sonic the Hedgehog are among the offerings. Newer titles like Spore Origins, Sudoku, Bejewled, Peggle, and several Sims games are also in stock. And there are video versions of old kitchen-table favorites like Monopoly, Uno, Scrabble, and Mah-jong.

Buying and downloading a game is just like buying anything else in the Store. Once you buy a game, it shows up in the Applications library in the Source list (click a purchased title to see accompanying directions). After you sync the game to your iPod, you can find it in iPod→Extras→Games. When you start the game, it transforms your iPod's scroll wheel and center button into game controls.

Unlike music or video files, however, you can play iPod games only on the iPod. They don't, alas, work in iTunes.

Buy iPod Touch Apps

The App Store hosts thousands of little programs you can add to your iPod Touch to make it a tiny pocket computer *and* a stylish media machine. Currency converters, 3-D video games, newsreaders, ebooks, blogging tools, guitar-chord programs, and mobile versions of popular sites like Facebook and eBay are among the many offerings.

Click the App Store menu in the main Store window to see the different program categories, like Sports or Finance. Many apps are free (each category's page has a list of freebies), and most for-pay programs cost less than $10.

You purchase apps just as you do music and movies: see, click, buy. Your programs sync up when you connect the Touch with iTunes. (You can also buy apps right on the Touch, as Chapter 3 explains.) Some programs for sale are intended for the iPhone and its hardware, though, so as with any software: check the system requirements before you buy.

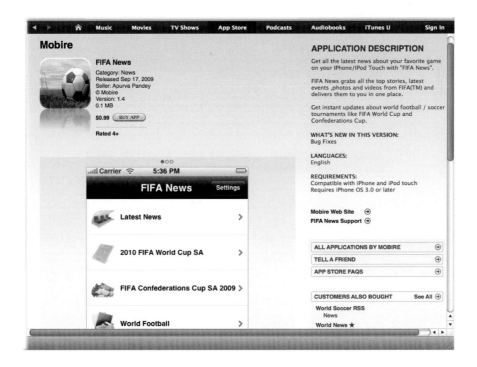

Download and Subscribe to Podcasts

The iTunes Store is host to thousands upon thousands of *podcasts,* those free audio (and video!) programs put out by everyone from big television networks to a guy in his basement with a microphone.

If you want to see what podcasts are available, click the Podcasts link at the top of the Store's main page. If you click the menu under the Podcasts list, you jump to just audio or video podcasts, or to podcasts on a specific topic. On the main Podcasts page, you can browse shows by category, search for podcast names by keyword (use the Search iTunes Store box), or click around until you find something that sounds good.

Many podcasters produce regular installments of their shows, releasing new episodes as they're ready. You can have iTunes keep a look out for fresh editions of your favorite podcasts and automatically download them. All you have to do is *subscribe* to the podcast: click the podcast you want, and then click the Subscribe button.

If you want to try out a single podcast, click the Get Episode link near its title to download just that one show. Some attention-needy podcast producers don't give you the single-episode download option; in those cases, you'll see a Subscribe Only link near the title.

Usage Rights: What You Can Do with Your Purchases

The stuff you buy at the iTunes Store is yours to keep (unless you rented it). You're not charged a monthly fee, and your digitally protected downloads don't go *poof!* after a certain amount of time. In April 2009, Apple removed the copy-protection and restrictions from most music tracks. But for older purchases, you are still bound by the usage agreement for the iTunes Store:

- You can play downloaded songs on up to five different iTunes-equipped Macs or PCs (in any combination) and you can burn them onto CDs (seven times for each playlist).

- You can watch movies, videos, and TV shows on any five computers, on as many iPods as you own, or piped over to the TV with an AV cable or via an Apple TV box.

- You can download music to a single iPod from up to five separate iTunes accounts, but the 'Pod won't accept files from a sixth account—a restriction designed to prevent someone from filling up their player with copyrighted content from the accounts of, say, their entire sophomore class.

You can burn backup CDs and DVDs of your purchases, but you can't burn an iTunes movie or TV show to a disc and watch it on your DVD player. (On the flip side, some newer DVDs now come with an "iTunes Digital Copy" that you can add to your library from the disc; instructions are in the package.)

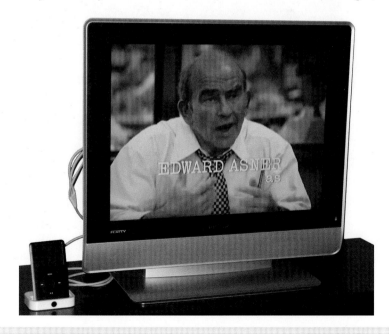

iTunes LPs

Music collectors old enough to remember the days when albums came on 12-inch round sheets of vinyl sometimes lament the decline of the long-playing record format. Audio-fidelity squabbles aside, album covers themselves were typically colorful works of art, often packed with extras like printed lyric sheets, liner notes, photos, or fold-out posters inside.

In an attempt to give iTunes customers a little more bang for their music buck (and recall those bountiful glory days of vinyl), Apple has come up with a format called *iTunes LP*. An iTunes LP comes with more than just songs—it includes extra bonus tracks, digital liner-note booklets, video documentaries, artist interviews, and other material.

Not every album is the Store is an iTunes LP and the extra treats vary by artist. But the price isn't outrageous—maybe $13 or $14 for the whole enchilada.

You can see what's available in the format by clicking the iTunes LP icon on the Store's main Music page or searching for *iTunes LP*. Albums in the category have a square blue iTunes LP badge on their Store page (circled below). While iTunes LPs may not provide the pure physical joy of, say, unfolding the original album cover for *Sgt. Pepper's Lonely Hearts Club Band*, that hard drive full of iTunes LPs is going to be a lot easier to haul than crates full of vinyl records when you have to move.

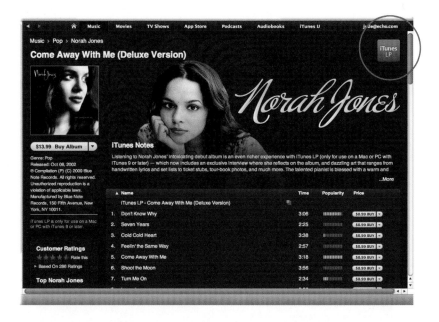

Other Cool iTunes Store Features

Apple's loaded the iTunes Store with plenty of unique, ear-inspiring special collections—all designed to separate you from your money. Just check the Quick Links box on the main page of each Store section. The Movies page, for example, has a link to current theatrical trailers that you can watch in peace without people yapping through them. Take some time and check out:

- **iTunes Extras.** Miss those bonus treats like cast interviews and deleted scenes that you get with movies on DVD? The iTunes Extras area of the Movies section lists all the films with additional material— they're sort of like iTunes LPs, except for movies. Happily, Extras don't cost extra.

- **iTunes Essentials.** Looking for a quick course in, say, the works of Johnny Cash or Jock Rock? Hit the Store's main Music page and click the Quick Link for iTunes Essentials to see the vast collection of specialized collections you can buy with a click and a credit card.

- **Free on iTunes.** While most of the content in the iTunes Store costs money, plenty of free things are also available to download. To see what won't cost you a buck, click the tab for the Music section of the Store. In the Quick Links box

on the right side of the page, click the Free on iTunes link. Here, you can find everything from free songs from up-and-coming indie bands to video podcasts from Hollywood film directors, all there for your cost-conscience downloading pleasure.

 Tip The iTunes U link on the main Store page leads to audio or video content from hundreds of schools around the country. Presentations, video tours, lectures, and more are all available at iTunes U—yay, rah, Fightin' Downloaders!

iTunes Gift Certificates: Buy 'Em and Spend 'Em

Gift certificates make perfect presents for people who have everything—especially when purchased by people who are lousy shoppers. These redeemable email coupons are also an excellent way to save face in potentially unpleasant situations. ("Honey, you may think that I forgot our anniversary again, but…check your email!")

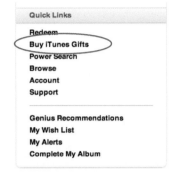

Buying

To buy one, click Buy iTunes Gifts on the main page of the iTunes Store and then click the type of gift you want to send. After you choose delivery by either email or in person (you can print gift certificates yourself) the process is like buying anything on the Web: you fill in your address, gift amount, personalized message, and so on.

If you already have an Apple ID, you can log in and request to have your credit card billed; if not, sign up for one. Once you complete all the pixel paperwork, your gift certificate will be on its way.

Spending

However they arrive, iTunes Store gift certificates are meant to be spent. Here's how they work:

- If you're lucky enough to be the recipient of an iTunes email gift, redemption is just a click away. Click the Redeem link in the iTunes Store window. Copy the Redeem Code from your email and paste it into the box provided. Click Redeem. Then start shopping.

- If the gift arrived by hand (or you received an iTunes Gift Card), start up iTunes and click iTunes Store in the Source list. On the Store's main page, click the Redeem link. Type in the confirmation number printed on the gift certificate and click Redeem.

If you already have an iTunes Store account, log in and start shopping. If you've never set your mouse pointer inside the Store before, you'll need to create an Apple Account. You have to provide your name and address, but you don't have to surrender a credit card number. If you choose None, you can use your gift certificate as the sole payment method—and end your shopping experience once you've burned through it.

Other Ways to Send iTunes Gifts

If you want something more personalized than an email message, you have two other options for giving someone an iTunes-themed gift.

The brightly colored prepaid iTunes Music Card is a fun spin on the gift certificate concept. Available in many different dollar amounts, givers can find cards at places like Amazon.com, Target, and Apple's own stores. You can also buy them in the iTunes Store (and have them mailed out by the Postal Service) by clicking the Buy iTunes Gifts link. Recipients can spend it all in one place—the iTunes Store—by clicking the link for Redeem on the Store's main page.

In a daring feat of bending a noun into a verb, the iTunes Store also lets you "gift" selections of music and videos to intended recipients, giving them the ability to download your thoughtful picks right from the Store onto their own computers. You can send songs and albums to any pal with an email address, as well as audio books, music videos, and TV shows. Click the triangle next to an item's Buy button and choose "Gift This…" from the menu.

If you're proud of a certain iTunes playlist you made yourself, you can send all the songs on it—if they're available in the Store—to a friend with a couple of clicks. Just select the playlist in the iTunes Source list and click the arrow that appears next to its name. A box pops up asking of you'd like to send it

as a gift or publish it as an iMix. Click the Give Playlist button, which takes you back to the iTunes Store to make it all happen over the Internet.

iTunes Allowance Accounts

Allowance accounts are a lot like iTunes gift certificates. You, the parent (or other financial authority), decide how many dollars' worth of Store goods you want to give to a family member or friend (from $10 to $50). Unlike gift certificates, however, allowance accounts automatically replenish themselves on the first day of each month—an excellent way to keep music-loving kids out of your wallet while teaching them to budget their money.

Both you and the recipient need to have Apple IDs, but you can create one for the recipient during the set-up process. To set up an allowance, from the iTunes Store's main page, click the Buy iTunes Gifts link, scroll down to the Allowances section and click "Set up an allowance now". Fill out the form. After you select the amount you want to deposit each month, fill in your recipient's Apple ID and password.

Once the giftee logs into the designated Apple Account, she can begin spending—no credit card required. Once the allowance amount has been spent, that's it for music until the following month. (Of course, if the recipient has a credit card on file, she can always put the difference on the card.) If you need to cancel an allowance account, click the Account link on the Store's main page to take care of the matter.

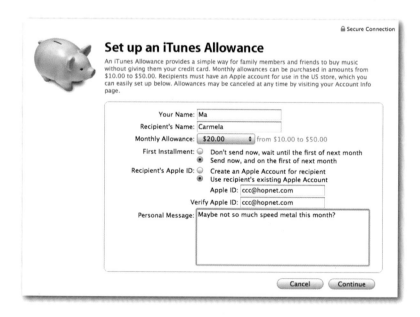

Make an iTunes Wish List

With no paper money flying about to remind you of reality, it's easy to rack up hefty credit card charges. Consider, then, making an iTunes *wish list* to help keep track of songs you want to buy…when your budget allows.

For iTunes customers still using dial-up Internet connections, the Wish List replaces the old Shopping Cart feature as a place to park your stuff before you're ready to download all your purchases at the end of your shopping session. (The 1-Click instant downloading of iTunes purchases can overhwhelm a poor dial-up modem if you aren't done shopping yet.)

Adding items to your iTunes Wish List is easy: when you see something you want, click the triangle next to the Buy button and choose Add to Wish List from the pop-up menu.

To see all the items you've piled up on it, visit the Quick Links box on the Store's home page and click the My Wish List link. If your wishes have changed since you added an item to the list, select the item and click the X that appears next to it to remove it.

When you're ready to buy something from the Wish List, click the Buy button next to the item. The file begins to download to your computer.

If you have been using the Wish List as a substitute Shopping Cart to hold all the songs until you are ready to download everything all at once at the end of your session, there's a special button just for you. It's the Buy All button up in the top right corner of the Wish List screen. Click it and let your dial-up modem have a few hours to itself downloading your purchases.

What to Do If Your Download Gets Interrupted

It's bound to happen sometime: You're breathlessly downloading a hot new album or movie from iTunes and the computer freezes, crashes, or your Internet connection goes on the fritz. Or you and your iPod Touch were in the middle of snagging an album from the iTunes Wi-Fi Store, and the rest of the gang decided it was time to leave the coffee shop.

If this happens to you, don't worry. Even if your computer crashes or you get knocked offline while you're downloading your purchases, iTunes is designed to pick up where it left off. Just restart the program and reconnect to the Internet.

If, for some reason, iTunes doesn't go back to whatever it was downloading before the incident, choose Store→"Check for Available Downloads" to resume your downloading business.

You can check for available purchases any time you think you might have something waiting, like a new episode from a TV Show Season Pass. You can also scoop up any digital booklets included with albums here—those don't download to your Touch from the Wi-Fi Store because they're PDF files meant to be viewed on your computer.

 Tip If you need help from a human at Apple you can either call (800) 275-2273 or email them. From the iTunes Store's main page, click the Support link. Your Web browser presents you with the main iTunes service and support page; click any link in the Customer Service area and then, at the bottom of the page that appears, fill out the Email Support form. Live online chat is also available for some issues.

Set Up Parental Controls for the Store

If you have children with their own Allowance Accounts, you may not want them wandering around the iTunes Store and buying just *anything*. With the Parental Controls feature, you can still give your children the freedom to spend and discover, but you can restrict the types of things they buy—without having to helicopter over them every time they click a Store link.

❶ In the iTunes Preferences box (Ctrl+comma [⌘-comma]) click the Parental Control tab.

❷ A box unfurls with all the things you can choose to limit. For Store material, you can block songs and other items tagged with the Explicit label, restrict movie purchases to a maximum rating (G, PG, PG-13, or R), and choose the highest TV Show content rating allowable for kids (TV-Y, TV-Y7, TV-G, TV-PG, TV-14, or TV-MA). Applications (including games) are subject to age restrictions of 4+, 9+, 12+, and 17 years and older.

❸ Click the lock to password protect the settings box so the kids can't change it themselves.

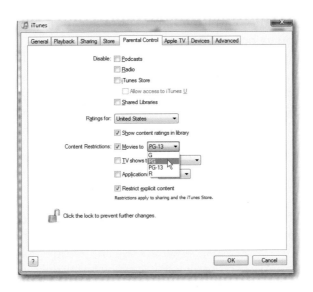

You can also block certain icons from appearing in the iTunes Source list, including Podcasts, Internet Radio, Shared Libraries, or even the entire iTunes Store itself. You can, however, make an exception for educational content from iTunes U to keep them learning instead of whining.

Play iTunes Purchases on Multiple Computers

The Home Sharing feature of iTunes 9, (described in Chapter 5) makes shuttling your iTunes purchases between computers at home easier than ever before. But not every computer you want to share with is at home on the same network—maybe you downloaded Season One of *Lost* on your office's fast fiber-optic network instead of your pokey redidential DSL line.

Apple's usage agreement lets you play Store purchases on up to five computers: PCs, Macs, or any combination. Although iTunes Plus songs and those sold after April 2009 don't have password-demanding copy-restrictions built in, music tracks purchased before 2009 and most videos still do.

For protected content, you must type in your Apple username and password on each computer to authorize it to play any songs, videos, or audio books purchased with that account. Each computer must have an Internet connection to relay the information back to Store headquarters. (You don't have to authorize each and every purchase; you authorize the computer once.)

You authorized your first machine when you initially signed up for an Apple Account. To authorize another computer:

❶ **On the computer you used to purchase an iTunes Store item, grab any file you've bought from iTunes.** You can drag the files right out of your iTunes window onto your desktop. You can also find all the song and video files in your iTunes Media (or iTunes Music) folder: Music→iTunes→iTunes Media (Home→Music→iTunes→iTunes Media). Copy-protected Store files are easily recognizable by their *.m4p* or *.m4v* file extensions. Movies are stored in a folder called Movies and so on.

❷ **Move the file to the second computer.** Copy the file onto a CD or USB drive, email it to yourself, or use whatever method you prefer for schlepping files between distant machines.

❸ **Deposit the file in the iTunes Media folder on the second computer. Then, import the copied file into iTunes on the second computer.** To import the file, you can either choose File→"Add to Library" (and then select and open the file), or just drag the file right into the iTunes window.

> **Tip** If all the iTunes Store goodies you want to copy have been synced to the iPod, you can transfer them right off the portable player to another iTunes-equipped computer. Flip ahead a couple pages to get the details.

❹ In your iTunes list, select a transferred file and click the Play button.
For protected content, iTunes asks for your Apple Account user name and password.

❺ Type your Apple ID and password, and click OK. This second computer is now authorized to play that file—and any other copy-protected songs or files you bought using the same Apple Account.

Another way of authorizing a computer before you transfer anything over to it is to choose Store→Authorize Computer.

> **Note** The copy-protection and restrictions are built into videos and some iTunes music tracks. Songs and other content in the high-quality iTunes Plus format are "DRM-free"—that is, free of the digital-rights management software that disables iTunes tracks after you hit your usage limits. In January 2009, Apple announced it was making iTunes Plus versions of just about all its 10 million songs. This means no computer-authorization or CD-burn limits; tracks will even work on non-iPod music players. But be careful about trading Store purchases around the Internet—the name and email address on your iTunes account are easily visible on the file's Summary screen (page 80).

Deauthorize Your Computer

Unless these are iTunes Plus tracks, you won't be able to play protected purchased music or video on a sixth computer if you try to authorize it. Apple's authorization system will see five other computers already on its list and deny your request. That's a drag, but copy protection is copy protection.

To play protected files on Computer Number 6, you have to deauthorize another computer. Choose Store→Deauthorize Computer from the computer about to get the boot, and then type in your Apple Account username and password. The updated information zips back to Apple.

Are you thinking of putting that older computer up for sale? Before wiping the drive clean and sending it on its way, be sure to deauthorize it, so your new machine will be able to play copy-protected files. Erasing a hard drive, by itself, doesn't de-authorize a computer.

If you forget to deauthorize a machine before getting rid of it, you can still knock it off your List of Five, but you have to reauthorize every machine in your iTunes arsenal all over again. To make it so, in the iTunes Store, click the Account link. On the Apple Account Information page, click the Deauthorize All button.

> **Tip** Want the hassle-free life of an iTunes Plus library? Go to the iTunes Store and click the Upgrade My Library link on the main page. You can upgrade your older tracks to iTunes Plus versions for 30 cents a pop—instead of having to buy them all over again at the full price.

Use Your iPod to Copy Purchases to Other Computers

You may love the convenience of buying music and movies from any Internet-connected Mac or PC—whether it's your regular computer or not. But what do you do if you buy Store stuff on a different computer (at work, say) and need an easy way to move it back to your main machine?

Sure, you can move the files as described a few pages earlier. But that's a hassle. If you have an iPod set to manually manage songs and playlists (page 106), though, you can just use that iPod to ferry Store purchases back to your regular computer. Both computers involved need to be authorized with the same iTunes account, but if you're just toting tunes around between your work and home PCs, that shouldn't be a problem. Here's what you do:

❶ Connect the iPod to Computer #1and load it up with the Store files you want to transfer.

❷ Eject the iPod from Computer #1 and connect it to Computer #2.

❸ In iTunes, choose File→"Transfer Purchases From iPod".

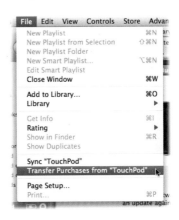

This painless transfer technique works only on Store-bought items, so you can't use it to, say, copy the player's entire library onto another computer.

 If you've purchased music or video at the iTunes Wi-Fi Store with your iPod Touch, iTunes automatically syncs the new content from the Touch with your computer's iTunes library when you connect the two. If for some reason it doesn't, choose File→"Transfer Purchases from iPod".

See Your iTunes Purchase History and Get iTunes Store Help

The iTunes Store keeps track of what you buy and when you buy it. If you think your credit card was wrongly charged, or if you suspect that one of the kids knows your password and is sneaking in forbidden downloads, you can contact the Store or check your account's purchase history page to see what's been downloaded in your name.

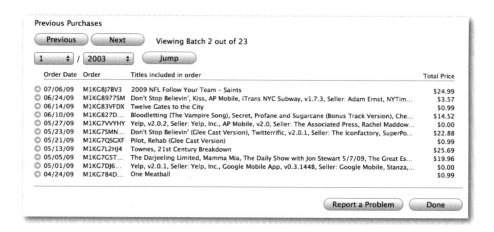

To do the latter, on the iTunes Store's main page, click the Account link, type in your password, and then click Purchase History. Your latest purchase appears at the top of the page, and you can scroll farther down to see a list of previous acquisitions. Everything billed to your account over the months and years is here, including gift-certificate purchases. If you see something wrong, click the "Report a Problem" link and say something.

If you have other issues with your account or want to submit a specific query or comment, the online help center awaits. From the iTunes Store's main page, click the Support link. Your Web browser presents you with the main iTunes service and support page; click the link that best describes what you want to learn or complain about. For billing or credit card issues, check out the iTunes Account and Billing Support link on that same Web page.

Buy Songs from Other Music Stores

There are many online music services out there and every one of 'em wants to sell you a song. But due to copy-protection, some of these merchants' songs don't work on the iPod. Some of them do, though. Thanks to recent moves by many stores to strip out the digital-rights management (DRM) protection on song files, their music has been liberated into the friendly MP3 play-anywhere format. Vive la musique!

Buying songs from somewhere other than the Store is as easy as supplying a credit card number and downloading the file using a Web browser. Once you have the file on your computer, use iTunes' File→"Add to Library" command to add it to your collection. Here are some of the online music services that now work with the iPod:

- **Napster.** You don't get the full Napster software and services, but Windows and Mac users can download and save MP3 files to your iTunes folder through the Napster Web site. (*www.napster.com*)

- **eMusic.** Geared toward indie bands, eMusic offers several subscription plans based on quantity: 16 bucks a month, for example, gets you 35 songs of your choice to download. (*www.emusic.com*)

- **Amazon MP3 Downloads.** From the main page, click Digital Downloads and then choose MP3 Downloads. Amazon has a free piece of software called the Amazon MP3 Downloader that takes half a minute to install and automatically tosses your purchases into iTunes for you. Click the link (circled below) at the top of the Amazon MP3 page to snag the Downloader program. (*www.amazon.com*)

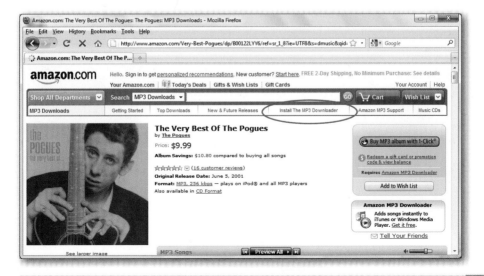

8

New This Week   New to Own   New to Rent   See All >

X-Men Origins: ...   Crank 2: High Vo...   Hannah Montana...   Twilight   Adventureland

It's Showtime: Video on the iPod

Video-playing iPods have been around since October 2005, when Apple's standard iPod arrived with a video chip inside and a video screen outside. These days, every iPod (except for the tiny, screen-less Shuffle) can handle moving pictures. But there's one iPod that plays video especially well: With its high-resolution 3.5-inch screen, the iPod Touch seems like it was *made* for video, even though it handles music and the Web just fine, too. And the Nanos of late 2009 don't just play video—they *shoot* it, too—mini-movies ready for YouTube, Facebook, or other video-sharing sites.

No matter which iPod you use, you're not stuck just watching two- or three-minute music videos. As explained in the previous chapter, the iTunes Store has all kinds of cinematic goodies you can buy: full-length Hollywood movies and episodes (or entire seasons) of TV shows. You can even get some videos in the super-sharp high-definition format, which looks great on your TV or computer screen. And yes, there are also thousands of music videos, just like the kind MTV used to play back when it, uh, played music.

This chapter shows you how to get videos from computer to iPod—and how to enjoy them on your own Shirt-Pocket Cinema.

Add Videos to iTunes

The iTunes Store is chock-full of videos, but sometimes you want to add your own flicks to your iTunes library. No problem, just drag the file from your desktop and drop it anywhere in iTunes' main window, or choose File→"Add to Library" to locate and import your files. Once you get videos into iTunes, you can play them there or copy them to your iPod.

Another way to add video files (or music files, for that matter) to iTunes is to drag them into the Automatically Add to iTunes folder. New to iTunes 9, this folder analyzes what you put inside it, and—based on the file extension—shelves it in the right spot for you. You find the auto-folder not through iTunes, but by navigating your system files. In Windows, it's usually in C:/Music→iTunes→iTunes Media→Automatically Add to iTunes (Home→Music→iTunes→iTunes Media→Automatically Add to iTunes). If iTunes can't match a file, it dumps it into a Not Added subfolder.

If you copy over a lot of videos from your Nano or other camcorder, an even easier route to this folder is through a desktop shortcut, so you can drag files directly to the shortcut, without having to root around your hard drive.

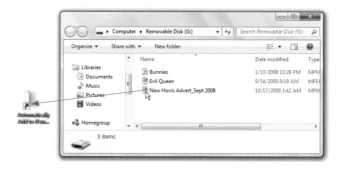

Tip ▸ Movies and TV shows get their own libraries in the iTunes Source list. If you import a video yourself and it's in the wrong place in the Source list, you may need to tweak the file's labeling info. Open the file's Get Info box (Ctrl+I [⌘-I]), click the Options tab, and then assign it a video format from the Video Kind drop-down menu: Music Video, Movie, TV Show, Podcast, or iTunes U file.

Play Videos in iTunes

Cranking up your iTunes movie theater is a lot like playing a song: Double-click your chosen video's title and iTunes starts playing it. When you click either the Grid or Cover Flow view buttons (circled), you see the videos represented by either a movie poster-type picture or a frame from the video. (Like album covers, videos you buy from the iTunes Store come with nice artwork.)

iTunes gives you a few video-viewing options. You can play the video in iTunes' artwork window, in the main window, opt to have it open in a separate, floating window (as shown here), or watch it full-screen on your computer.

To choose your screen size, go to the iTunes Preferences box (Ctrl+comma [⌘-comma]) and then click the Playback tab. Use the drop-down menus for Movies and TV Shows, and for Music Videos.

You can also pick a variety of window sizes under iTunes' View→Video Size menu, including Half Size, Actual Size, Double Size, Fit to Screen, and Full Screen.

Transfer Videos to Your iPod

Chapter 1 gives you the lowdown on syncing all kinds of files between iTunes and your trusty iPod. If you don't feel like flipping back there, here's a quick summary:

- **Synchronization.** Connect your iPod to your computer and click its Source pane icon in iTunes. Click the Movies tab and turn on the "Sync movies" checkbox. You can also choose to sync only certain movies to save space on your iPod. If you have TV programs in your iTunes library, click the TV Shows tab and adjust your syncing preferences there.

- **Manual management.** Click the appropriate library in the Source list (Movies, TV Shows, Podcasts, etc.), and then drag the files you want from the main iTunes window onto your connected iPod's icon.

If you made any video playlists in iTunes, you can copy those over to your iPod just as you would a music playlist. In case you haven't tried it, making a video playlist is just like making a music playlist. Chapter 6 has the details on making and modifying playlists.

Video Formats That Work on the iPod

As described in Chapter 7, the iTunes Store now sells movies, music videos, and TV shows. You can also import your own home movies and downloaded movie trailers and other videos into iTunes, as long as the files have one of these file extensions at the end of their name: *.mov*, *.m4v*, or *.mp4*.

Other common video formats, like *.avi* or Windows Media Video (*.wmv*), won't play in iTunes, but you can convert them with Apple's $30 QuickTime Pro software or any of the dozens of video-conversion programs floating around the Web. (If you're unsure whether a file's compatible, it's always worth trying to drag it into iTunes' main window and then choosing Advanced→"Create iPod or iPhone Version".)

Here are a few popular video-conversion tools:

- **PQ DVD to iPod Video Converter Suite**. This $40 program for Windows converts TiVo recordings, DVD video, DivX movies, Windows Media Video, RealMedia files, and AVI files to the iPod's video format (*www.pqdvd.com*).

- **Videora iPod Converter**. With this free software, you can gather up all those *.avi* and *.mpg* video clips stashed away on your PC and turn them into iPod video clips. Find it at *www.videora.com*.

- **ViddyUp!** Mac OS X owners can convert their movies, even those in *.avi* and DivX formats, with this $10 shareware program (*www.splasm.com*).

- **HandBrake.** Now available in versions for Windows and Mac OS X, this easy-to-use bit of freeware converts DVD movies and other files for the iPod. You can get it at *http://handbrake.fr*.

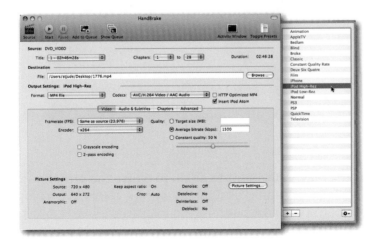

Play Videos on the Nano or Classic

Videos you buy from the iTunes Store (as well as other iTunes-friendly videos) appear in your iPod's Videos menu after you copy them onto the device. To watch a music video, TV show, or movie, scroll through the various Video sub-menus (Movies, Rentals, and so on) until you find something you like.

Say you want to watch a TV Show. Select TV Shows from the main Videos menu. The next screen lists all your iPod's TV shows by title. Scroll to the show you want and click the center button. The resulting menu lists all the *episodes* you have for that show. Scroll to the one you want and press the Play/Pause button to start the show. If you have a new Nano, turn it sideways for maximum viewing pleasure.

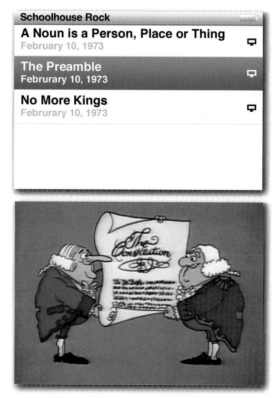

Here's a quick tour of the iPod's main video playback controls:

- **Press the Play/Pause button again to pause the program.** Pausing on the iPod works just like hitting Pause on a VCR or TiVo so you can get more Doritos. Press the button again to pick up where you left off.

- **To increase or decrease a video's volume, run your finger along the scroll wheel.** Adjusting the volume of a video works the same way as controlling the volume of a song.

- **To fast-forward or rewind through part of a video, tap the Select button twice.** A time code bar appears along the bottom of the screen. Use the scroll wheel to advance or retreat through a big chunk of the video. For moving forward and backward in smaller increments, hold down the Fast-Forward and Rewind buttons on the click wheel (see page 20).

When your video ends, the iPod flips you back to the menu you were on before you started watching your show. If you want to bail out before the movie's over, press the Menu button.

Some videos come in letterbox format, which leaves a strip of black above and below your video window. If you're not into widescreen HamsterVision, visit the Settings area of the Videos menu and turn on the "Fit to Screen" option.

 Tip Want your video file to remember its position when you pause or stop it? Easy. In iTunes, select the video and then press Ctrl+I (⌘-I). Click the Options tab and turn on the checkbox next to "Remember playback position".

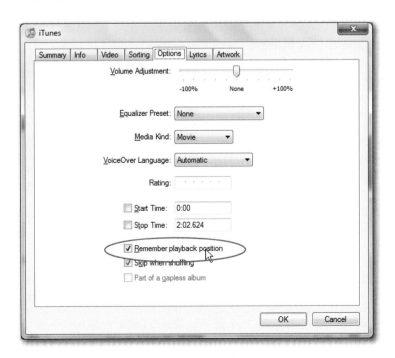

Shoot Video on the iPod Nano

The Nanos of 2009 can do something no other iPod can: make movies. Through its tiny lens on the back, this little iPod can shoot standard-definition video—or VGA video H.264 wth AAC audio at 30 frames per second, if you want to get technical about it. While the NanoCam works best outdoors and doesn't shoot high-def video like some of those other pocket cams out there, let's see the *those* camcorders play the Stones or deal up a hand of Solitaire.

Record a Video

Shooting a movie on the Nano is pretty much a point-and-shoot process. Here's how:

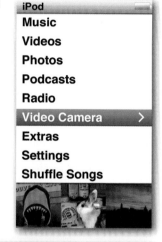

❶ **Choose iPod→Video Camera.** An animated lens shutter opens on-screen.

❷ **Aim the back of the Nano at your subject.** You can shoot video either in portrait or landscape mode. If you're holding the iPod horizontally in your right hand with the click wheel under your thumb, the camera's lens and microphone are in the upper-right corner of the back—be mindful of your fingers curling around and blocking the lens.

❸ **Press the center button to start recording.** The red "recording" dot in the top-right corner of the screen blinks as the time counter ticks along.

❹ **Press the center button again to stop recording.** You can record clips up to 2-gigabytes in size at a time. After those 2 GB, you have to start a new clip. You can record as many videos as you can fit on your have drive (along with everything else you've got).

 Tip If reality is too boring for you, you can add one of the Nano's 16 special-effects filters to your clip. They make your video look like it was shot on grainy film stock or through the eyes of the Terminator. You have to turn the filters on *before* you start shooting. To select one, choose iPod→Video Camera and hold down the center button to get to the effects menu, which shows samples. Scroll to the effect you want and click the center button. Press the center button to start recording.

Play a Video Clip—or Delete It

When you finish recording, you can play the clip back immediately: just press the Menu button on the click wheel to go to the Camera Roll menu. Scroll to the clip you want and press the Play/Pause button to start it up.

Your iPod groups videos by the date you shot them. If you shot multiple clips on the same day, click the center button and scroll to select the thumbnail for the video you want to review. Press the center button again to play the video. You can also get to your videos by choosing iPod→Videos→Camera Videos.

If you find your iPod getting overstuffed with home-grown footage (or you have a lot of dud clips where the baby refused to take that first step while your Nano was at the ready), you can delete all or some of the clips. Choose iPod→Videos→Camera Videos, select the clip you want to get rid of, and hold down the center button until a menu appears. Here, you can choose Delete (for just this clip) or Delete All (for *all* the clips you've shot; choose wisely).

Import Video to Your Computer

Unfortunately, the videos you shoot on the Nano don't sync back to iTunes when you connect your 'Pod to the computer. You have to grab the files yourself. To do this, you need to enable your iPod for use as an external disk—see page 206 for instructions on how to do that.

❶ **Connect your Nano to your computer in disk mode (see page 206).** Double-click its icon on your desktop to open it.

❷ **Choose iPod→DCIM→000Apple.** Your videos are those numbered *IMG_000.mp4* files.

❸ **Drag your clips from the iPod to your computer.** Once on your hard drive, you can import the videos into your favorite movie-making software, edit the dull parts, add background music, and upload the results to sites like YouTube and Facebook for sharing.

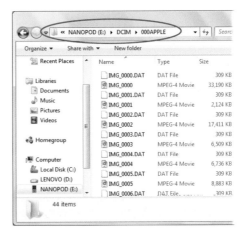

If you use iPhoto on a Mac, you can import videos like pictures: open iPhoto, select the Nano in the Device list, and import the desired clips. When you click a video thumbnail in iPhoto to play it, the clip opens in the QuickTime player for your movie-watching enjoyment.

Play Videos on the iPod Touch

To play a video on the Touch, find the one you want in the Videos menu and tap it to start playback. But how do you run the show on an iPod that has no physical controls? Easy; the playback buttons are *on the screen*.

When you watch video, *anything* else on the screen distracts you, so Apple hides these controls. Tap the screen once to make them appear, and again to make them disappear. Here's what they do:

- **Done.** Tap this blue button, in the top-left corner, to stop playback and return to your master list of videos.

- **Scroll slider.** This progress indicator at the top of the screen is exactly like the one you see when you play music. It displays the elapsed time, the remaining time, and a little white, round handle that you can drag to jump forward or backward in a video.

- **Zoom/Unzoom.** See the little ⬚ or ⬚ button in the top-right corner of the screen? Tap it to adjust the zoom level of the video, as described on the facing page.

- **Play/Pause (▶/❙❙).** These buttons do the same thing during video playback as they do during music playback: they alternate between playing and pausing your media.

- **Previous, Next (❙◀◀, ▶▶❙).** Hold down your finger to rewind or fast-forward the video. The longer you hold, the faster the zipping. (When you fast-forward, you even get to hear the sped-up audio, at least for the first few seconds.)

If you're watching a movie you bought from the iTunes Store, you may be surprised to discover that it comes with predefined chapter markers, just like a DVD does. Internally, your movie is divided into scenes. Tap the ⏮ or ⏭ buttons to skip to the previous or next chapter marker—great for long movies.

- **Volume.** You can drag the round, white handle of this scroll bar (bottom of the screen) to adjust playback volume.

Zoom/Unzoom

The iPod Touch's screen is bright, vibrant, and stunningly sharp. (It's got 480×320 pixels, crammed so tightly together that there are 163 of them per inch, nearly twice the resolution of a computer screen.) It's not, however, the right shape for videos.

Standard TV shows are squarish, not rectangular. So when you watch TV shows, you get black letterbox columns on either side of the picture.

Movies have the opposite problem. They're *too* wide for the iPod screen. So when you watch movies, you wind up with *horizontal* letterbox bars above and below the picture.

Some people are fine with that. After all, HDTV sets have the same problem, and people get used to it. Console yourself with the knowledge that, with letterbox bars on-screen, you're seeing the scene as the director composed it.

Other people, however, can't stand the bars. You're already watching a pretty small screen, so why sacrifice precious real estate to black bars?

Fortunately, the Touch gives you a choice. If you double-tap the video as it plays, you zoom in, magnifying the image so that it fills the entire screen. If the playback controls are visible, you can also tap ⬈ or ⬋.

Truth is, part of the image is now off the screen; you're not seeing the entire composition as originally created. You lose the top and bottom of TV scenes, and the left and right edges of movie scenes.

If this effect winds up chopping off something important—say some text on the screen—restoring the original letterbox view is just a double-tap away.

 Tip Both iTunes and the iPod can play videos that have closed-captioned text on-screen for the hearing-impaired. To turn it on in iTunes, open the Preferences box (Ctrl+comma [⌘-comma]), click the Playback tab, and then put a check in the box next to "Show closed captioning when available". On the Classic or Nano, choose iPod→Videos→Settings→Captions. On the iPod Touch, tap your way to Home→Settings→Video to get to the controls.

YouTube Videos on the iPod Touch

YouTube, of course, is the stratospherically popular video-sharing Web site, where people post short videos of every stripe: funny clips from TV, homemade blooper reels, goofy short films, musical performances, bite-sized serial dramas, and so on. Of course, you already have a Web browser on your Touch—Safari. So why not just point it to YouTube, the way millions of people do?

In a word, Flash. Most YouTube movies come in a format called Flash, which the Touch doesn't recognize. Apple, however, convinced YouTube to re-encode its millions of videos into H.264, a *much* higher-quality video format than Flash—*and* one you can play on your iPhone, iPod Touch, and on Apple TV.

Finding a Video to Play

The YouTube program works much like the iPod's Music and Videos menus; it's basically a collection of lists. Tap one of the icons at the bottom of the screen to find videos in any of these ways:

- **Featured.** A scrolling, flickable list of videos hand-picked by YouTube's editors. You get to see the name, length, star rating, and popularity (viewership) of each one.

- **Most Viewed.** A popularity contest. Tap the buttons at the top to look over the most-viewed videos *Today*, *This Week*, or *All* (meaning "of all time"). Scroll to the bottom of the list and tap Load 25 More to see the next chunk of the list.

- **Search.** Makes the Touch's keyboard appear, so you can type a search phrase. YouTube produces a list of videos whose titles, descriptions, keywords, or creator names match what you typed.

- **Favorites.** A list of videos you've flagged as your own personal faves, as described in a moment.

If you tap More, you get three additional options:

- **Most Recent.** These are the very latest videos posted on YouTube.

- **Top Rated.** When someone watches a video on YouTube, they can give it a star rating. (You can't rate videos when you view them on the Touch, however.) This list rounds up the highest-rated videos. Beware, though— you may be disappointed in the taste of the masses.

- **History.** This is a list of videos you've viewed recently on the Touch—and a Clear button that nukes the list (so people won't know you've been watching that "Charlie Bit My Finger" video).

If you have a free account with YouTube, you can also tap into the last three options: My Videos (for your own creations), Subscriptions, and Playlists.

Each YouTube video listing offers a ⊙ button at the right side. Tap it to open a Details screen for that video, featuring a description, date, category, tags (keywords), uploader name, play length, number of views, links to related videos, and so on.

That same Details screen offers an Add to Favorites button you can use to put the video in your list of personal favorites. Tap the Bookmarks button at the bottom of the screen to see the list.

Playing YouTube Videos

To play a video, tap its row in any of the lists. Turn the Touch 90 degrees counterclockwise—all videos play in horizontal orientation. The video begins playing automatically; you don't have to tap the ▶ button.

When you first start playing a video, you get the usual iPod controls, like ▶▶|, |◀◀, ||, the volume slider, and the progress bar that lets you move to a different spot in the movie. Here again, you can double-tap the screen to magnify the video, just enough to eliminate the black bars on the sides of the screen (or tap the ▨ button at the top-right corner to do the same).

The controls fade away after a moment, so they don't block your view. You can make them appear and disappear with a single tap on the screen.

Finally, there are two other icons on these controls: The first is the ⊞ button, which adds the video you're watching to your Bookmarks list, so you won't have to hunt around for it later. The second is the ✉ button, which lets you share your discovery by e-mail. A quick tap attaches a YouTube link to a fresh message in Touch Mail (see page 61).

Finally, there's a **Done** button at the top-left corner. It takes you out of the video you're watching and back to the list of YouTube videos.

Play iTunes and iPod Videos on Your TV

Movies on the iPod and computer screen are great, but watching them on a bigger screen is often even more gratifying. In case you were wondering, you *can* watch all those movies and videos on your TV screen—you just need to connect your computer or iPod to your television. *What* you connect them with depends on the hardware involved.

If you're connecting your computer to the TV, here are your best options:

- Connect computers that have S-video connections with an S-video cable; that pipes high-quality video to your TV. For the audio side of things, a $10 Y-shaped cable with a stereo mini-plug on one end and the red and white RCA plugs on the other provide the sound.

- If you have a computer-friendly television (the kind that can double as a computer monitor thanks to VGA or DVI ports), you can just plug your laptop right into the TV.

To mate your iPod with your TV, your options depend on which generation iPod you have.

- **Early video iPods (the ones that came out before Apple dubbed the model the "Classic").** You can connect these iPods to your TV with a

> **Tip** Not sure which iPod you have? Apple has a handy illustrated chart of almost every 'Pod that ever scrolled the Earth at *http://support.apple.com/kb/HT1353*. And if you're not sure which ones support TV Out, see *http://support.apple.com/kb/HT1454*.

special cable like the Apple iPod AV Cable, available at *http://store.apple.com* and other places. This $19 cord has a stereo mini-plug on one end (for the iPod's headphones jack), and red, white, and yellow RCA plugs on the other end that link to the audio and video ports on your TV. Some similar camcorder cables may also work, as do third-party cables from Belkin and Monster Cable, or special iPod video docks from DLO and other companies.

- **The iPod Classic, video Nano, or iPod Touch.** You, new iPod owner, need a different cable—one that can unlock the iPod's ability to pipe video to your TV. (Older iPod cables and many third-party offerings won't work with these models, unless you're using them with one of Apple's Universal Docks for iPods.)

The easiest place to find these cables is the Apple Store (*www.apple.com/ipodstore*). Here, you can find the Apple Composite AV Cable for TVs with older video inputs. You can also find the Apple Component AV Cable, made for high-end TVs and widescreen sets that can handle higher-quality video and audio connections. Both versions of the cable cost about $50, but that includes an integrated AC adapter to make sure your 'Pod is powered for a whole-weekend movie marathon.

Several third-party companies also make video docks and cables for the iPod; see Chapter 12 to get an idea of who's selling what. If you go with a non-Apple product, make sure it's rated to work with your particular iPod make and model.

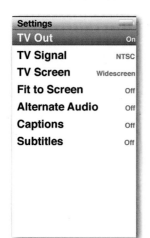

Once you connect your iPod to your TV, set it up so the video appears on the big screen: choose iPod→Videos→Settings and set TV Out to "On". (The TV Out settings on the iPod Touch are at Home→Settings→Video.)

The other Settings options are pretty self-explanatory. (The exception: TV Signal. Choose NTSC if you live in the U.S. or Japan, or pick PAL if you're connecting to a European or Australian TV set).

Once you get the iPod or computer hooked up to play movies, be sure to select the alternate video source on your television set, just as you would to play a DVD or game.

9

Picturing Your Photos on the iPod

Who needs an overstuffed wallet with cracked plastic picture sleeves to show off your snaps? If you have an iPod Nano, Touch, or Classic, you can quickly dump all your favorite shots right onto your iPod and show them on the glossy color screen. The picture-perfect fun doesn't stop there, either. Like earlier versions of the iPod and Nano, this trio of 'Pods can create a mini-slideshow of your images, right there in the palm of your hand. And you can plug most modern iPods into your TV set to fire up the show on a big living-room screen. This chapter shows you how to do everything except microwave the popcorn.

Setting Up: Get Ready to Put Photos on Your iPod

In addition to a computer loaded with iTunes and an iPod outfitted with a color screen, you need a few other things to move pictures to a 'Pod:

- **Compatible photo software for Windows or a Mac—or a folder of photos on your hard drive.** iPods can sync with several popular photo programs that you may already have. Windows mavens can grab pictures from Adobe Photoshop Album or the more versatile Adobe Photoshop Elements. On the Mac, there's Aperture or iPhoto 6 or later. You can also transfer pictures from a folder of photos on your computer, like the Pictures folder on a Windows system or the Mac's iPhoto Library folder for those who haven't upgraded past iPhoto 6.

- **Digital photographs in the proper format.** iTunes plays well with the photo formats for most digital cameras, Web pages, and email programs, along with a few others. In Windows, you can use JPG, GIF, TIF, BMP, PSD, SGI, and PNG formats on the iPod. On the Mac, JPG and GIF files, as well as images in the PICT, TIFF, BMP, PNG, JPG2000, SGI, and PSD formats, work just fine.

There are a couple of other things to remember when you add images to your iPod. For one, you can't import pictures from one of those photo CDs from the drugstore or a backup disc you made yourself—iTunes needs to pull the photos directly from your hard drive. Photos stored on DVDs or CDs won't cut it, either. The solution in both cases? Transfer the pix from disk to computer, and *then* they're ready for your iPod.

When it comes to photos, the iPod allies itself with just a single computer. Unlike manual music management, where you can grab songs from several different computers, you can only synchronize pictures between one iPod and one computer. If you try to load photos from a different computer, iTunes replaces all the photos on your iPod with the ones from that new machine. Ouch.

You also can't dump photos directly into the iPod from your digital camera— you need to go through iTunes, unless you have a much older iPod and a gadget like the iPod Camera Connector that siphons photos from the camera's memory card over to the iPod's hard drive (available for $40 at *Amazon. com*). This device doesn't work with the iPod Nano, though, nor do they work on the iPod Classic or Touch.

Get Pictures onto Your iPod

Okay, so you've got the right iPod and a bunch of pictures in iTunes-friendly format on your hard drive. How do you get those photos from your hard drive to your iPod? They get there just like your music does—through iTunes.

First, you need to set your preferences in iTunes and on the iPod so they can copy the photos you want to carry around, like so:

❶ Connect your iPod to your PC or Mac with the iPod's USB cable.

❷ Once the iPod shows up in the iTunes Source list, click its icon to select it.

❸ In the middle of the iTunes tabs for your iPod, click the one for Photos.

❹ Turn on the checkbox next to "Sync photos from" and then choose your photo program or photo-storage folder; that lets iTunes knows where to find your pix. You can copy everything over or just the *albums* (sets of pictures) you select.

❺ Click Sync (or Apply, if this is your first time syncing photos) after you make your selections.

If you don't use any of the programs listed in the "Sync photos from" menu and you just want to copy over a folder of photos on your hard drive, select "Choose folder" from the menu and then navigate to the desired folder. You can sync just the photos in your chosen folder, or include the photos tucked away in folders *inside* your chosen folder, too.

Select the "All photos and albums" option if you want iTunes to haul every single image in your photo program's library over to your iPod. (If you don't want to copy over those bachelorette-party snaps, opt for "Selected albums" and choose only the collections you want from your photo program.)

If you use a Mac with iPhoto '09 and have taken advantage of the program's face-recognition feature, you can also sync photos according to who's in the pictures. Just scroll down on the photo-sync preferences page to the Faces area and turn on the checkboxes next to the names of your favorite people. You can sync individual iPhoto events here as well.

Whenever you connect your iPod to your computer, iTunes syncs the photo groups you designated, adding any new pictures you stored in these groups since you last connected. During the process, iTunes displays an "Optimizing photos…" message in its display window, like the one shown here.

Don't let the term "optimizing" scare you: iTunes hasn't taken it upon itself to touch up your photographic efforts. The program simply creates versions of your pictures that look good on anything from your tiny iPod screen to your TV screen (in case you end up connecting your iPod to it). Then it tucks all of these copies away on your hard drive before adding them to your iPod.

Once you have some pictures on your Classic or Nano, your iPod randomly selects images and displays them in a floating slideshow of its own devising on the right side or bottom of your screen when you have the Photos menu selected.

 Tip Want to take a snap of some cool thing on your iPod Touch's screen? Hold down the Home button and press the Sleep/Wake button as thought it were a camera shutter. The resulting screenshot lands in Photos→Saved Photos. You can transfer it back to your computer the next time you sync. In fact, if your computer has a program that senses when you connect a digital camera, it will likely leap up and offer to pull in the Touch's screenshots just as it would regular photos.

Digital Photographer Alert: Storing Full-Quality Photos on Your iPod

When iTunes optimizes your photos for iPoddification, it streamlines the images a bit instead of copying the big, full-resolution files. But if you want, you can copy over the full-size photos instead. That way, you can transfer them to another computer—good news if you're a photographer and want to haul around a big, print-ready photo collection from one machine to another.

Just follow these steps:

❶ Connect your iPod Nano or Classic and select it in the iTunes Source list. Make sure you've set up your iPod as a portable hard drive (see Chapter 10 for details). The short version: in your iPod's Settings page in iTunes, click the Summary tab and then turn on the "Enable disk use" checkbox.

❷ Click the Photos tab in the iTunes window.

❸ Turn on the "Include full-resolution photos" checkbox. (Mac fans with videos stored in iPhoto can sync those up as well by turning on the "Include videos" checkbox right above.)

After you sync, full-resolution copies of your photos sit happily in the Photos folder on the iPod's hard drive. (The Photos folder has a subfolder called Thumbs that's full of iPod-optimized images all scrunched up in special .ithmb files; you can safely ignore these.)

View Photos on the iPod Classic or Nano

Once you get your photos freed from the confines of your computer, you'll probably want to show them off to your pals. To get to the goods, choose Photos→All Photos from your iPod's main screen. Or, if you opted for individual photo albums when you set up the synchronization preferences, scroll to the album you want to view and then press the round center button.

The iPod pops up a screen filled with tiny versions of the pictures in the group you select. Use the scroll wheel to maneuver the little yellow highlight box, and then zoom along the rows until you get to the picture you want to see. If you have hundreds of pee-wee pix to plow through, tap the Previous and Next buttons to advance or retreat by the screenful.

Here are some other navigational tips:

- Highlight the photo and press the center button to call up a large version of the photo—it'll fill your iPod screen.

- Press the Previous and Next buttons—or scroll the click wheel in either direction—to move forward or backward through pictures in an album.

- If you have a Nano, hold it sideways to see photos in landscape view.

- Press the Menu button to go back to the screen full of tiny photos.

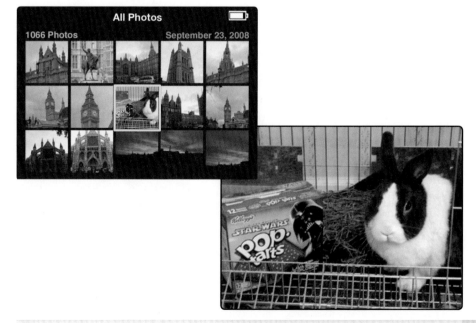

View Photos (in a Pinch) on Your iPod Touch

With its big color screen, the iPod Touch shows off your photos better than other iPods—and lets you have more fun viewing them because it's literally a hands-on experience.

To see the pictures you synced from your computer, tap the Photos icon on the iPod Touch's Home screen. Then tap Photo Library to see your pictures in thumbnail view. If you chose to copy over specific photo albums, tap the name of the album you want to look at. To get back to your library, tap the Photo Albums button at the top of the screen.

To see a full-screen version of a picture, tap the thumbnail image of it. The Touch displays photo controls for a few seconds; tap the photo to make them go away. Double-tap a photo to magnify it. You can also rotate the Touch to have horizontal photos fill the width of the screen.

Here are some other things you can do with your photos on the iPod Touch:

❶ Tap the left- and right-arrow keys to move through the photos in your collection.

❷ Tap the triangle icon at the bottom of the thumbnails screen (shown above) to start a slideshow. Flip to the next page to learn about slideshow settings.

❸ To set a photo as the wallpaper for your Touch (you know, that background picture you see on-screen when you wake the Touch from a nap), tap the 📤 icon in the lower-left corner. Then tap the Use As Wallpaper button. This icon also leads to buttons to email photos over the Touch's WiFi connection, send pictures to your MobileMe account (if you have one), and assign a photo to someone in your Touch contacts list.

❹ Spread and pinch your fingers on-screen (those fancy Touch moves described in Chapter 3) to zoom in and out of a photo. Drag your finger around on-screen to pan through a zoomed-in photo.

❺ Flick your finger horizontally across the screen in either direction to scroll through your pictures at whizzy speeds. You can show off your vacation photos *really* fast this way (your friends will thank you).

While tapping the 📤 icon with a single photo on-screen attaches that one picture to an email message, tapping the 📤 icon from the *thumbnails* screen lets you attach multiple photos to a single message—tap all the pictures you want to include, address your email, type a note if you like, and then tap the Send button.

> **Tip** Want to use a certain photo for your Touch wallpaper, but wish that guy making faces in the backgound wasn't there? You can crop in on photos with the ol' spread, pinch, and drag moves to suit yourself. Once you like what you see, tap the icon in the bottom-left corner and then choose the Use As Wallpaper option.

Play Slideshows on Your iPod

A photo slideshow takes all the click-and-tap work out of your hands, freeing you up to admire your pictures without distraction. To run a slideshow on an iPod, you need to set up a few things, like how long each photo appears on-screen and what music accompanies your trip to Disneyland.

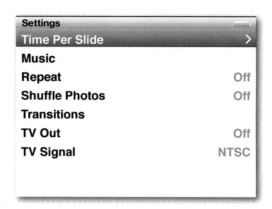

Slideshow Settings on a Classic or Nano

Start by choosing Photos→Settings. You'll see a slew of options to shape your slideshow experience.

- Use the Time Per Slide menu to set how much time (from 2 to 20 seconds) each photo stays on the screen. (During the slideshow, you can also go to the next image manually, with a tap of the click wheel.)

- Use the Music menu to pick a song from your iPod's playlists to serve as the soundtrack for your slideshow (assuming you want one). You may even want to create a playlist in iTunes to use with a particular slideshow.

- As with music tracks, you can repeat and shuffle the order of your photos. You can also add fancy Hollywood-style scene transitions by choosing

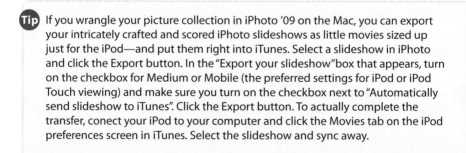

Tip If you wrangle your picture collection in iPhoto '09 on the Mac, you can export your intricately crafted and scored iPhoto slideshows as little movies sized up just for the iPod—and put them right into iTunes. Select a slideshow in iPhoto and click the Export button. In the "Export your slideshow" box that appears, turn on the checkbox for Medium or Mobile (the preferred settings for iPod or iPod Touch viewing) and make sure you turn on the checkbox next to "Automatically send slideshow to iTunes". Click the Export button. To actually complete the transfer, conect your iPod to your computer and click the Movies tab on the iPod preferences screen in iTunes. Select the slideshow and sync away.

Photos→Settings→Transitions. Pick from several dramatic photo-changing styles, including "Zoom" and "Fade Through Black". The latest iPod Nano even includes a "Ken Burns" effect, a gentle pan-and-zoom method used by the famous documentarian (and iPhoto users everywhere).

- To make sure your slideshow plays on your iPod's screen, turn the TV Out setting to Off, which keeps the signal in your iPod. (Turn the page if you want to project your slideshow on a TV.) Alternatively, you can select Ask, so that each time you start a slideshow, the iPod inquires whether you intend to run your photos on the big or small screen.

Once you get your settings just the way you want them, select the album or photo you want to start with, and then press the Play/Pause button on the click wheel to start the show. Press the Play/Pause button during playback to temporarily stop the show, and press it again to continue.

The show's time-per-slide, music, and transitions should all match the settings you chose. If you get impatient, you can use the click wheel's Previous and Next buttons to manually move things along.

Slideshow Settings On an iPod Touch

To customize the way your photos slide by on your Touch screen, press the Home button and then tap Settings→Photos. Your options include:

- **How long each picture stays on-screen.** Tap the time shown to get a menu of choices.

- **The transition effect between photos.** Dissolves, wipes, and all the usual styles are here.

You can also choose to repeat the show endlessly or to have your iPod shuffle the photos within it by tapping the Off or On buttons in the Settings area. Now, press the Home button and go back to Photos to start the slideshow.

 Note The iPod Touch doesn't include a slideshow music option in its settings. To get a soundtrack going for Touch Theater, hit the Home button, tap the Music icon and tap up a song or playlist. When the music starts, jump back to Photos and start your slideshow.

Play Slideshows on Your TV

Flip back to the previous chapter if you need help connecting your iPod to a television set so you can view your digital goodies on the big screen.

 Note As explained in the last chapter, the type of iPod you have dictates the equipment required to display photos and videos on your TV. First-generation video iPods that came out between 2005 and 2006 can use the older iPod AV cable that connects through the headphone port or Line Out jack on an iPod dock. Newer Classics, Nanos, and Touches connect through the Apple Universal Dock, the Apple Composite AV Cable, the Apple Component AV Cable, or a compatible third-party offering. In any case, it's going to cost you a few bucks.

Once you make the iPod-TV link, you're almost ready to start the show. You need to adjust a few more things on the iPod.

For Classics, Nanos, and Older Video iPods:

❶ **Choose Photos→Settings→TV Out→On.** The On option tells your iPod to send the slideshow *out* to a TV screen instead of playing it on its own screen. (You can also set your 'Pod to Ask if you want it to pester you about what screen to use.) If you have a Classic or Nano and use one of Apple's AV cables, the TV Out option automatically gets set to "On".

❷ **Select your local television broadcast standard.** If you're in North America or Japan, choose Photos→Settings→TV Signal→NTSC. If you're in Europe or Australia, choose Photos→Settings→TV Signal→PAL. If you're in an area not listed above, check your television's manual to see what standard it uses or search the Web for "world television standards."

❸ **Turn on your TV and select the video input source for your iPod.** You select the input for the iPod's signal the same way you tell your TV to display a signal from a DVD player or VCR. Typically, you press the Input or Display button on your TV's remote to change from the live TV signal to the new video source.

Now, cue up a slideshow on the iPod and press the Play/Pause button. Your glorious photographs—scored to the sounds of your selected music, if you wish—appear on your television screen. (Because television screens are horizontal displays, vertical shots end up with black bars along the sides.)

Your pre-selected slideshow settings control the show, though you can advance through it manually with your thumb on the click wheel. If you have the iPod Universal Dock, you can also pop through shots with a click of its tiny white Apple remote control. Although just one photo at a time appears on the TV, if you're driving the iPod Classic, your iPod shows not only the current picture, but the one before it and the one after, letting you narrate your show with professional smoothness: "OK, this is Shalimar *before* we had to get her fur shaved off after the syrup incident...."

For the iPod Touch:

❶ **Tap Settings→Video.** When you connect an AV cable to the Touch, your slideshow automatically appears on your TV set instead of on your iPod. In the TV Out section here, you can toggle Widescreen On or Off.

❷ **In the TV Signal area, select your local television broadcast standard.** If you're in North America or Japan, choose NTSC. If you're in Europe or Australia, choose PAL.

❸ **Turn on your TV and select the video input source for the Touch.** You select the input for the iPod's signal the same way you tell your TV to display the signal from a DVD player or VCR. Typically, you press the Input or Display button on your TV's remote to change from the live TV signal to the new video source.

❹ **On the Touch, navigate to the slideshow you want.** Press the Play triangle at the bottom of the screen, and the show begins.

10

The iPod as Personal Assistant

The early chapters in this book are all about showing you how your iPod works and how to fill it up with music, movies, photos, and more. But if you think that's *all* the iPod can do, think again. For instance, that gorgeous color screen is happy to display a copy of your computer's address book and calendar. And that's just for starters.

If you're looking for a handsome timepiece, the iPod can function as a world clock when you're on the road, and as a stopwatch when you're on the track. Modern iPods can now record your thoughts—if you speak them out loud into the iPod's microphone. The Nano can even count your steps and tell you how many calories you burned by just walking around.

If you've got a Nano, a Shuffle, or a Classic iPod, you can easily use it as an external hard drive for hauling around monster files, like PowerPoint presentations and quarterly reports. So if you've mastered the iPod's AV Club talents and you're ready for new challenges, this chapter shows you even more ways to use your iPod.

iPod as an Address Book

Putting a copy of your contacts file—also known as your computer's address book—onto your iPod is quite easy, as long as you use up-to-date software. Windows users need to have their contacts stored in Outlook Express, Outlook 2003 (or later), Windows Contacts, or the Windows Address Book (used by Outlook Express and some other email programs).

Mac folks need to use at least Mac OS X 10.4 (Tiger) and the Mac OS X Address Book (shown here), which Apple's Mail program uses to stash addresses. You can also use Entourage 2004 or later, but you first have to *link* before you *sync*: in Entourage, choose Preferences and click Sync Services. Then turn on the checkboxes for sharing contacts (and calendars) with Address Book and iCal (Apple's calendar program). Entourage shares the info, and Address Book and iCal sync it up.

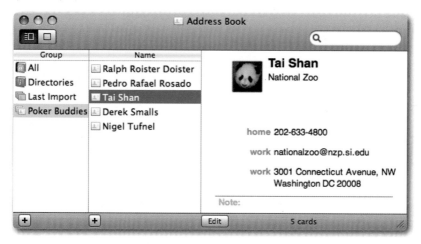

To turn your iPod into a little black book, follow these steps:

❶ Connect your iPod to your computer and click its icon when it shows up in iTunes' Source list. (If you use Outlook or Outlook Express, launch that now, too.)

❷ In the main part of the iTunes window, click the Contacts tab on a Classic or Nano; go for the Info tab on the Touch.

❸ Windows owners: Turn on the checkbox next to "Sync contacts from" and then use the drop-down menu to choose the program you want to copy contacts from. Mac owners: turn on the "Sync Address Book contacts" checkbox. If you want to sync contact groups, select them from the "Selected groups" box. You can also choose to import the photos in your contacts files.

❹ Click the Apply button in the lower-right corner of the iTunes window.

The iPod updates itself with the contact information stored in your address book. If you add new contacts while you have your iPod plugged in, choose File→Update iPod or click the Sync button in iTunes to manually move the new data over to your pocket player. When you decide someone doesn't deserve to be in your contacts list anymore, you delete them from your computer's address book and the person will disappear from your iPod the next time you sync it to your computer.

To look up a pal on the iPod Nano or Classic, choose iPod→Extras→Contacts and scroll to the name of the person. Press the center button and the address card for that person pops up on-screen. Touch owners: tap the Contacts icon on the Home screen and flick your way to whichever contact you're looking for. Tap the name to see the details. You can even send the contact info off by email—just tap the Share Contact button.

> **Tip** The iPod Touch offers some extra features in iTunes' Info tab. First, you have the option to sync contacts stored in both Google Gmail and Yahoo! Mail address books. Click the Configure button to enter your Gmail or Yahoo user name and password (you need an Internet connection to sync). Second, because you can enter contacts directly on your Touch, the Info settings give you the option to say which group you'd like to add your Touch-created contacts to when you return home.

The iPod as Calendar

Just as iTunes can pluck contacts off your computer, so it can snag and display a copy of your daily or monthly schedule on your iPod—*if* you happen to use Outlook on your PC or iCal on your Mac. (You can use Entourage 2004 or later by choosing, in Entourage, Preferences→Sync Services and checking off the option to have Entourage share its event info with iCal.)

To get your calendar connected, fire up iTunes and then:

❶ Connect the iPod to your computer and click the iPod's icon when it shows up in the Source list.

❷ In the main part of the iTunes window, click the Contacts tab (or the Info tab if you have a Touch). Scroll down past Contacts to Calendars.

❸ Turn on the checkbox next to "Sync calendars from Microsoft Outlook" (Windows) or "Sync iCal calendars" (Mac). If you have multiple calendars, select the ones you want to copy to your 'Pod.

❹ In the lower-right corner of the iTunes window, click the Apply button.

❺ If your iPod doesn't automatically start updating itself with your date book, choose File→Sync iPod. If you haven't changed any settings but are just updating info, the Apply button in the corner of iTunes turns to Sync, and you can click that instead of going up to Menuville.

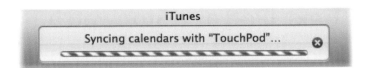

iTunes

Syncing calendars with "TouchPod"...

To look up your busy schedule on an iPod Classic or Nano, choose iPod→Extras→Calendars. Select the name of the calendar you want to examine and press the round center button. The skinny Nano screen gives you a calendar grid with dots on the days you have stuff scheduled, with the names of events listed below. On the Classic, you get a blue-and-gray grid with tiny red flags planted on the squares when you have something scheduled for that day. In both models, use the scroll wheel to navigate to a particular day and press the center button to see details on the day's events.

On the iPod Touch, tap the Calendar icon on the Home screen. Tap List, Day, or Month to see your schedule in the short or long term, or tap the Today button to see what's in your immediate future. List view shows all your upcoming appointments one after the other. In Month view, your Touch represents events with black dots and lists them below the calendar grid. Tap the black triangles on either side of the month name to advance forward or backward through the months. Tap the **+** button to add an event.

A few other calendar-keeping tips:

- If you make use of the To Do list function in your calendar program, those action items appear in their own place on the Classic and Nano. Choose iPod→Extras→Calendars→To Do.

- Your iPod can also pester you if you request a reminder of an upcoming event. To turn on the portable Nag Alerts, choose iPod→Extras→Calendars→Alarms. You have your choice of Off, Beep, or None (which just displays a silent message on-screen). The Touch flashes a beeping on-screen alert keyed to the event reminders in your synced calendar. You can set your own alert on the Touch by selecting an event and tapping the Edit button. Tap the Alert screen and pick a suitable amount of time for an advance-warning message.

Track Time: iPod as a Stopwatch

The iPod Nano, Classic, and Touch all have a Stopwatch feature riding alongside their great music and video capabilities. Using the iPod stopwatch is not unlike using a regular stopwatch, except that it can be a very expensive timer. As with most things, the Touch does things its own touchy-feely way.

iPod Touch

To get to the Touch's stylish full-screen stopwatch, tap your way through Home→Clock→Stopwatch. To start timing yourself, tap the green Start button. The timer starts counting and the Start button changes to a red Stop button. (Tap that when you're done timing.) If you're running a series of laps, tap the gray Lap button each time you finish one. The Touch records your time for that lap and then starts timing your next one.

The Touch displays the time for the lap-in-progress above the overall session timer. It lists the time for completed laps below the timer, so you can track your workout. The timer keeps ticking, even if you tap your way into another program to, say, pick a new playlist. When you tap the Clock icon again on the Home screen, you return to the Stopwatch, still ticking away.

If you need to pause the timer, tap the Stop button and then tap Start again to have it pick up where it left off counting. When you're finally done with your exercise, tap the Stop button to halt the clock. Then hit the gray Reset button to clear the times from the screen.

> **Tip** The iPod Touch has the Nike + iPod software built right into it. All you have to do is tap Home→Settings→Nike + iPod to turn it on. You still need to buy the special Nike shoes and shoe sensor that transmits your steps to the iPod. Nanos need the snap-on reciever ($29 for the kit at *www.apple.com/ipod/nike*), but once enabled, the iPod keeps track of your workout more scientifically than any personal trainer ever could—*and* you get to play your own music.

iPod Nano or Classic

The Stopwatch feature on these two iPods not only clocks your time around the track, it also *keeps* track of your running sessions. To turn your Classic or Nano into a timer, choose Extras→Stopwatch. Here's what you do from there:

- Press the Play/Pause button to begin. The iPod begins to clock you by hours, minutes, seconds, and milliseconds.

- If you're timing each lap around the track, tap the iPod's center button to record that lap time; the iPod lists that time underneath the overall session time. The screen displays up to three lap times.

- Press Play/Pause to stop the clock. When you're done timing, press the Menu button. This takes you back to the Stopwatch menu. Here, you can click on Resume to start up the clock again.

- If you want a new session with the Stopwatch, select New Timer.

The iPod stores logs of your last several workouts. To review your progress, scroll to Extras→Stopwatch, where you see your past exercise sessions listed by date and time of day. Scroll and select a session to see a list of your lap times, with the shortest, longest, and average lap noted on top. Press the iPod's center button to delete the log.

- If you have a lot of old logs cluttering up the screen, select Extras→Stopwatch→Clear Logs to wipe them all out.

- If you're in the middle of a session, go to Extras→Stopwatch→Current Log to see your current state of progress.

Stopwatch Log	
Sep 25 2009	**6:30 AM**
Total	**00:17:05.8**
Shortest	**00:02:57.1**
Longest	**00:05:01.2**
Average	**00:04:16.4**
Lap 1	00:04:32.2
Lap 2	00:05:01.2
Lap 3	00:02:57.1
Lap 4	00:04:35.0

 Tip Attention all cooks! The Touch's Timer is great for keeping track of that bubbling bouillabaisse. Nestled right next to the Stopwatch, the Timer works just as you'd expect: pick your countdown time using the virtual spinwheels and press Start.

Count Steps: iPod Nano as Pedometer

In addition to the Stopwatch feature, the latest iPod Nanos include another treat for fitness buffs: a colorful pedometer that tells you how many steps you've taken—since you turned on the pedometer, anyway. (It measures steps based on readings from the iPods built-in motion sensor.) The pedometer also displays how many calories you burn in the process. And all this careful bookkeeping is intended to help you with your workout goals.

To set up the pedometer for the first time:

❶ Choose iPod→Extras→Fitness→Pedometer.

❷ Use the click wheel to scroll up your weight. (If you need to change your weight later, go to iPod→Extras→ Fitness→Settings→Weight.)

❸ Press the center button to start the Nano counting your steps. A little shoe icon in the Nano's menu bar tells you that the pedometer's on and counting away.

❹ Press the center button again when you're done counting steps to see your total steps (and calories burned) for the day.

You can see a history of your recorded steps by choosing iPod→Extras→ Fitness→History. When the calendar screen appears, use the click wheel to scroll to a particular day. Press the center button to see a thorough breakdown of your stepping session (or sessions) on that date. (Press the Next or Previous buttons to jump to the next or last month.)

The session history lists your workout duration, stop and start times, calories burned, and total steps for the day and week. For exciting bar-chart action, turn the Nano sideways to see the data displayed on a graph.

You can fine-tune the pedometer's behavior by choosing iPod→Extras→ Fitness→Settings. Scroll and click to select an item. In Pedometer, you can have it Always On, or only activated when you feel like it with the Manual option. Also in Settings, you can set a daily step goal to aspire to, change your weight, or change the orientation of the screen to Vertical, Left, or Right.

> **Tip** As with the Touch, the $29 iPod + Nike Sport Kit (*www.apple.com/ipod/nike*) works with the Nano. It adds more gym tech with a special shoe sensor, workout data uploads to Nike's Web site, and plenty of power music mixes to inspire you.

Voice Memos: iPod as Audio Recorder

The Nano, Touch, and 160-gigabyte iPod Classic don't just *play* sound, they *record* it, too, thanks to the Voice Memos feature. If you have the Classic or the 8-gigabyte version of the Touch, however, you need to invest in Apple's optional Earphones with Microphone and Remote, (available for $29 at *www.apple.com/ipodstore*) or a compatible third-party microphone.

Once you have your microphone in place (the Nano's mic is built-in), you can start your recording session:

❶ On the Nano, choose iPod→Extras→Voice Memos. On the Classic, choose iPod→Voice Memos. On the Touch, tap the Voice Memos icon on the Home screen.

❷ To start recording, press the center button or Play/Pause on the Nano, choose Voice Memos→Start Recording on the Classic, or tap the red dot on the Touch's screen (circled). You can pause your recording by pressing the Play/Pause button on the click wheel or tapping the Touch's onscreen pause icon. Choose Resume on the Nano or Classic, (or tap the Pause icon on the Touch screen) to start recording again. On the Nano, press the center button to set audio-book-like chapter markers in the recording; these let you jump to each chapter using the Previous and Next buttons.

❸ When you finish recording, press the Nano's Menu button and choose Stop and Save from the Menu. Choose Stop and Save on the Classic. On the Touch, tap the black square on the right side of the screen to stop the recording session.

To play a recording, select it from the Voice Memos menu on a Nano or Classic, or tap the ☰ icon on the Touch. To delete a chosen recording on the Nano or Classic, press the center button to select it and choose Delete from the menu. On the Touch, select it on the Voice Memos menu and press the Delete button. The Touch has a Share button on the same screen that lets you send the selected recording as an email attachment.

If your iPod is set to sync, iTunes copies your recordings to its Voice Memos playlist. You can find the audio files on Nanos or Classics enabled for disk use, (skip ahead a few pages) in the iPod's Recordings folder.

Tick-Tock: iPod as a World Clock

As discussed earlier in this book, all iPods (except for the screenless Shuffle) have built-in clocks with a simple alarm feature. But that's *so* last week. These power Pods let you set multiple clocks, in different time zones, each with their own alarms. If you travel frequently, you can simply create a clock for each destination instead of constantly fiddling with time zone settings. Cool.

The iPod should already have one clock—the one you created when you first set it up and selected your time zone.

Add a Clock on Your iPod Touch

❶ Tap Home→Clock→World Clock.

❷ Tap the plus (**+**) button in the upper-right corner of the screen.

❸ When the keyboard pops up, start typing in the name of any large city.

❹ Tap the name of the city to add its clock to your list.

If you want to rearrange your list of clocks, tap the Edit button and use the three-stripe gripstrip (≡) to drag them into the order you want.

To delete a clock, tap the Edit button, tap the ⊖ icon next to the clock's name, and then tap the Delete button to whack that clock from the list.

Add a Clock to Your iPod Classic or Nano

❶ Go to iPod→Extras→Clocks and tap the iPod's center button.

❷ You have one clock there. Click the center button again to choose Add. (Choose Edit if you want just one clock, but want to change it.)

❸ On the next screen, select a world region, like North America, Europe, Africa, or Asia. Some categories on the Region menu are less obvious: Select Atlantic if you live in Iceland or the Azores; choose Pacific if you live in Hawaii, Guam, or Pago Pago.

❹ Select a region and the next screen takes you to a list of major cities and the current time in that part of the world. Scroll and select the city of your choice. Once you do, the iPod creates a clock labeled with the city's name and showing the local time. It adds the clock to your Clock menu.

If you want to change a clock, select it and press the iPod's center button to bring up the on-screen options for Edit and Delete. Choose Edit, which takes you back through the whole "pick a region, pick a city" exercise.

If you decide you have too many clocks and don't need that Tora Bora clock after all, select the unwanted clock from the list. Press the center button on the iPod, scroll down to Delete, and press the center button again to erase time.

 To make adjustments, like changing to Daylight Saving Time or to change the iPod's current time zone, choose iPod→Settings→Date & Time on a Classic or Nano. On the Touch, hit the Home screen and then tap Settings→General→Date & Time to get to the time controls.

iPod as a Portable Hard Drive

If being a portable entertainment system and organizer isn't enough, your iPod can also serve as a portable disk to shuttle documents, presentations, and other files from one computer to another. (The Touch doesn't naturally work as an external drive unless you use utility programs like TouchCopy, mentioned back in Chapter 5.)

To give your iPod these file-toting powers:

❶ Plug your 'Pod into your computer.

❷ When its icon shows up in the Source list, select it and then click the Summary tab in the main iTunes window.

❸ Turn on the checkbox next to "Enable disk use" in the Options area of the Summary screen. (If you have an iPod Shuffle, use the on-screen slide to designate just how much of your 2 or 4 gigabytes you want to use for music and how much for files.)

❹ In the lower-right corner of the iTunes window, click the Apply button. If you forget and try to move on to something else, iTunes reminds you that you modified an iPod setting and prompts you to OK the change.

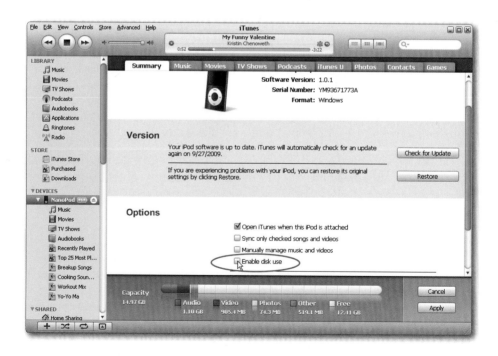

Your iPod now shows up in the My Computer area of Windows or on the Mac desktop. You can drag files on and off the iPod just as you would with any other drive connected to your computer: Drag files onto the

iPod's icon, or double-click the icon and create folders to put your files into. Delete files by dragging them to the Trash or Recycle Bin. Steer clear of the folders labelled Calendars, Contacts, and Photos; the iPod uses those to store the eponymous items. The next page shows you how to use the Notes folder.

Keep in mind that once you turn your iPod into an external hard drive, you have to treat it like one by formally ejecting the drive from iTunes before disconnecting your 'Pod. (Do so by clicking the Eject icon next to the iPod's name in the iTunes Source list and you'll avoid huffy alert boxes from your operating system about improper device removal.)

Your iPod keeps music, movies, and other iTunes stuff in a special, invisible area of the player, so copying regular computer files onto the iPod doesn't affect those files. (And syncing your music with a PC or Mac doesn't affect the computer files, either.) But remember that the more you fill up your iPod with entertainment, the less room you have for data files—and vice versa.

 Note Windows can't read the Mac disk format, but a Mac can read a Windows-formatted iPod or iPod Nano. If you want to use your iPod with both systems, plug it into the PC first and let iTunes format your 'Pod for Windows. The Shuffle and the Touch automatically work with both PCs and Macs.

Read Text Files on Your iPod

The squint factor may be a little much, but the iPod Classic or Nano can display text files, which comes in handy if you want to review class notes while you're relaxing or if you want to skim talking points before a presentation.

You create iPod Notes from plain text files (with a *.txt* extension) like those from Windows NotePad or TextEdit on a Mac. You can't use full-fledged word-processing documents from Microsoft Word or AppleWorks, unless you save them as plain text files.

To use the iPod's Notes feature:

❶ Connect your iPod to your computer as an external disk. (Flip back two pages to find out how.)

❷ Once you save your text files in the proper plain-text format, open your iPod by double-clicking its icon in the Computer window for Windows (the My Computer window on Windows XP) or on the Mac desktop.

❸ Drag the files into the Notes folder on your iPod.

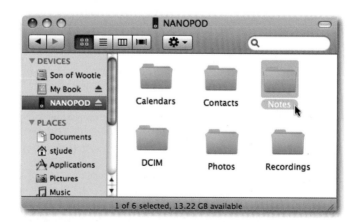

 By itself, the iPod can only display short text files—those under 4 kilobytes in size. But there's plenty of shareware around the Web that lets you read much longer files on your iPod. Hit the links at *www.missingmanuals.com* to see a few options.

❹ After you copy your files, eject the iPod from iTunes by clicking the Eject button next to its name in the Source list (or use the Eject button in the corner of the iTunes window).

❺ When you're ready to start reading, choose Extras→Notes. You'll see the names of your text files listed in the Notes menu. Scroll to the one you want and click the iPod's center button to bring it up on-screen.

As you read, you can use the scroll wheel to page up and down through the file. Press the Menu button to close the file and return to the list of Notes files. If you can't find a document you're looking for in the Notes menu, open the Notes folder on your iPod and make sure it is indeed a *.txt* file.

Boswell's Life of Johnson highlights.txt

Mr. Cambridge, upon this, politely said, 'Dr. Johnson, I am going, with your pardon, to accuse myself, for I have the same custom which I perceive you have. But it seems odd that one should have such a desire to look at the backs of books.' Johnson, ever ready for contest, instantly started from his reverie, wheeled about, and answered, 'Sir, the reason is very plain. Knowledge is of two kinds. We know a subject ourselves, or we know where we can find information upon it. When we enquire into any subject, the first thing we have to do is to know what books have treated of it. This leads us to look at catalogues, and the backs of books in libraries.'

Using the iPod as a text reader is a handy way to bring along your grocery list so you can rock while you shop. If you want to browse more challenging prose than "Buy Pampers," swing by Project Gutenberg's Web site at *www. gutenberg.us*. Here, you can download thousands of public-domain literary works as plain text files and transfer them to your iPod's Notes folder for a little Shakespeare, Schopenhauer, or Sun Tzu.

Tip The iPod Touch may not be able to double as an external hard disk (and thus, a pocket ebook reader) without help from third-party software, but if you've got a Wi-Fi signal, who needs a hard disk? Since you, Touch owner, have the Web in the palm of your hand, just point your mini-Safari directly at *gutenberg.us* or *books. google.com* to do your reading. If you've got an online text storage locker like Google Docs (*docs.google.com*), you can stash personal files and notes there and then tap them to open and read them when you log into your Google account. If you keep text in the Notes feature in Microsoft Outlook for Windows or Mac OS X 10.5 Mail, you can copy that info over to the Touch's own Notes program via your iPod sync preferences (Chapter 5). Don't forget the 99-cent classics in the Books section of the iTune App Store. Or the free Shakespeare app, where you can get the complete works of The Bard in less than 3 megabytes of precious Touch space.

Surfing the Web with iPod Touch

I f you have an iPod Touch, you have something that no other iPod has: the power of the World Wide Web, right in your pocket. The Web on the iPod Touch looks like the Web on a desktop or laptop computer, and that's one of Apple's greatest accomplishments. You see the real deal—the actual fonts, graphics, and layouts—not the stripped-down, bare-bones mini-Web you usually get on cellphone screens.

The iPod Touch's Web browser is a lite version of Safari, the browser that, in its full-blown version, comes with every Macintosh and is now available for Windows. Safari Lite is fast, simple to use, and very pretty indeed. This chapter will show you how to get online with your Touch, and what to do once you get there.

Get Your Wi-Fi Connection

Before you can get surfin' with Safari, you need to get the iPod Touch connected to the Internet. That means connecting it to a *Wi-Fi* network. Wi-Fi, known to geeks as 802.11 and to Apple fans as AirPort, means wireless networking. It's the same technology that lets laptops the world over get online at high speed in any Wi-Fi *hot spot*. Hot spots are everywhere these days: in homes, offices, coffee shops (notably Starbucks), hotels, airports, and thousands of other places.

When you're in a Wi-Fi hot spot, your Touch has a very fast connection to the Internet, as though it's connected via a cable modem or DSL. In fact, if you connect your iPod Touch to your own home wireless network, it's actually using the same cable or DSL connection the other computers around the house share.

When you launch any of the Touch's programs that require an Internet connection—Safari or YouTube, for example—the iPod tries to get online in this sequence:

- First, it sniffs around for a Wi-Fi network you've used before. If it finds one, it connects quietly and automatically. You're not asked for permission, a password, or anything else.

- If it can't find a previous hot spot but it detects a *new* one, a message appears on the screen. It displays the new hot spot's name; tap it to connect. (If you see a 🔒 icon next to the hot spot's name, then it's been protected by a password, which you need to know; you'll have to enter on the keyboard that pops up.)

Silencing the "Select a Wi-Fi Network" Messages

Every now and then, you might be bombarded by those "Select a Wi-Fi Network" messages at a time when you have no need to be online. You might want the iPod to stop bugging you—to *stop* offering Wi-Fi hot spots.

In that situation, from the Home screen, tap Settings→Wi-Fi and turn off "Ask to Join Networks". When this option is off, your iPod never blurts out the names of new networks you might want to join. But each time you want join a new network, you have to visit this settings screen and select one, as described next.

The List of Hot Spots

At some street corners in big cities, Wi-Fi signals bleeding out of apartment buildings·sometimes give you a choice of 20 or 30 hot spots to join. But whenever the iPod invites you to join a hot spot, it suggests only a couple of them: the ones with the strongest signal and, if possible, no password requirement.

There may be times, however, when you want to see the complete list—maybe because the iPod-suggested hot spot is flaky. To see the full list, from the Home screen, tap Settings→Wi-Fi. Tap the network you want to join.

Commercial Hot Spots

Tapping the name of the hot spot you want to join is generally all you have to do—if it's a home Wi-Fi network. Unfortunately, joining a *commercial* Wi-Fi hot spot—one that requires a credit-card number (in a hotel room or airport, for example)—requires more than just connecting to it. You also have to *sign into* it, exactly as you'd do if you were using a laptop.

To do that, return to the Home screen and open Safari. You'll see the "Enter your payment information" screen either immediately, or as soon as you try to open a Web page of your choice.

Supply your credit-card information or (if you have a membership to the Wi-Fi chain, like Boingo or T-Mobile) your name and password. Click Submit or Proceed, try *not* to contemplate how this $8 per hour is pure profit for somebody, and enjoy your surfing.

Going on a Safari Tour

You get onto the Web by tapping the Safari icon on the Home screen (below, left); the very first time you do this, a blank browser window appears (below, right). To type a Web address into the browser, tap the address bar and the keyboard pops up on-screen ready for your input.

Safari has most of the features of a desktop Web browser: bookmarks, auto-complete (for Web addresses), cookies, a pop-up ad blocker, and so on. (It's missing niceties like multimedia plug-ins—especially Adobe Flash for video.)

When you go to a Web page, mini-Safari behaves just like a desktop browser. It highlights the address bar as it loads all the elements on the page, and even gives you Apple's circular "Wait! Wait! I'm loading the page!" animated icon at the top of the screen.

> The iPod Touch runs pretty much the same operating system as the iPhone and Apple usually releases updates to the software a few times a year. While some updates can simply be security-related fixes, the company does occasionally make bigger overhauls, like redesigning the Safari interface. If your copy of Safari doesn't look exactly like what's pictured here, odds are you're running a version released before or after iPhone/iPod Touch OS 3.1.1. You can see what version you have by tapping Home→Settings→General→About→Version.

Here's a quick tour of the main screen elements, starting from the upper left:

- **Address bar.** This empty white box is where you enter the *URL* (Web address) for a page you want to visit. (URL is short for the even less self-explanatory Uniform Resource Locator.)

- **✕, ↻ (Stop, Reload).** Click the ✕ button on the address bar to interrupt the download of a Web page you just requested (if you made a mistake, for instance, or if it's taking too long).

  Once a page finishes loading, the ✕ button turns into a ↻ button. Click this circular arrow if a page doesn't look or work quite right, or if you want to see the updated version of a Web page that changes constantly (such as a breaking-news site). Safari re-downloads the Web page and reinterprets its text and graphics.

- **Search box.** Just like the big browsers, Safari has a separate little box for typing in search terms. Tap here and the keyboard pops up. Type in your keywords and tap the blue Google (or Yahoo) button that appears in the bottom-right corner.

- **◀, ▶ (Back, Forward).** Tap the ◀ button to revisit the page you were just on.

  Once you tap ◀, you can then tap the ▶ button to return to the page you were on *before* you tapped the ◀ button.

- **✚ (Add Bookmark).** When you're on a page that you might want to visit later, bookmark it by tapping this button.

- **▢ (Bookmarks).** This button brings up your list of saved bookmarks (skip ahead a few pages to read more about bookmarks).

- **▢, ▢ (Page Juggler).** Safari can keep multiple Web pages open, just like any other browser. The number indicates how many open pages you've got.

Zoom and Scroll Through Web Pages

These two gestures—zooming in on Web pages and then scrolling around them—have probably sold more people on the iPhone and the iPod Touch than any other feature. It all happens with a fluid animation, and a responsiveness to your finger taps, that's positively addicting. New owners often spend time just zooming in and out of Web pages simply because they can.

When you first open a Web page, you get to see the *entire thing*. Unlike Web browsers on most cellphones, the Touch crams the entire site onto its 3.5-inch screen, so you can get the lay of the land.

At this point, of course, you're looking at .004-point type, which is too small to read unless you're a microbe. So the next step is to magnify the *part* of the page you want to read.

The iPod Touch offers three ways to do that:

- **Rotate the iPod.** Turn the device 90 degrees in either direction. The Touch rotates and magnifies the image to fill the wider view.

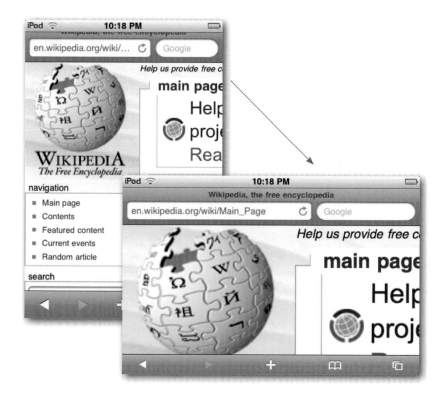

- **Do the two-finger spread.** Put two fingers on the glass and spread them apart. The Web page stretches before your very eyes, growing larger. Then pinch to shrink the page back down again. (Most people do several spreads or several pinches in a row to achieve the degree of zoom they want.)

- **Double-tap.** Safari is intelligent enough to recognize different *chunks* of a Web page. One article might represent a chunk, for example, a photograph another chunk. When you double-tap a chunk, Safari magnifies *just that chunk* to fill the whole screen. It's smart and useful.

Double-tap again to zoom back out.

Double-tap —

Once you've zoomed out to the proper degree, you can scroll around the page by dragging or flicking with your finger. You don't have to worry about "clicking a link" by accident; if your finger's in motion, Safari ignores the tapping action, even if you happen to land on a link. It's awesome.

To go ahead and actually click a link, simply tap it with your finger.

Tip Every now and then, you'll find, on a certain Web page, a *frame* (a column of text) with its own scroll bar—an area that scrolls independently of the main page. (If you have a MobileMe account, for example, the Messages list is such a frame.)

The Touch has a secret, undocumented method for scrolling one of these frames without scrolling the whole page: the *two-finger drag*. Check it out.

The Safari Address Bar

As on a computer, the Touch's browser offers four ways to navigate the Web:

- Type an address into the Address bar.

- Choose a bookmark.

- Return to a site you visited recently using the History list.

- Tap a link.

The following pages cover each of these methods in turn.

The Address bar is the strip at the top of the screen where you type in a Web page's address. And it so happens that *three* of the iPod Touch's greatest tips and shortcuts all have to do with this important navigational tool:

- **Insta-scroll to the top.** You can jump directly to the Address bar, no matter how far down a page you've scrolled, just by tapping the very top edge of the screen (on the status bar). That "tap the top" trick is timely, too, when a Web site *hides* the Address bar.

Tap anywhere on this strip...   *...to jump back to the top of the page.*

- **Don't backspace to delete.** There *is* an ⊗ button at the right end of the Address bar, whose purpose is to erase the entire current address so you can type another one. (Tap inside the Address bar to make it, and the keyboard, appear.)

  In the latest version of the iPod Touch software, tapping the URL inside the address bar also brings up the Select and Select All buttons—or Paste, if you have text copied to the Touch's clipboard (Chapter 3).

- **Don't type *http://www or .com.***
  Safari is smart enough to know that most Web addresses begin and end with those terms—so you can leave all that stuff out, and it will supply them automatically. Instead of *http://www.cnn.com*, for example, just type *cnn* and hit Go. (If the suffix you seek is .net, .edu, or .org, press and hold the .com button and slide across to the one you need, as shown at right.)

Otherwise, this Address bar works just like the one in any other Web browser. Tap inside it to make the keyboard appear. (If the Address bar is hidden, tap the top edge of the Touch's screen.)

Flip the page for more about using the Touch keyboard.

Use the Touch Keyboard

The iPod Touch has no physical keys—heck, it barely has any actual buttons. A virtual keyboard, therefore, is the only possible system for entering text.

The keyboard appears automatically whenever you tap in a place where typing is possible, mainly in the address bar of the Web browser or within a Web page itself. You can also use it when emailing (Chapter 3) and to enter calendar appointments and contact information (Chapter 10).

To use it, just tap the key you want. As your finger taps the glass, a "speech balloon" appears above your finger, showing an enlarged version of the key you actually hit (since your finger is now blocking your view of the keyboard).

In darker gray, surrounding the keyboard letters, you'll see these special keys:

❶ **Shift (⇧).** When you tap this key, it glows white, to indicate that it's in effect. The next letter you type appears as a capital. Then the ⇧ key automatically returns to normal, meaning that the next letter will be lowercase.

❷ **Backspace (⌫).** This key actually has three speeds.

- Tap it once to delete the letter just before the blinking cursor.

- Hold it down to "walk" backward, deleting each letter as you go.

- If you hold down the key long enough, it starts deleting *words* rather than letters, one whole chunk at a time.

❸ **?123** . Tap this button when you want to type numbers or punctuation. The keyboard changes to offer a palette of numbers and symbols. Tap the same key—which now says ABC—to return to the letters keyboard. (Fortunately, there's a much faster way to get a period—touch the **?123** key, drag your finger to the number you need, and then let go.)

Once you're on the numbers/symbols pad, a new dark gray button appears, labeled **#+=**. Tapping it summons a *third* keyboard layout, containing less frequently used characters, like brackets, the # and % symbols, bullets, and math symbols.

When you're typing in a Web form (or someplace that's not a Web address), the keyboard also adds a Return key. Tapping this key moves to the next line, just as on a real keyboard.

Surfing on the Safari Keyboard

In Safari, (as with other typing apps) you can *rotate* the keyboard into landscape orientation. This is a big deal; when it's stretched out the wide way, you get much bigger, broader keys, and typing is much easier and faster. Just remember to rotate the iPod *before* you tap the Address bar or text box; once the keyboard is on the screen, you can't rotate it.

As you probably know, there are no spaces allowed in Internet addresses; therefore, in the spot usually reserved for the Space bar, this keyboard has three keys for things that *do* appear often in Web addresses: a period, a / key, and ".com". These nifty special keys make typing Web addresses a lot faster.

Finally, tap the blue Go key when you're finished typing the address. That's your Enter key. (Or tap Cancel to hide the keyboard *without* "pressing Enter.")

As you type, a handy list of suggestions appears beneath the Address bar. These are all Web addresses that Safari already knows about, either because they're in your Bookmarks list or in your History list (meaning you've visited them recently). If you recognize the address you're trying to type, by all means tap it instead of typing out the rest of the URL. The time you save could be your own.

Create and Use Safari Bookmarks

Amazingly enough, Safari comes pre-stocked with bookmarks (Favorites)— that is, a list of Web sites you might want to visit and re-visit without having to remember and type in their URLs. Even more amazingly, all of these canned bookmarks are interesting and useful to *you* in particular! How did it know?

Easy—it copied your existing desk-top computer's browser bookmarks from Internet Explorer (Windows) or Safari (Macintosh and Windows) when you synced the Touch. Sneaky, eh? (Flip ahead a few pages if you haven't synced.)

Anyway, to see the bookmarks, tap the button at the bottom of the screen. You see the master list of bookmarks. Some may be "loose," and many more are probably organized into folders, or even folders *within* folders. Tapping a folder shows you what's inside, and tapping a bookmark immediately begins opening the corresponding Web site.

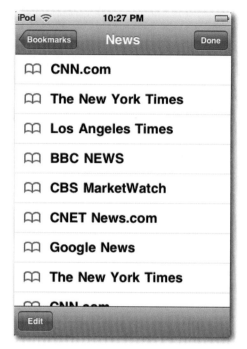

Tip The iPod Touch has a Caps Lock feature, but you have to request it. Press the Home button and go to Settings→General→Keyboard and turn on "Enable caps lock." From now on, if you double-tap the ⇧ key, it turns blue. You're now in Caps Lock mode, and you'll now type in ALL CAPITAL LETTERS until you tap the ⇧ key again. (If you can't seem to make Caps Lock work, try double-tapping the ⇧ key *fast.*)

You can also turn on (or off) the Auto-Capitalization feature here, plus the shortcut that inserts a period followed by a space when you tap the space bar twice.

Adding New Bookmarks

You can add new bookmarks right on your iPod. Any work you do here is copied *back* to your computer the next time you sync the two machines.

When you find a Web page you might like to visit again, tap the **+** button (bottom center of the screen). Tap the Add Bookmark option. The Add Bookmark screen appears. You have two tasks:

- **Type a better name.** In the top box, you can type a shorter or clearer name for the page than the one that it comes with. Instead of "Bass, Trout, & Tackle—the Web's Premiere Resource for the Avid Outdoorsman," you can just call it "Fish site."

  The box below this one identifies the underlying URL, which is totally independent of what you've *called* your bookmark. You can't edit this one.

- **Specify where to file this bookmark.** If you tap the button that says Bookmarks >, you open Safari's hierarchical list of bookmark folders, which organize your bookmarked sites. Tap the folder where you want to file the new bookmark.

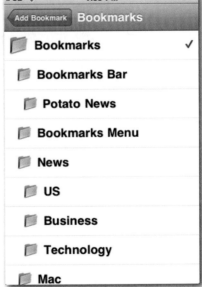

> **Tip** If you make a mistake as you tap in a URL and don't notice it right away, you don't have to backspace all the way to the typo. Press your finger down on the text until a magnifying glass and a flashing insertion cursor appear, then drag your finger to the error, lift your finger, and correct the mistake. Then go back to where you were.

Edit and Organize Bookmarks and Folders

It's easy enough to massage your Bookmarks list—to delete favorites that aren't so favorite any more, to make new folders, to rearrange the list, to rename a folder or a bookmark, and so on.

The techniques are the same for editing bookmark *folders* as they are for editing the bookmarks themselves—after the first step. To edit the folder list, start by opening the Bookmarks list (tap the ⌘ button), and then tap Edit.

To edit the bookmarks themselves, tap the ⌘ button, tap a folder, and *then* tap Edit.

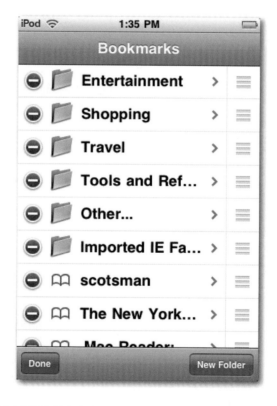

> **Tip** Want to add your favorite Web site to your Home screen? Tap the + button at the bottom of your browser and choose "Add to Home Screen". The site's icon is now right on the Touch's main screen. And don't worry about filling up your Home screen pages—you can have up to nine of 'em and finger-flick between them.

Now you can:

- **Delete something.** Tap the ⊖ button next to a folder or bookmark, and then tap Delete to confirm.

- **Rearrange the list.** Drag the grip strip (≡) up or down in the list to move the folders or bookmarks up or down. (You can't move or delete the History folder, however.)

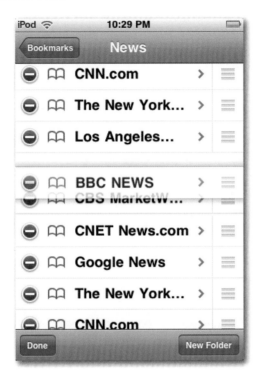

- **Edit a name and location.** Tap a folder or bookmark name. If you tap a folder, you arrive at the Edit Folder screen, which lets you edit the folder's name and, if this folder's *inside* another folder, you can reassign it. If you tap a bookmark, you see the Edit Bookmark screen, where you can edit the link's name and the URL it points to.

  Tap the Back button (upper-left corner) when you finish.

- **Create a folder.** Tap the New Folder button in the lower-right corner of the Edit Folders screen. You're offered the chance to type a name for it and whether you want to file it inside another folder.

Tap Done when you finish.

Syncing Bookmarks with iTunes

Bookmarks—those helpful little point-and-click shortcuts that have saved us all countless hours of mistyping Web site addresses—are a reflection of your personality, because they generally tend to be sites that are important to *you*. Fortunately, you can copy any bookmarks you have on your computer to your iPod Touch. In fact, any bookmarks you create on your iPod can make the trip back to your computer, too. It's a two-way street.

iTunes can transfer your bookmarks from Internet Explorer or Safari. Just plug in your Touch, click its icon in iTunes, and click the Info tab. Scroll down past Contacts, Calendars, and Mail Accounts until you get to the section called Web Browser. Then:

- **In Windows,** turn on *Sync bookmarks from:*, and then choose either *Safari* or *Internet Explorer* from the pop-up menu. Click Apply or Sync.

- **On the Mac,** turn on *Sync Safari bookmarks* and click Apply or Sync.

If you ever want to blow away all the bookmarks on your Touch and start over with a fresh set of bookmarks from your computer, scroll down to the Advanced area of the Info screen (where it says "Replace information on this iPod"). Then put a check in the box next to Bookmarks before you sync again.

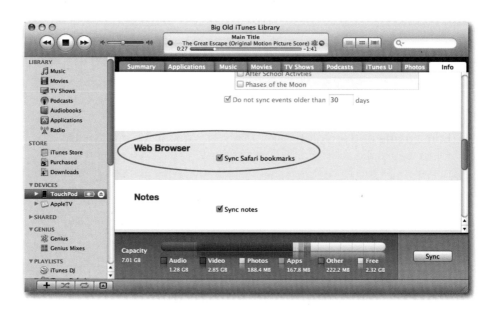

Special Instructions for Firefox Fans

If Mozilla's Firefox browser is your preferred window to the Web, you can still move those foxy favorites over to your iPod, but you'll have to do it the long way—by importing bookmarks from Firefox into Safari. And while this setup will get your bookmarks onto your Touch, it won't establish a *two-way* sync; new bookmarks you add on the iPod won't get synced back to Firefox.

- **Windows.** Download a free copy of Safari (*www.apple.com/safari*), start it up, and let it import your Firefox bookmarks during the setup process. Once it does, press Ctrl+Shift+B to see all your bookmarks, weed out the ones you don't want, and then set the iPod Touch to sync with Safari.

- **Macintosh.** You already have Safari. If you have your whole bookmarked life in Firefox, grit your teeth and open that dusty Safari anyway, then choose File→Import Bookmarks. Navigate to your Firefox book-marks file, which is usually in your Home folder→Library→Application Support→Firefox→Profiles→*weird scrambled-named folder like e9v01wmx. default* folder. Inside, double-click the file called bookmarks.html.

  You've just imported your Firefox bookmarks. Now, in Safari, press ⌘-Shift-B to show all your bookmarks on-screen. Delete the ones you don't want on the Touch, and then set the iPod to sync with Safari.

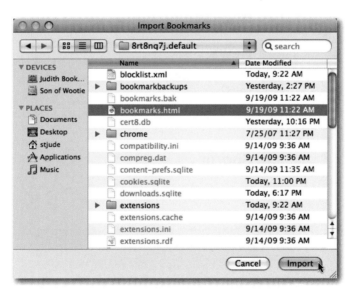

Actually, *most* other browsers can export their bookmarks. You can use that option to export your bookmarks file to your desktop, and then use Safari's File→Import Bookmarks menu to pull it in from there.

The Safari History List

Behind the scenes, Safari keeps track of the Web sites you've visited in the last week or so, neatly organized into subfolders like "Earlier Today" and "Yesterday". It's a great feature when you can't recall the URL for a Web site you visited recently—or when you remember that it had a long, complicated address and you get the psychiatric condition known as iPod Touch Keyboard Dread.

To see the list of recent sites, tap the 🕮 button, and then tap the History folder, whose icon bears a little clock to make sure you know that it's special. Once the History list appears, just tap a bookmark (or a folder name and *then* a bookmark) to revisit a Web page.

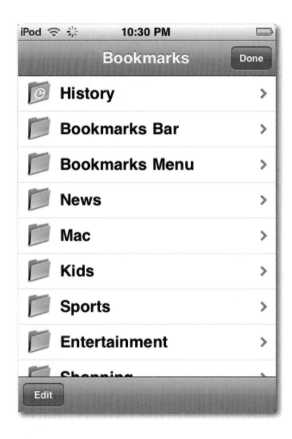

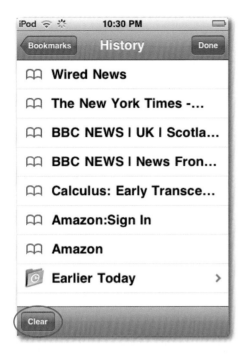

Erasing the History List

Some people find it creepy to have Safari maintain a complete list of every Web site they've recently seen, right there in plain view of any family member or co-worker who wanders by. They'd just as soon not have their wife/husband/boss/parent/kid know what they've been up to, Web-wise.

You can't delete just one particularly incriminating History listing. You can, however, delete the *entire* History list, thus erasing all your tracks. To do that, tap Clear; confirm by tapping Clear History.

Congratulations! You've just rewritten History.

Tapping Links

You'd be surprised at the number of iPod Touch newbies who stare dumbly at the screen, awestruck at the beauty of full-blown Web pages—but utterly baffled as to how to click links.

The answer: Tap with your finger.

Just tap the links on the screen, much the way you'd click them if you had a mouse. As you know from desktop-computer browsing, not all links are blue and underlined. Sometimes, in fact, they're graphics.

 Tip If you hold your finger on a link for a moment—touch it rather than tap it—a box pops up identifying the link's full Web address and offering three buttons: you can open the linked page, open it in a new browser page, or copy it to the Touch's clipboard to paste it elsewhere. Chapter 3 has more on moving Touch text around.

Mapping Your Way with Wi-Fi

People who bought the first version of the iPod Touch had to use Safari for all their map work and driving directions. Owners of 2008 and 2009 iPod Touches (and those who paid Apple $10 or $20 to upgrade their software on their 2007 models) can use the built-in Maps app instead. Like Safari, though, Maps needs a Wi-Fi connection to pull its data down from the Web, so it's not the best thing in the world for emergency directions when you're lost in the bad part of town.

To plot your course, tap the Maps icon on the Home screen. Here are some of the things you can do with Maps and a network connection:

- **Find yourself.** Tap the icon in the bottom-left corner (circled) to have the Touch pinpoint your current location within a few hundred yards. (While the Touch doesn't have a GPS chip inside, it does have software that calculates your position based on a big database of Wi-Fi hotspots.)

- **Find an address.** In the Address box at the top of the screen, type in an address—or tap the 🔄 icon to call up your Contacts list, where you can select the friend or business you want to map. Tap the Search button to see a red pushpin drop onto that location.

- **Find your way.** Tap the Directions button at the bottom of the screen. A two-field box appears. If you don't want to use your current location, tap the ⊗ in the Start box and type in a point of origin. In the End box, type in the destination address. Press the Route button. This gives you a map to follow, but if you want text-based instructions, tap the icon on the bottom right corner (circled) to peel back the screen. Here, tap List to get a written explanation of your route. You can also choose the look of your map: a regular cartographic version, a satellite image, or a hybrid of both. Tap Show Traffic if you want to see current road congestion and maybe take that antacid *before* you leave the house.

Search the Web

You don't have to look far to find a search engine on the Touch's version of Safari. Just tap the little Search box to the right of the main Address Bar to open up a new bar with plenty of room to type in keywords.

That's an awfully handy shortcut. It means that you can perform a Google search without having to go to Google.com first. Just tap into that box, type in your search phrase, and then tap the big blue Google button in the lower-right corner.

 At first glance, the Touch keyboard may look like it can't handle accented letters like é or ü, but looks can be deceiving. The trick to getting those graves, acutes, umlauts, tildes, and other diacritical marks on your typed characters? As shown above, hold down the letter key for an extra second or two and a whole world of accents appears on screen. Just slide your fingertip over to the one you want. Voilà!

Changing Your Default Search Engine

But say, for some reason, you don't like Google. You're a Yahoo fan and would rather do your exploring with your preferred search engine.

Are you stuck with Google on your iPod Touch? Nope, not at all.

You can tell the iPod to use Yahoo's search feature instead of Google's if you like. From the Home screen, tap Settings→Safari→Search Engine. Once you get there, tap Yahoo. If you ever want to change it back to Google, just return to the Settings menu.

 Tip There are all kinds of cool things you can type into the Google search bar to get immediate feedback from Google—special terms that tell Google, "I want *information,* not Web-page matches."

For example, you can type in a movie name and zip code or city/state (*The Titanic Returns 10024*) to get an immediate list of today's showtimes in theaters near you. Get the forecast by typing *weather chicago* or *weather 60609*. Stock quotes: just type the stock symbol (*amzn*). Dictionary definitions: *define schadenfreude*. Unit conversions: *liters in 5 gallons*. Currency conversions: *25 usd in euros*.

Then tap the blue Google button to get instant results. And, yes, many of the same shortcuts work on Yahoo as well.

Audio and Video on the Web

In general, streaming audio and video on the Touch is a bust. The Touch doesn't recognize RealPlayer or Windows Media file formats, nor does it understand Flash. All of this means that the iPod can't easily play the huge majority of online video and audio recordings.

But the Touch isn't *utterly* clueless about streaming online goodies. It can play some QuickTime movies, like movie trailers, as long as they've been encoded (prepared) in certain formats (like H.264). It can also play MP3 and WAV audio files right off the Web. Here are a few sites to sample:

- **BBC News.** The Beeb's podcasts stream nicely and you can search shows by radio station, genre, or get an A to Zed list. *http://www.bbc.co.uk/podcasts/*

- **New York Times podcasts.** A whole page of different news shows that start streaming when you tap the MP3 link. *www.nytimes.com/podcasts*

- **"Meet the Press" audio stream.** An MP3 edition of the venerable Sunday-morning talk show can be found here: *http://podcast.msnbc.com/audio/podcast/MSNBC-MTP.xml*

Actually, any old MP3 file plays fine right in Safari. If you've already played through your 8, 32, or 64 gigabytes of music synced from your computer, you can always do a Web search for *free mp3 music*.

As for video, you have more to watch on the Web than just Touch-friendly streaming videos you can tap into back at Home→YouTube. Apple, in addition to making iPods and Macs, hosts a huge collection of movie trailers on its site at *www.apple.com/trailers*. Tap a movie poster to get started.

> **Tip** If you're dreaming of streaming Internet radio over the Touch's Wi-Fi waves, check out the App Store. There, you can find free Touchable versions of Pandora Internet Radio, the Minnesota Public Radio player, and AOL Radio (200 music stations and 150 CBS Radio stations with plenty of news, talk, and sports).

Social Networking on the iPod Touch

With your iPod Touch, you can keep connected to all your favorite social networking sites whenever you can hop onto a wireless network. But if you find the Web versions of Facebook, MySpace, or Twitter a little unwieldy on the Touch screen, you have another option: App Store editions of your online hangouts.

Chapter 7 has info about the Store and Chapter 3 has instructions on how to install iPod Touch apps. Once you're ready, here's some of what's out there:

- **Facebook** and **MySpace.** Both mega-popular destinations have free mobile applications, right there in the App Store. Customized with easy-to-read text and big, tappable icons, these mobile versions are designed to look good on the iPhone and iPod Touch. Once you download and install an app, you just need to fire it up and log in like you do on the regular site.

Facebook

- **Twitter.** Using this widely popular micro-blogging service is much more fun on the iPod Touch than trying to text out pithy thoughts on a tiny mobile phone keypad (unless, of course, it's an iPhone). Several free Twitter-friendly programs are available in the App Store, including *Twitterific*, *Tweetie*, and *EchoFon*. For a global perspective, the *Twittervision* program lets you see tweets from around the world.

Flickr for iPhone

- **Flickr.** Browsing the pictures on this massive photo-sharing site is nice and easy with *Flickr for iPhone*, which neatly arranges images in a grid on the Touch screen, with full-screen views a tap away. Once you log into your Flickr account on the iPod Touch, you can easily get you all your photo sets and tags from icons at the top of the screen. You can also choose to see your images listed vertically, with photo name and comments in full view.

- **LOLCats.** Those wacky felines have at least two applications to show off their ungrammatical exploits as submitted by hundreds of cat owners. If you need to take a break and have a laugh at kitty's expense, try *LOLCats* or *LOLCats Free*.

LOLCats Free

Manipulate Multiple Pages

Like any self-respecting browser, Safari can keep multiple pages open at once, making it easy for you to switch between them. You can think of it as a miniature version of *tabbed browsing*, the feature you find on Safari Senior, Firefox, and Internet Explorer, which keeps a bunch of Web pages open simultaneously—in a single, neat window.

The beauty of this arrangement is that you can start reading one Web page while the others load into their own tabs in the background. On the iPod Touch, it works like this:

- **To open a new window,** tap the ⧉ button in the lower right. The current Web page shrinks into a mini version. Tap New Page to open a new, untitled Web-browser page; now you can enter an address.

Note Touch Safari can handle eight open Web pages at once. If you try to go for that ninth one, it starts replacing the current open page with the new one.

- **To switch back to the first window,** tap 🗗 again. Now there are two dots (••) beneath the miniature page, indicating that you have *two* windows open. (The boldest, whitest dot indicates where you are in the horizontal row of windows.) Bring the first window's miniature onto the screen by flicking horizontally with your finger. Tap it to open it full-screen.

  You can open a third window, and a fourth, and so on, and jump between them, using these two techniques. The 🗗 icon sprouts a number to let you know how many windows are open; for example, it might say 🗗.

- **To close a window,** tap 🗗. Flick over to the tiny window you want to close, and then tap the ⊗ button at its top-left corner.

 Sometimes, Safari sprouts a new window *automatically* when you click a link. That's because the link you tapped is programmed to open a new window.

Pop-up Blockers, Cookies, and Security

Internet criminals will try to rip you off, no matter what Web browser you use. Phishing—when a devious Web site masquerades as a legitimate site to dupe people into entering personal information—has long been a problem. Mini-Safari now has a Fraud Warning setting, which alerts you when you *might* be on a fishy, phishy site. You can turn it on in Settings→Safari.

And the world's smarmiest advertisers have been inundating us with pop-up and pop-under ads for years—nasty little windows that appear in front of a browser window or, worse, behind it, waiting to jump in when you close your window. They're often deceptive, masquerading as alerts or dialog boxes, and they'll do absolutely anything to get you to click them.

Fortunately for you, Safari comes set to block those pop-ups so you don't see them. It's a war out there—but at least you have some ammunition.

The thing is, though, pop-ups are sometimes legitimate—notices of new banking features, seating charts on ticket-sales sites, and so on. Safari can't tell these pop-ups from ads—and so it stifles those pages, too.

What to do? If a site you trust says "Please turn off pop-up blockers and reload this page," you know you're probably missing out on a *useful* pop-up message. In those situations, you can turn off Safari's pop-up blocker. From the Home screen, tap Settings→Safari. Where it says "Block Pop-ups," tap the On/Off switch.

Cookies

Cookies are something like Web page preference files. Certain Web sites—particularly commercial ones like Amazon.com—deposit them on your hard drive like little bookmarks, so the site remembers you the next time you visit. Ever notice how Amazon.com greets you "Welcome, Leroy" (or whatever your name is)? It's reading its own cookie, left behind on your hard drive (or in this case, on your iPod).

Most cookies are perfectly innocuous—and, in fact, are extremely helpful, because they help Web sites remember your tastes. Cookies also spare you the effort of having to type in your name, address, and so on, every time you visit these sites.

But fear is widespread, and the media fans the flames with tales of sinister cookies that track your movement on the Web. If you're worried about invasions of privacy, Safari is ready to protect you.

To check all this out, from the Home screen, tap Settings→Safari. The options here are like a paranoia gauge. If you click Never, you create an acrylic shield around your iPod. No cookies can come in, and no cookie information can go out. You'll probably find the Web a very inconvenient place; you'll have to re-enter your information upon every visit, and some Web sites may not work properly at all. The Always option means, "oh, what the heck—just gimme all of them."

A good compromise is From Visited, which accepts cookies from sites you *want* to visit, but blocks cookies deposited on your Touch by sites you're not actually visiting—cookies you get, say, from an especially evil banner ad that's been planted on a page by hackers. There are quite a few of those these days.

The Safari settings screen also offers a Clear Cookies button (it deletes all the cookies you've accumulated so far), as well as Clear History and Clear Cache buttons.

A *cache* is a little patch of the Touch's storage area where your iPod retains bits and pieces of Web pages you visit—graphics, for example. The idea is that the next time you visit the same page, the iPod won't have to download those bits again. It's already got them on board, so the page appears much faster.

If you worry that your cache eats up space, poses a security risk, or is confounding a page (by preventing the most recent version of the page from appearing), tap this button to erase it and start over.

RSS: The Missing Manual

In the beginning, the Internet was an informational Garden of Eden. There were no banner ads, pop-ups, flashy animations, or spam messages. Back then, people thought the Internet was the greatest idea ever.

Those days, alas, are long gone. Web browsing now entails a constant battle against intrusive advertising and annoying animations. And with the proliferation of Web sites of every kind—from news sites to personal blogs—just reading your favorite sites can become a full-time job.

Enter RSS, a technology that lets you subscribe to *feeds*—summary blurbs sent out from thousands of sources around the world, from Reuters to Apple to your nerdy neighbor next door. The result: You spare yourself the tediousness of checking sites for updated news and information manually, plus you get to read short summaries of new articles without ads and blinking animations. If you want to read a full article, you just tap its headline.

Safari, as it turns out, doubles as a handy RSS reader. Whenever you tap an "RSS Feed" link on a Web page, or whenever you type the address of an RSS feed into the Address bar (it often begins with *feed://*), Safari automatically displays a handy table-of-contents view that lists all of the news blurbs on that page.

Scan the summaries—and when you see an article that looks intriguing, tap its headline. You go to the full-blown Web page to read the full-blown article.

 Tip It's worth bookmarking your favorite RSS feeds. A great one for tech fans is *feed:// www.digg.com/rss/index.xml*, a constantly updated list of the coolest and most interesting tech and pop-culture stories of the day. Most news publications offer news feeds, too. (The humble author of this chapter has his own daily *New York Times* feed at *http://pogue.blogs.nytimes.com/?feed=rss2*.)

Find Other Mobile-Friendly Sites

If looking at regular Web pages on your iPod's browser is too much sensory overload, and RSS is a little too sparse, there's a middle ground. Many Web site publishers have *optimized* their sites for use on mobile devices, like cellphones, wireless PDAs, iPhones, and Touch iPods.

These sites offer large type (all the better to read on pee-wee screens) and a quick-loading graphic or two. But how do you find these little treasures?

Some big Web sites can automatically sense when you're coming in on a mobile browser and serve you up the simplified version. Others swap out the *www* part of their URL with an *m* (for mobile), as in *m.nytimes.com*.

Here are a few sites with mobile browsers in mind:

- Google (of course) has mobile versions of many of its features, like Gmail and Picasa online photo albums, at *www.google.com/mobile*.

- The British Broadcasting Corporation has a streamlined version of its main news site at *www.bbc.co.uk/mobile*.

- Yahoo has its own mobile offerings, including streamlined search, sports, and stock quotes, at *m.yahoo.com*.

- There are also Web pages that round up links to the mobile editions of popular sites. Here are two worth bookmarking in your Touch browser: *www.cantoni.mobi/* and *mobile.palm.com*.

Use MobileMe to Keep Data in Sync

As long as you're in range of a wireless network, your iPod Touch can serve as a pocket-sized little window to your email and the Web, no matter where you are. But in these days when practically everything is connected to the Internet, wouldn't it be great if *all* your devices talked to each other, too? Like if you make a calendar appointment on your laptop while you're on a business trip—and your spouse's iPod Touch back home magically updates itself with the new information? Or if someone sends you an email message, you get it on all your computers and handhelds?

With Apple's MobileMe service, you can do all that and more.

First, a little bit about MobileMe: it's a $100-a-year subscription service you buy from Apple, and for that annual Benjamin, you get a whole bunch of tools and services designed to make life online just a little bit easier. For instance, you get an *@me.com* email address; an online gallery page to post your favorite photos and videos; a chunk of space on Apple's servers called an iDisk that you can use to back up or share large files; and an online parking space for your contacts and calendars. You start out with 20 gigabytes of space for all this stuff, but Apple will gladly sell you more room if you find you need it.

So how do you get started with MobileMe? Easy. Just connect your Touch to your computer and click the Info tab in iTunes. In the MobileMe area, click the Lean More button (Windows) or Set Up Now (Mac).

iTunes whisks you away to the MobileMe sign-up area, where you supply your credit-card number, pick out a user name and password, and download any necessary software, like the MobileMe control panel for Windows.

Once you're all signed up and have that software installed, it's time to set up your computer and then the Touch. The next page explains how to do both.

Set Up MobileMe on a PC or Mac

Now that you have a MobileMe account to sync your data between machines, you have to tell MobileMe what you want to sync.

❶ In Windows, choose Start→Control Panel→Network and Internet→ MobileMe. On a Mac, choose →System Preferences→MobileMe.

❷ Click the Account tab and sign in with your username and password.

❸ Click the Sync tab. Turn on the checkbox next to "Sync with MobileMe" and choose how often you want your MobileMe data pushed out to the Touch and any other computers you plan to use with the service. Most people choose the "Automatically" option.

❹ Next, choose the info on your computer, like contacts, bookmarks, and appointments, you want to sync to your Touch over the airwaves.

❺ Click The Sync Now button to upload your computer's info to Apple's servers.

Click OK to close the box. Okay, that part's done. Now set up the Touch to accept all the data pushed to it from MobileMe.

Set Up MobileMe on the Touch

❶ On the Touch, choose Settings→Mail, Contacts, Calendars.

❷ Tap Fetch New Data. On the next screen make sure Push is set to On.

❸ Tap the icon in the top left corner to go back to the previous screen. Now tap Add Account, choose MobileMe, and fill in your MobileMe username and password.

❹ Turn on Mail, Contacts, Calendars, and Bookmarks. You can even activate Find My iPod Touch—which maps the location of a lost or stolen Touch at *www.me.com* if it's on a Wi-Fi network.

12

iPod Out Loud

Now that you've spent all this time getting your iPod fully loaded with cool entertainment, you probably want to listen to your play-lists, albums, audio books, and podcasts wherever you happen to be—in a car, on your big booming home stereo, in the bathroom, wherever. If you can load it onto your iPod, you can channel it through most any sound system—and at pretty reasonable cost, too. This chapter explains the simple procedures you follow to play your iPod through the woofers and tweeters in your life. (If you want to play iPod movies on your TV, flip back to Chapter 8.)

One note of caution before you plunk down your hard-earned cash on a fancy audio gizmo: Apple has made a lot of different iPod models over the years, and not every add-on or accessory works with all iPods. To be safe (especially if you recently bought a new iPod), check the product's fine print to make sure it and your iPod will be happy together.

Taking Your iPod on the Road

Since the glorious days of crackly AM radio, music and driving have gone hand in hand. These days, a stereo system with an AM/FM radio and a CD player is the bare minimum for most cars, and late-model vehicles now cruise around with all sorts of high-end equipment, from MP3-compatible CD players to satellite radio. (Whether the music you play on them has improved over the years is subject to debate.)

If having your playlists with you is your idea of paradise by the dashboard light, there are several inexpensive ways to integrate your iPod with your car's stereo. Whatever method you choose, you have to consider two factors:

- **How to connect your iPod to your existing audio system.** You have your pick of a cable or a wireless connection.

- **How to power your iPod.** Of course, your iPod can run fine on its battery for short trips. If you're retracing historic Route 66, however, you'll probably want to invest in an adapter that can power your iPod from your car's electrical system.

You can choose from four main ways to get your iPod's sounds piping through your car speakers, some of them more expensive than others. (You can get most of the gear discussed here from sites listed at the end of the chapter.) Here are the typical options:

❶ **Via an FM transmitter.** These inexpensive devices let you borrow an empty FM frequency from your car's radio and play the iPod's music over the airwaves—with no cables snaking across the dashboard, although some include iPod charger cords for the car's 12-volt port. Setup is easy: scan your FM dial for an unused channel through which you can pipe your iPod's audio, connect the transmitter to your iPod, and push Play. *Advantages:* Convenience; everybody's got an FM radio. *Disadvantages:* Long road-trippers constantly have to search for new frequencies. Urban dwellers may find it tough finding available signals. *Audio quality:* Fair.

If it involves getting the iPod to play in the car, odds are Griffin Technology has a product for it. From the left: $50 iTrip FM Transmitter, the $10 DirectDeck wired casette adapter, and the $10 auxilary audio cable. You can find all these items (and more iPod-related goodies) at www.griffintechnology.com.

❷ **Using a wired adapter.** Another option—if your car still has a cassette player—is getting one of those cassette-shaped gadgets that slips into your tape deck and offer a 3.5 mm miniplug for the iPod's headphones port. Griffin Technology, Belkin, and Monster all make 'em.
Advantages: Simplicity; insert cassette and you're good to go.
Disadvantages: Not everyone's got a cassette deck anymore.
Audio quality: Fair.

❸ **Using the auxiliary jack.** If your car's stereo console has a 3.5 mm jack as an auxiliary input, you can use a simple male-to-male miniplug audio cable to connect your iPod. Radio Shack, Griffin Technology, or Monster Cable can help you out here for less than $10.
Advantages: High-quality sound.
Disadvantages: You still have to run your iPod using its controls.
Audio quality: Great.

❹ **Using a special iPod aftermarket kit or custom installation.** If you really want fine sound and have the budget for it, several companies now offer kits that add an iPod-friendly cable to your existing in-dash stereo system. Apple has a list of resources based on car manufacturer at *www.apple.com/ipod/car-integration* so you can see what's available for your ride. Equipment-wise, if you have an Alpine stereo, you may be able to use the $30 iPod Interface KCA-422i cable (*www.alpine-usa.com*), while Pioneer Electronics owners can find a slew of compatible iPod cables, adapter boxes, and accessories at *www.pioneerelectronics.com*.
Advantages: Great sound, easy to control.
Disadvantages: None, aside from price.
Audio quality: Great.

The popularity of the iPod over the past few years has even led major auto manufacturers to include iPod cables wired right into their new cars. So if you're in the market for new wheels anyway, why not ask about getting your *click wheel* on the road, too?

You can connect your iPod to several Pioneer car stereo systems with the Pioneer CD-IB100II iPod Interface Adapter. The dashboard display even shows the track titles and lets you shuffle songs. Check it out at www.pioneerelectronics.com.

Connect the iPod to a Home Entertainment System

CD players that can play discs full of MP3 files cost less than $100. But if you have an iPod, you already have a state-of-the-art MP3 player that can connect to your existing stereo for under $20—or spend a little more and get the full iPod AV Club experience.

Connecting with an Audio Cable

To link your iPod to your stereo, you need the right kind of cable and a set of input jacks on the back of your receiver. Most audio systems come with at least one extra set of inputs (after accounting for the CD player, cassette deck, and other common components), so look for an empty jack labelled "AUX".

The cable you need is a Y-shaped cord with a 3.5 mm (1/8") stereo miniplug on one end and two bigger RCA plugs at the other end. The stereo miniplug is the standard connector for iPod-style headphones (and for speakers and microphones); RCA plugs are standard red-and-white connectors for linking stereo components together.

Plug the miniplug into the iPod's headphone jack, and the RCA plugs into the left and right speaker jacks on the back of your stereo. Most online iPod superstores like XtremeMac, Griffin Technology, DLO, and Belkin sell their own version of the Y-shaped cable. There's a list of sites that sell helpful iPod stuff at the end of this chapter.

Connecting with an iPod Dock

Investing in an iPod dock is another way to link your portable to your permanent home-entertainment system. A typical dock provides a notch for your iPod to sit upright, with cable jacks on the back for tethering the dock to your stereo or receiver. As a bonus, you usually get a remote to control the iPod from across the room. Apple sells its $50 iPod docks and $50 AV cables at *http://www.apple.com/ipodstore*. You can also find fancier gear like DLO's HomeDock HD, ($200 at *www.dlo.com*) that let you pipe your video files up to your HDTV screen when you're not blasting audio through the stereo's speakers.

iPod Speaker Systems

You can hook up your iPod to a home audio system to share your sounds, but sometimes it's more convenient to get the iPod a set of speakers to call its own. Some speakers connect to the iPod's headphone jack with a stereo miniplug cable, while others connect via an iPod dock.

Some iPod sound systems even use wireless signals and remote speakers to play the iPod's music in many rooms at once. With many of these systems, you don't even need to have an existing wireless network in place, either.

The price and quality of iPod speakers can range from $15 cheap plastic things at the grocery store to $300 systems from high-end audio companies like Bose, Altec Lansing, Sony, Tivoli, and others. Wireless speaker systems range from about $200 to $700. Here are a few speakers to sample, but check the list at the end of the chapter for more places to find supersonic iPod accessories.

- **DLO iBoom Jukebox.** With a curvy shape that brings to mind an old Wurlitzer jukebox, DLO's iBoom (shown here) lets you see what you're cranking up from across the room, thanks to a remote with its own color screen. The iBoom Jukebox sells for $200 at *www.dlo.com*.

- **Altec Lansing Mix.** With rumbling bass, specially engineered tweeters, and a 7-band equalizer, the Mix is ready for any party. And it comes with its own remote and jacks to connect two more audio players alongside your iPod. You can find it for $300 at *www.alteclansing.com*.

- **Eos Wireless.** For $200, you get an iPod base station with its own set of speakers, plus another set of remote speakers. To spread the sound around, you can scatter up to four additional wireless speakers—in either black or white to match your decor—in other rooms for about $100 a pop, all on the system's own wireless network. (*www.eoswireless.com*)

- **Sony Wireless Music System for iPod.** This $700 package is pricey, but you get a glossy iPod dock (shown at right) and two remote speaker units—plus the thing brings its own wireless network to the party. For big houses, you can buy up 8 more speakers to use with the dock. Each satellite speaker unit also has a FM tuner for real, live radio. (*www.sonystyle.com*)

Stream iTunes Music with AirPort Express

What do you get when you mix an existing home Wi-Fi network with iTunes and Airport Express (Apple's portable wireless base station)? Music anywhere you want it. Stream your songs throughout your home by plugging one of these coaster-sized devices anywhere you've got a stereo. If you don't have an AirPort Express, you can buy one for $99 at *http://store.apple.com* and other places. Here's how to get started:

❶ **Plug the AirPort Express into an electrical outlet near the stereo (or near a pair of powered speakers).**
Repeat this step in any other room you want to beam your music.

❷ **Connect your stereo system or powered speakers to the AirPort Express.**
After you plug the Airport Express into the wall, use a Y-shaped cable (the one with the two RCA plugs on one end and the miniplug on the other, mentioned on page 248) to connect the AirPort Express to your stereo system or to a pair of powered speakers. If your system has a digital Toslink port, you can also use a digital fiber optic cable to connect the two for better sound. (Speakers that use a USB connection don't work with AirPort Express.)

❸ **Install the AirPort Utility software from the CD in the box.** The Utility program (Start→All Programs→Airport [Applications→Utilities→Airport]) walks you through the setup process, automatically picking up your Wi-Fi settings and prompting you to name the Airport Express. Naming it something like "Living Room Stereo" is helpful when it comes to using iTunes, as you'll see in the next step.

❹ **Open iTunes and look for a pop-up menu with the name of your AirPort Express.** Once you start up iTunes with the AirPort Express running, you'll notice a little pop-up menu at the bottom of the iTunes window (circled, facing page). If you've installed multiple Expresses, you'll see each one of them listed in the pop-up menu.

❺ Press Play. With everything connected and turned on, select the Airport Express base station in the iTunes pop-up menu and click the Play button on your iPod to blast your playlists across your home. To play music through more than one set of speakers, choose Multiple Speakers and then put a checkmark next to each base station's name you want to use.

Using the iPod Touch as a Remote

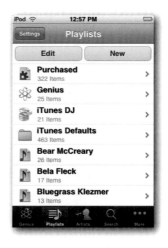

If you don't want to be tied to your computer to manage the tunes—and you have a Touch—there's a cool program called Remote in the iTunes App Store. Tapping into your Wi-Fi network, Remote lets you control your music from anywhere in the house. Even better, it's free.

Install the Remote app from the iTunes Store (Chapter 7) on your Touch. Tap the Remote icon and, on the next screen, tap Add Library. An icon for Remote appears in the iTunes Devices list. Click it and type in the four-digit code displayed on the Touch into the corresponding four boxes on the iTunes screen. Click OK and your iTunes library and playlists appear on the Touch screen. You can now play, pause, skip, and jump through your music library to your heart's content.

If you have trouble geting Remote to show up in the iTunes window, open up Edit (iTunes)→Preferences→Devices and make sure there's a check mark in the box next to "Look for iPhone & iPod touch Remotes".

 If you don't have a Wi-Fi network but are ready to join the wireless revolution, you're in luck. The AirPort Express also works as a full-fledged Wi-Fi router. Just follow the AirPort Utility's setup instructions for creating a wireless network *and* for activating AirTunes (Apple's name for this whole streaming-music scenario).

Find a Power Source for Your iPod

Your car's cigarette lighter can serve a far healthier role than its original purpose: It can breathe life into an iPod battery. You won't ever again have to worry about the iPod conking out in the middle of your favorite song when you're on the road. Several companies make travel-worthy chargers, including four well-known iPod accessory mavens:

- **PowerJolt SE.** This $20 doodad from Griffin Technology powers 'Pods on the road. It comes with a coiled cable to string between the PowerJolt and the iPod. It works with most modern dock-connecting iPods, including the Nano and the Touch; you can find it at *www.griffintechnology.com*.

- **DLO AutoCharger.** This stylish appliance powers your player and recharges it through the car's cigarette lighter, using three color-coded lights that let you keep tabs on your iPod's charging status. The $20 charger comes in either black or white and has a coiled cord that can stretch out to about five feet. You can get one at *www.dlo.com*.

- **Xtreme Mac InCharge Travel.** No matter whether you move about by plane, train, or automobile, the InCharge Travel global charging kit keeps your iPod powered up. This $50 collection of cords and adapters includes a car charger, an Empower adapter for commercial airline electrical systems, and a regular electrical power adapter that you can use anywhere from an Amtrak train to a Japanese hotel room—plug adapters and voltage converters included. The company also sells a tubular $20 charger just to use in the car; all models are at *www.xtrememac.com*.

- **Belkin Mini Surge Protector.** Ever been in an airport or hotel room with minimal electrical outlets? Plug the travel-sized Belkin Mini Surge Protector into the wall and make three outlets out of one. It also has two powered USB ports on the end just waiting for you to plug in your iPod's USB cable for charging alongside your laptop and other devices. It sells for $25 in the iPod accessories area at *www.belkin.com*.

Where to Find Cool iPod Stuff

Since the iPod's arrival in 2001, its accessories market has been growing by leaps and bounds. There are several online iPod superstores with a huge selection of merchandise, from stylish cases to snap-on FM radios. If you want to see what's out there without having to leave your desk, the bigger Pod-focused Web shops include:

- **The Apple Store** (*http://www.apple.com/ipodstore*). Apple has pages and pages of products for all its iPod offspring. You can shop the store based on the model of iPod you have—which should help ease any compatability worries you have, as in "Hmmm, I wonder if this groovy speaker system will work with my fabulous new iPod Touch....?"

- **Digital Lifestyle Outfitters** (*www.dlo.com*). One of the first makers of iPod accessories, DLO makes and sells a variety of cases, docks, car chargers, and even the iBoom box. The company also sells Surface Shields—thin sheets of clear, stick-on plastic—to help protect glossy iPod screens from scuffs and scratches.

- **Belkin** (*www.belkin.com*). With fashionable cases, chargers, and a spider-like attachment called the Rockstar that lets you attach five sets of headphones to one iPod, Belkin sells a variety of fun—and functional—iPod extras. There's even an external microphone that brings voice-memo recording powers to older iPods (Chapter 10).

- **XtremeMac** (*www.xtrememac.com*). XtremeMac has a healthy amount of iPod merchandise. It's notable for its SportWrap armband cases for active iPod lovers, creative charging solutions, and a compact iPod alarm clock so you can wake up to your own music.

- **Griffin Technology** (*www.griffintechnology.com*). With its iTrip line of FM transmitters and its DirectDeck, Griffin's forte is products that get your iPod thumping through car and home stereo speakers. The company also sells a handful of cases and items like the RadioShark, which is designed to add recordable broadcast radio to your computer and iPod.

Other companies like Kensington (*www.kensington.com*) and Monster Cable (*www.monstercable.com*) have healthy iPod accessory sections on their sites, especially if you're looking for cables, docks, FM transmitters, and the like.

Computer and electronics stores like Fry's and Best Buy usually have a section devoted to iPod cases and speakers. And as a sign of the iPod's mainstream cultural significance, even all-purpose suburban bazaars like Target include a rack or two of iPod stuff for sale.

13

What to Do When the iPod Isn't Working Right

I t's bound to happen sometime: your iPod locks up, freaks out, or just isn't its usual cheerful self. Luckily, you can solve many iPod problems with a button-tap here or a battery charge there. Then your portable Pod Life is back to normal.

Of course, an iPod is a little mini-computer in its own right, and there can be bigger issues that are more involved or require the help of a technical expert. Figuring out what your iPod is trying to tell you when it's sick is the first step in getting it back to good health. This chapter explains what to do if your iPod starts acting weird—and where to go if you need more information or can't fix it yourself.

Apple's Alphabet: The 5 "R"s of iPod Repair

As posted in the growing iPod support section of its Web site (*www.apple.com/support/ipod/five_rs*) Apple recommends trying "The 5 Rs" when you encounter trouble with a Classic, Nano, or Shuffle. The Touch, unique among iPods, has its own "R"s—listed here at the bottom of the page.

Here's what each "R" stands for, along with a few more helpful details:

- **Reset** your iPod, as explained on the next page.

- **Retry** your iPod connection by plugging it into a different USB port on your computer.

- **Restart** your computer and check for any software updates you may need to download and install.

- **Reinstall** your iPod and iTunes software with fresh versions downloaded from *www.apple.com/itunes*.

- **Restore** your iPod's software (also explained later in this chapter).

If you have an iPod Touch, the "R"s vary a bit:

- **Recharge.** Make sure your Touch has gas in its battery tank.

- **Restart.** Press the Sleep/Wake button until the red Off/On slider appears. Slide the Touch off, then press Sleep/Wake to turn it on again. If that doesn't do much, try resetting the Touch as described on the next page.

- **Remove.** Synced content may be sinking your Touch. Connect your iPod to iTunes and remove recently added stuff and resync.

- **Reset Settings.** Tap Settings→General→Reset→Reset All Settings. The option to erase all content and settings may also work, but it's drastic. If it seems to be an Internet connectivity issue, the Reset Network Settings button here may help set things straight.

- **Restore.** Connect your Touch to iTunes and click Restore to reformat it.

The next few pages cover these steps and more, so you can avoid that sixth, painful "R": *Ramming* your head into the wall when your iPod won't work.

Reset Your iPod

If your iPod Classic or Nano seems frozen, confused, or otherwise unresponsive, you can *reset* it without losing your music and data files. You might not be able to save some settings, like Bookmarks in long audio book files and On-The-Go playlists, but at least you can get things running again with this easy, quick fix:

❶ Make sure you charge your iPod battery, and then slide the Hold switch on and off again.

❷ Press and hold down the Menu and center Select buttons simultaneously until you see the Apple logo appear on the screen. This could take up to 10 seconds, and you may have to do it twice, but keep at it until you see the Apple logo.

If the technology gods are smiling, your iPod will go through its little start-up sequence and then return you to the main menu.

The reset procedure for the iPod Touch is easy to remember. Just hold down the two buttons that are *not* the volume rocker: the Sleep/Wake button on top and the Home button on the front. Let go when you see the Apple logo.

A stalled or befuddled iPod Shuffle may also need a good firm reset from time to time, but like the Shuffle itself, resetting it is a bit simpler than wrestling with the other iPods: Turn the On/Off switch to the Off position, wait 10 seconds or so, and then flip it back to the On position.

Download and Reinstall iTunes and iTunes Updates

If iTunes is acting up, you may need to download and install a fresh version of the program. The latest version's always waiting at *www.apple.com/itunes/download*. Your iTunes program itself may also alert you to a new version—or you can make sure it does so in the future:

- If you use iTunes for Windows and installed the Apple Software Update utility when you added iTunes, an alert box appears whenever an iTunes update is ready and offers to install it for you. If you skipped installing the utility, choose Edit→Preferences→General and turn on "Check for updates automatically." If you prefer to check manually, choose Help→"Check for Updates". In either case, you're prompted to snag any available updates.

- The Mac's Software Update program is designed to alert you, via a pop-up dialog box, about new updates for iTunes. If you turned Software Update off (in System Preferences), however, you can run it manually by choosing Software Update from the Apple menu.

As with any software update, once you download the software, double-click the installer file's icon and follow along as the program takes you through several screens of upgrade excitement. If the version of iTunes you're installing is newer than the one you've got, you get "Upgrade" as a button option when you run the installer—and it usually takes less time to do the job.

If you're installing the same version of the program, the iTunes installer may politely ask if you want to either *Repair* or even *Remove* the software. Choosing Repair can often fix damaged files or data that iTunes needs to run properly. It can also be a quicker fix than fully removing the program and reinstalling it all over again.

Use the Diagnostics Tools in iTunes for Windows

With different PC hardware manufacturers out there and multiple versions of Windows in the mix, the PC side of the iTunes/iPod fence can be a little unpredictable. To help sort things out, iTunes 9 for Windows includes a feature called Diagnostics, which helps troubleshoot four categories of woes. Your choices include:

- **Network Connectivity.** These tests check your computer's Internet connection and its ability to access the iTunes Store.

- **DVD/CD Drive.** If you're having trouble importing music to iTunes from a CD—or you can't burn your own discs—these tests inspect your PC's disc drive for problems and incompatibilities.

- **iPhone/iPod Connectivity.** These diagnostics don't actually test the iPod's own hardware or software, but they do examine the way your PC connects to your iPod.

- **iPhone/iPod Touch Sync.** These tests actually *do* test the iPod Touch's hardware and software to make sure it can transport the data you're trying to sync.

To run this battery of tests, choose Help→Run Diagnostics, select a category, and then follow along on-screen. Each diagnostic program runs tests and then displays a red, yellow, or green light. Click the Help button next to a red or yellow light to get troubleshooting help from Apple's Web site. (Green means groovy.) Once the tests are done, you can copy the results to the clipboard or save them to a text file for sharing with techies.

Update the iPod's Software

Updating the iPod's internal software—which Apple does occasionally to fix bugs and add features—is much easier than it used to be, thanks to iTunes. No matter which iPod model you have, iTunes 9 and later handles all software updating chores.

If your iPod Nano or Classic is formatted for Windows, update it on a Windows PC; likewise, update a Mac-formatted iPod on a Macintosh. You can tell which system your iPod is formatted for by choosing, on the iPod, Settings→About. Press the Select button twice to get to the screen with the format info. You can update a Touch from either machine. (If you have a Shuffle or any iPod that's set to autosync with a computer, update it on the machine it's synced with to avoid erasing your iPod.)

To make sure you have the latest version of the iPod software, follow these steps:

❶ Connect your iPod to the computer and select it in the Source list.

❷ On the Summary tab, click the "Check for Update" button in the Version area. If your iPod is up to date, iTunes tells you so.

❸ If iTunes finds new iPod software, you'll be prompted to download it. Click the Downloading icon in the Source pane to monitor your download progress (shown below). Sometimes iTunes will have already downloaded the new iPod software. In that case, just click the Update button in the iTunes main window.

❹ Follow the instructions on-screen.

Older iPod models may require the use of an AC adapter to finish the update, but newer iPods mainly just sit there quietly with a progress bar and an Apple logo on-screen. Once all that goes away, your iPod screen returns to normal and iTunes displays a message box letting you know it's completed the update.

If you're updating your iPod Shuffle, play close attention to the progress bar on the iTunes screen and follow any instructions given. Since the Shuffle has no screen, iTunes is the place to go to see when iTunes finishes the update—usually by returning the Shuffle's icon to the Source list when it's good to go.

 The section of Apple's Web site devoted to iPod support has grown tremendously since the first iPod was released in 2001. You can find troubleshooting guides, tutorials, and more for each iPod model at *www.apple.com/support/ipod*. If it's an out-of-warranty hardware problem, try a specialized iPod repair shop like *www.iresq.com* or *http://www.techrestore.com/ipod*. And when it does come time to upgrade or replace your 'Pod, you can learn about Apple's recycling policy at *www.apple.com/recycling/*.

Start Over: Restoring Your iPod's Software

Just like the operating system that runs your computer, your iPod has its own software that controls everything it does. *Restoring* the iPod software isn't the same thing as updating it. Restoring is a much more drastic procedure, like reformatting the hard drive on your PC or Mac. For one thing, restoring the software *erases everything on your iPod*.

So restore with caution, and do so only if you try all the other troubleshooting measures in this chapter. If you've decided to take the plunge, first make sure you have the most recent version of iTunes (flip back a page for information on that), then proceed as follows:

❶ Start iTunes, and connect your iPod to your computer with its cable.

❷ When the iPod appears in the iTunes Source list, click its icon to see the Summary information (in the main area of the iTunes window).

❸ In the Summary area, click the Restore button.

Note Now, just because you've sucked the life out of your iPod doesn't mean that all your songs, videos, and so on are gone from iTunes. That's the beauty of the iPod-iTunes partnership: By storing everything in iTunes, you can always re-load it onto your iPod, as described on the next page.

❹ If you have an iPod Touch, iTunes gives you the chance to back up your settings—like your preferences for contacts and calendar syncing and other personalized data on your iPod. This means much less work getting your Touch all re-personalized after you reinstall its software. If you want to wipe every trace of your existence from the Touch, skip the backup.

❺ Because restoring erases everything on your iPod, you get a warning message. If you're sure you want to continue, click Restore again.

❻ If you use a Mac, enter an administrator password; a progress bar appears on your iPod's screen. Leave the iPod connected to your computer to complete the restoration process. You may also see an Apple logo appear on-screen.

After iTunes finishes the restore process, its Setup Assistant window appears asking you to name your iPod and choose your syncing preferences—just like when you connected your iPod for the first time. Let the iPod automatically update your files, or add your songs, photos, and videos back manually and see if this little procedure has fixed the iPod's ailment.

 If you manually manage your music and you restore the iPod's software, you'll lose any songs that aren't stored in your iTunes library. (For example, you may have copied a song from a friend's computer that you no longer have access to.) In that case, you may want to get yourself a program that lets you harvest your songs off the iPod (*www.ilounge.com* lists several and Chapter 5 has suggestions).

Understanding the iPod's Battery Messages

Remember how you were taught that certain kinds of batteries (in laptops and camcorders, say) worked better if you occasionally fully drained and then recharged them? Forget it. You want to keep the iPod's lithium-ion battery charged *always*, or else you'll lose your clock, date, and other settings.

The color screen on the iPod Classic, Nano, and Touch shows a green battery that depletes as you use the player. When the battery icon turns red, it's time to recharge, because you have less than 20 percent of your iPod's power left. The screenless Shuffle communicates its battery needs through a small colored light: green for a good charge, amber for partially drained, and red for a battery that needs juice pronto.

Some imperiled iPods display a dull gray charging icon and won't turn on when the battery has run all the way down. This means the poor thing doesn't even have the energy to show its battery-charging color icon. On other models, you may see a yellow triangle icon next to a colorless battery graphic and the stern message, "Connect to Power".

Plug your iPod into your computer, or an optional AC adapter, and give it about half an hour of power to get back to its regular screen graphic. When the battery gets this depleted, you may also have to charge it up for a while to even get the iPod to show up in iTunes.

> **Note** If you had your iPod plugged in all night and it still barely shows a charge, it's probably because something else went to sleep besides you: the computer. An iPod won't charge properly when your computer goes into sleep, hibernation, or standby modes, so adjust your machine's power settings to make sure it doesn't conk out before your iPod gets juiced up. An AC adapter, available at most iPod accessory shops (Chapter 12), lets you skip the whole computer-charging thing.

Apple's Tips for Longer iPod Battery Life

Apple has posted various recommendations on its Web site for how to treat an iPod battery to ensure a long life:

- Don't expose your iPod to extreme hot or cold temperature ranges. (In other words, don't leave it in a hot, parked car, and don't expect it to operate on Mt. Everest.)

- Use your iPod regularly (not that you wouldn't). And be sure to charge it at least once a month to keep that battery chemistry peppy.

- Put the iPod to sleep to conserve battery power. (Press the Play/Pause button until the iPod display goes blank and the iPod settles into slumber; on the Touch, click the Sleep/Wake button on top.)

- Take the iPod out of any heat-trapping cases before you charge it up.

- Use the Hold switch when you're not actively fiddling with the iPod's controls. This keeps it from getting bumped on automatically.

- When you see the Low Battery icon or message, plug your iPod into the computer or an electrical outlet with the AC adapter. The iPod battery indicator shows roughly how much charge is left in the battery.

- Features like the backlight and the equalizer—or jumping around within your media library—can make the battery drain faster, as can using big, uncompressed file formats like AIFF.

- That wireless chip inside the iPod Touch saps power even if you're not trawling the Web. Save energy by turning it off when you don't need it at Settings→Wi-Fi. Lowering the frequency with which you check email or have data pushed to the Touch from the Internet can save some energy as well—you can make those adjustments by choosing Settings→Mail, Contacts, Calendars.

Replace Your iPod's Battery

The iPod uses a rechargeable lithium-ion battery. Unlike players that run on Duracells, you can't easily pop out the old battery and replace it when the cell wears out after repeated charging-and-use cycles.

Which is not to say you *can't* replace the iPod's battery. It just takes a little more time and effort. If your battery is too pooped to power your 'Pod, here are some options:

- You get a full one-year warranty on your iPod battery (two years with the optional AppleCare Protection Plan). But Apple itself offers an out-of-warranty battery replacement service for $49 to $79, (depending on the iPod model) at *www.apple.com/support/ipod/service/battery*.

- Laptops For Less (*www.ipodbattery.com*), offers do-it-yourself iPod battery replacement kits for less than $20.

- Other World Computing sells high-capacity NewerTech iPod batteries for all models of iPods. The company has instructional videos on their Web site, but will also replace the battery for you if you send them your iPod (*http://eshop.macsales.com/shop/ipod*).

- PDASmart.com will replace your iPod's ailing battery for $50 (parts and labor included) at *www.pdasmart.com/ipodpartscenter.htm*. The company can also fix broken screens and hard drives.

AppleCare—What It Is and Whether You Need It

You probably have an insurance policy on your house and car, so why not get one for your iPod? That's the logic behind getting the AppleCare Protection Plan for your iPod. The price for this peace of mind? The plan for the iPod Classic and Touch sells for $59, while coverage for the Nano and Shuffle is $39.

When you buy a brand-new iPod, you automatically get free telephone support to fix one problem within your first 90 days of iPod ownership, plus a year-long warranty on the hardware. If the iPod starts acting weird or stops working altogether, Apple will fix it for free or send you a replacement 'Pod.

If you buy the AppleCare Protection Plan (available in many places where you buy iPods or at *www.apple.com/support/products/applecareipod.html*), you get:

- Two full years of free telephone support from the date of your iPod purchase

- Two full years of hardware protection from the date of your iPod purchase

If you need a repair or replacement, your iPod's covered, and he plan covers your iPod's earphones, battery, and cables, too. Paying an extra $39 or $59 to get the extended warranty may not appeal to everyone, but if you want a little peace of mind with your new iPod, it's a small price to pay.

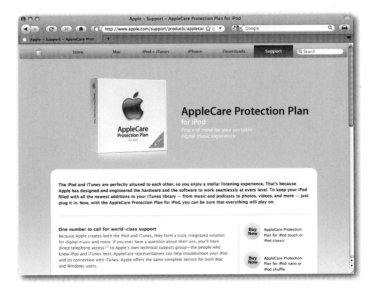

Index

H

HandBrake, 169
hard drive, portable, iPod as, 206–207
headphone jack, location of, 21
help, for using iTunes Store, 162
hiding album covers (iTunes), 76
Hold switch, 21, 28
Home button, 23, 53
home entertainment systems,
    connecting iPod to, 248
Home screen (iPod Touch), 53, 60
Home Sharing, 90–91
home Wi-Fi-network
  AirPort Express and, 250–251
horizontal orientation, for videos, 177
hot spots (Wi-Fi), 212, 213

I

`Done` button (YouTube), 177
iCal, syncing with, 198–199
icons
  on Touch's Home screen, 51, 60
  rearranging, on Touch, 53
images, copying, 100
iMixes (published playlists), 125
importing
  existing songs into iTunes, 10
  specific songs from CDs, 78–79
  videos to computer, 173
indicators, iTunes import process, 79
Info tab (iPod Touch), 105
installing
  iTunes, 8
  new apps, on Touch, 70
Internet radio, 89
interrupted downloads (iTunes
    Store), 156
iPhone
  apps for, 147
  iPod Touch, differences from, 5
  Podcasts menu, 34
iPhoto
  importing videos using, 173
  slideshows from, 190
  syncing with, 182

iPod
  adding playlists to, 117
  as address book, 196–197
  as alarm clock, 41
  as calendar, 198–199
  as audio recorder, 203
  charging, 45
  clock, setting, 40
  contents of, viewing, 103
  copying iTunes Store purchases to
      other computers using, 161
  copying music to iTunes, 110
  ejecting from iTunes, 106
  Extras menu, 35
  game playing on, 47
  illustrated chart of, 178
  information about, in iTunes, 103
  locking, 49
  menu customization, 39
  menus, 29
  Music menu, 30
  operating, 27
  Photos menu, 33
  as portable hard drive, 206–207
  Settings menu, 36–37
  size of, finding, 103
  syncing preferences, adjusting,
      104–105
  transferring videos to, 168
  turning on/off, 28
  unpacking and setting up, 9
  Videos menu, 32
  volume adjustments, 44
  as world clock, 204–205
iPodAccess, 110
iPod Camera Connector, 183
iPod Classic
  about, 6
  autosync feature, 12
  calendars on, 199
  controls for, 20
  finding music, 24–25
  games for, 47, 146
  Genius Mixes on, 124
  Genius playlists on, 122
  main menu, customizing, 39
  manual music loading, 13

Windows
 address books from, 196
 Audible Download Manager, 145
 formatting iPod with, 207
 Vista, file locations in, 108
 XP, file locations in, 108
Windows Media Audio (WMA)
  format, 10
wired adapter, for car stereo system, 247
wireless networking. *See* Wi-Fi;
  Wi-Fi networks
wireless speaker systems, 249
Wish Lists (iTunes Store), 155
WMA format, 10
world clock, 204–205

X

X button (Safari browser), 215
XtremeMac, 253
Xtreme Mac InCharge Travel, 252

Y

Yahoo! Mail
 setup, on Touch, 61
 syncing contacts with, 197
YamiPod, 110
YouTube icon, 60
YouTube, watching videos from, on iPod
  Touch, 176–177

Z

zooming
 finger gestures for, 62
 Web pages, 216–217
Zoom/Unzoom (video control), 174, 175

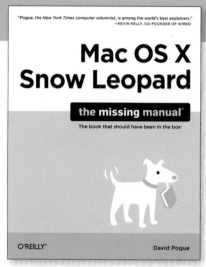

Buy this book and get access to the online edition for 45 days—for free!

iPod: The Missing Manual

By J. D. Biersdorfer with David Pogue
October 2009, $19.99
ISBN 9780596804312

With Safari Books Online, you can:

Access the contents of thousands of technology and business books

- Quickly search over 7000 books and certification guides
- Download whole books or chapters in PDF format, at no extra cost, to print or read on the go
- Copy and paste code
- Save up to 35% on O'Reilly print books
- **New!** Access mobile-friendly books directly from cell phones and mobile devices

Stay up-to-date on emerging topics before the books are published

- Get on-demand access to evolving manuscripts.
- Interact directly with authors of upcoming books

Explore thousands of hours of video on technology and design topics

- Learn from expert video tutorials
- Watch and replay recorded conference sessions

To try out Safari and the online edition of this book FREE for 45 days,
go to **www.oreilly.com/go/safarienabled** and enter the coupon code LKHJZAA.
To see the complete Safari Library, visit safari.oreilly.com.

Spreading the knowledge of innovators   safari.oreilly.com

Get even more for your money.

Join the O'Reilly Community, and register the O'Reilly books you own. It's free, and you'll get:

- 40% upgrade offer on O'Reilly books
- Membership discounts on books and events
- Free lifetime updates to electronic formats of books
- Multiple ebook formats, DRM FREE
- Participation in the O'Reilly community
- Newsletters
- Account management
- 100% Satisfaction Guarantee

Signing up is easy:

1. **Go to: oreilly.com/go/register**
2. **Create an O'Reilly login.**
3. **Provide your address.**
4. **Register your books.**

Note: English-language books only

To order books online:
oreilly.com/order_new

For questions about products or an order:
orders@oreilly.com

To sign up to get topic-specific email announcements and/or news about upcoming books, conferences, special offers, and new technologies:
elists@oreilly.com

For technical questions about book content:
booktech@oreilly.com

To submit new book proposals to our editors:
proposals@oreilly.com

Many O'Reilly books are available in PDF and several ebook formats. For more information:
oreilly.com/ebooks

O'REILLY®

Spreading the knowledge of innovators   www.oreilly.com